Robert Dodsley, William Shenstone

The Works of William Shenstone in Verse and Prose

Robert Dodsley, William Shenstone

The Works of William Shenstone in Verse and Prose

ISBN/EAN: 9783744691857

Printed in Europe, USA, Canada, Australia, Japan

Cover: Foto ©Thomas Meinert / pixelio.de

More available books at **www.hansebooks.com**

The WORKS,

IN VERSE AND PROSE,

OF

WILLIAM SHENSTONE, Efq;

In THREE VOLUMES. With DECORATIONS.

——————— Sæpe ego longos
Cantando puerum memini me condere foles. VIRG.

IMITATION.
Right well I call to mind
When (yet a Boy) whole funs and lengthen'd days
I oft employ'd in chaunting fylvan lays.

The SIXTH EDITION. —— VOL. I.

ADVERTISEMENT

To the READER.

TO this Edition is subjoined (for the sake of those Readers to whom it may not prove unwelcome) an Explanation, or rather, in most Places, a liberal Imitation, of all the Latin Inscriptions and Quotations throughout this Work, by Mr. HULL. That Gentleman's well-known Friendship for Mr. SHENSTONE, and Willingness to oblige, being his sole Inducements to this (as *he* chooses to have it called) *trifling* Addition, the Editor thinks it no more than a just Return of Gratitude to let his Purchasers know to whom they are beholden for it. Be it remembered however that it was executed in a Country Retirement, where our eminent Translators of the Classics were not at hand to be consulted.

PREFACE.

A Great part of the poetical works of Mr. SHENSTONE, particularly his Elegies and Paſtorals, are (as he himſelf expreſſes it) " The exact tranſcripts of the ſituation of his own mind;" and abound in frequent alluſions to his own place, the beautiful ſcene of his retirement from the world. Excluſively therefore of our natural curioſity to be acquainted with the hiſtory of an author whoſe works we peruſe with pleaſure, ſome ſhort account of Mr. SHENSTONE's perſonal character, and ſituation in life, may not only be agreeable, but abſolutely neceſſary, to the reader; as it is impoſſible he ſhould enter into the true ſpirit of his writings, if he is entirely ignorant of thoſe circumſtances of his life, which ſometimes ſo greatly influenced his reflections.

I could wiſh however that this taſk had been allotted to ſome perſon capable of performing it in that maſterly manner which the ſubject ſo well deſerves. To confeſs the truth, it was chiefly to prevent

vent

vent his remains from falling into the hands of any one still lefs qualified to do him juftice, that I have unwillingly ventured to undertake the publication of them myfelf.

Mr. SHENSTONE was the eldeft fon of a plain un-educated gentleman in SHROPSHIRE, who farmed his own eftate. The father fenfible of his fon's extraordinary capacity, refolved to give him a learned education, and fent him a commoner to PEMBROKE College in OXFORD, defigning him for the church: but tho' he had the moft aweful notions of the wifdom, power, and goodnefs of God, he never could be perfuaded to enter into orders. In his private opinions he adhered to no particular fect, and hated all religious difputes. But whatever were his own fentiments, he always fhewed great tendernefs to thofe who differed from him. Tendernefs, indeed, in every fenfe of the word, was his peculiar characteriftic; his friends, his domeftics, his poor neighbours, all daily experienced his benevolent turn of mind. Indeed, this virtue in him was often carried to fuch excefs, that it fometimes bordered upon weaknefs; yet if he was convinced that any of thofe ranked amongft the number of his friends, had treated him ungeneroufly, he was not eafily reconciled. He ufed a maxim, however, on fuch occa-

fions,

sions, which is worthy of being obferved and imitated; " I never (faid he) will be a revengeful enemy; but I cannot, it is not in my nature, to be half a friend." He was in his temper quite unfufpicious; but if fufpicion was once awakened in him, it was not laid afleep again without difficulty.

He was no œconomift; the generofity of his temper prevented him from paying a proper regard to the ufe of money: he exceeded therefore the bounds of his paternal fortune, which before he died was confiderably encumbered. But when one recollects the perfect paradife he had raifed around him, the hofpitality with which he lived, his great indulgence to his fervants, his charities to the indigent, and all done with an eftate not more than three hundred pounds a year, one fhould rather be led to wonder that he left any thing behind him, than to blame his want of œconomy. He left however more than fufficient to pay all his debts; and by his will appropriated his whole eftate for that purpofe.

It was perhaps from fome confiderations on the narrownefs of his fortune, that he forbore to marry; for he was no enemy to wedlock, had a high opinion of many among the fair fex, was fond of their fociety,

and

- and no ſtranger to the tendereſt impreſſions. One,
which he received in his youth, was with difficulty
ſurmounted. The lady was the ſubject of that
ſweet paſtoral, in four parts, which has been ſo
univerſally admired; and which, one would have
thought, muſt have ſubdued the loftieſt heart, and
ſoftened the moſt obdurate,

His perſon, as to height, was above the middle
ſtature, but largely and rather inelegantly formed: his
face ſeemed plain till you converſed with him, and
then it grew very pleaſing. In his dreſs he was
negligent, even to a fault; though when young,
at the univerſity, he was accounted a BEAU. He
wore his own hair, which was quite grey very early,
in a particular manner; not from any affectation of
ſingularity, but from a maxim he had laid down,
that without too ſlaviſh a regard to faſhion, every
one ſhould dreſs in a manner moſt ſuitable to his
own perſon and figure. In ſhort, his faults were
only little blemiſhes, thrown in by nature, as it
were on purpoſe to prevent him from riſing too
much above that level of imperfection allotted to
humanity.

His character as a writer will be diſtinguiſhed by
ſimplicity with elegance, and genius with correct-
neſs.

nefs. He had a fublimity equal to the higheft attempts; yet from the indolence of his temper, he
chofe rather to amufe himfelf in culling flowers at
the foot of the mount, than to take the trouble of
climbing the more arduous fteeps of PARNASSUS.
But whenever he was difpofed to rife, his fteps,
though natural, were noble, and always well fup-
ported. In the tendernefs of elegiac poetry he hath
not been excelled; in the fimplicity of paftoral, one
may venture to fay he had very few equals. Of
great fenfibility himfelf, he never failed to engage
the hearts of his readers: and amidft the niceft attention to the harmony of his numbers, he always
took care to exprefs with propriety the fentiments of
an elegant mind. In all his writings, his greateft
difficulty was to pleafe himfelf. I remember a paffage in one of his letters, where, fpeaking of his
love fongs, he fays,—" Some were written on oc-
" cafions a good deal imaginary, others not fo; and
" the reafon there are fo many is, that I wanted to
" write ONE good fong, and could never pleafe
" myfelf." It was this diffidence which occafioned
him to throw afide many of his pieces before he had
beftowed upon them his laft touches. I have fup-
preffed feveral on this account; and if among thofe
which I have felected, there fhould be difcovered
fome little want of his finifhing polifh, I hope it
will

will be attributed to this caufe, and of courfe be ex-
cufed: yet I flatter myfelf there will always appear
fomething well worthy of having been preferved.
And though I was afraid of inferting what might in-
jure the character of my friend, yet as the fketches
of a great mafter are always valuable, I was unwilling the public fhould lofe any thing material of
fo accomplifhed a writer. In this dilemma it will
eafily be conceived that the tafk I had to perform
would become fomewhat difficult. How I have ac-
quitted myfelf, the public muft judge. Nothing,
however, except what he had already publifhed, has
been admitted without the advice of his moft judicious
friends, nothing altered, without their particular
concurrence. It is impoffible to pleafe every one;
but 'tis hoped that no reader will be fo unreafonable,
as to imagine that the author wrote folely for his
amufement: his talents were various; and though
it may perhaps be allowed that his excellence chiefly
appeared in fubjects of tendernefs and fimplicity, yet
he frequently condefcended to trifle with thofe of humour and drollery: thefe, indeed, he himfelf in fome
meafure degraded by the title which he gave them of
LEVITIES; but had they been entirely rejected, the
public would have been deprived of fome JEUX
D'ESPRITS, excellent in their kind, and Mr.
SHENSTONE's character, as a writer, would have
been but imperfectly exhibited.

But

But the talents of Mr. Shenstone were not confined merely to poetry; his character, as a man of clear judgment, and deep penetration, will beſt appear from his proſe works. It is there we muſt ſearch for the acuteneſs of his underſtanding, and his profound knowledge of the human heart. It is to be lamented indeed, that ſome things here are unfiniſhed, and can be regarded only as fragments : many are left as ſingle thoughts, but which, like the ſparks of diamonds, ſhew the richneſs of the mine to which they belong; or like the foot of a HERCULES, diſcover the uncommon ſtrength, and extraordinary dimenſions of that hero. I have no apprehenſion of incurring blame from any one, for preſerving theſe valuable remains : they will diſcover to every reader, the author's ſentiments on ſeveral important ſubjects. And there can be very few, to whom they will not impart many thoughts which they would never perhaps have been able to draw from the ſource of their own reflections.

But I believe little need be ſaid to recommend the writings of this gentleman to public attention. His character is already ſufficiently eſtabliſhed. And if he be not injured by the ina-
bility

bility of his editor, there is no doubt but he will
ever maintain an eminent ftation among the beft of
our Englifh writers.

R. DODSLEY.

A PRE-

A

PREFATORY ESSAY

ON

ELEGY.

IT is observable, that discourses prefixed to poetry are contrived very frequently to inculcate such tenets as may exhibit the performance to the greatest advantage. The fabric is very commonly raised in the first place, and the measures, by which we are to judge of its merit, are afterwards adjusted.

There have been few rules given us by the critics concerning the structure of elegiac poetry; and far be it from the author of the following trifles, to dignify his own opinions with that denomination. He would only intimate the great variety of subjects, and the different * styles in which

the

---

* This essay was written near twenty years ago.

the writers of elegy have *hitherto indulged them-*
selves, and endeavour to shield the following ones
by the latitude of their *example.*

If we consider the etymology of * *the* word, *the*
epithet which † Horace *gives it, or the confes-*
sion which ‡ Ovid *makes concerning it, I think*
we may conclude *thus much however ; that* elegy,
in its true and genuine acceptation, includes *a ten-*
der and querulous idea: that it looks upon this *as its*
peculiar characteristic, and so long as this *is tho-*
roughly sustained, admits of a variety of subjects ;
which by its manner of treating them, it renders
its own. It throws its melancholy stole *over pretty*
different objects ; which, like the dresses at a fune-
ral procession, gives them all a kind of solemn and
uniform appearance.

It is probable that elegies were written at first
upon the death of intimate friends *and* near rela-
tions; celebrated beauties, *or* favourite mis-
tresses;

* ι-λιγειν, ι-particulam dolendi.
† Miferabiles elegos.   Hor.
‡ Heu nimis ex *vero* nunc tibi nomen erit.
                    Ovid. de Morte Tibulli.

treffes; beneficent governors *and* illuftrious men: *one may add perhaps, of all thofe, who are placed by* VIRGIL *in the laurel-grove of his Elyfium, (Vide* HURD's *Differtation on* HORACE's *Epiftle)*

Quique fui memores alios fecere merendo.

After thefe fubjects were fufficiently exhaufted, and the feverity of fate difplayed in the moft affecting inftances, the poets fought occafion to vary their complaints; and the next tender fpecies of forrow that prefented itfelf, was the grief of abfent *or* neglected *lovers. And this indulgence might be indeed allowed them; but with* this *they were not contented. They had obtained a fmall corner in the province of love, and they took advantage, from thence, to over-run the whole territory. They fung its fpoils, triumphs, ovations, and rejoicings *, as well as the captivity and exequies that attended it. They gave the name of* elegy *to their pleafantries as well as lamentations; 'till at laft, through their abundant fondnefs*

---

* Dicite Io Pæan, & Io bis dicite Pæan.   OVID.

ness for the myrtle, they forgot that the cypress was their *peculiar garland*.

In this it is probable they deviated from the original *design* of elegy; and it should seem, that any kind of *subjects*, treated in such a manner as to diffuse a pleasing melancholy, might far better *deserve* the name, than the facetious mirth and libertine festivity of the successful votaries of love.

But not to dwell too long upon an opinion which may seem perhaps introduced to favour the following performance, it may not be improper to examine into the use and end of elegy. The most important end of all *poetry* is to encourage virtue. Epic and tragedy chiefly recommend the public virtues; elegy is of a species which illustrates and endears the private. There is a truly virtuous pleasure connected with many pensive contemplations, which it is the province and excellency of elegy to enforce. This, by presenting suitable ideas, has discovered sweets in melancholy which we could not find in mirth; and has led us with success to the dusty urn, when we could draw no plea-

sure

sure from the sparkling bowl; as pastoral conveys
an idea of simplicity and innocence, it is in particular the task and merit of elegy to shew the innocence and simplicity of rural life to advantage:
and that, in a way distinct from pastoral, as much
as the plain but judicious landlord may be imagined
to surpass his tenant both in dignity and under-
standing.. It should also tend to elevate the more
tranquil virtues of humility, disinterestedness,
simplicity, and innocence: but then there is a
degree of elegance and refinement, no way incon-
sistent with these rural virtues; and that raises
elegy above that merum rus, that unpolished
rusticity, which has given our pastoral writers
their highest reputation.

Wealth and splendor will never want their proper weight: the danger is, lest they should too much
preponderate. A kind of poetry therefore which
throws its chief influence into the other scale, that
magnifies the sweets of liberty and independence,
that endears the honest delights of love and friendship, that celebrates the glory of a good name after death, that ridicules the futile arrogance of

birth,

birth, that recommends the innocent amusement of letters, and insensibly prepares the mind for that humanity it inculcates, *such a kind of poetry may chance to please; and if it please, should seem to be of service.*

As to the style *of elegy, it may be well enough determined from what has gone before.. It should imitate the voice and language of grief, or if a metaphor of dress be more agreeable, it should be simple and diffuse, and flowing as a mourner's veil. A versification therefore is desirable, which, by indulging a free and unconstrained expression, may admit of that simplicity which elegy requires.*

Heroic metre, with alternate rhime, seems well enough adapted to this species of poetry; and, however exceptionable upon other occasions, its inconveniencies appear to lose their weight in shorter *elegies; and its advantages seem to* acquire *an* additional *importance. The world has an admirable example of its beauty in a collection of elegies ** not

---

* N. B. This preface was written near twenty years ago.

not long *since* publifhed ; *the product of a gen-tleman of the moft exact tafte, and whofe untimely death merits all the tears that elegy can fhed.*

- *It is not impoffible that fome may think this metre too lax and profaic : others, that even a more diffolute variety of numbers may have fuperior advantages. And, in favour of thefe laft, might be produced the example of* MILTON *in his* LYCIDAS, *together with one or two recent and beautiful imitations of his verfification in that monody. . But this kind of argument, I am apt to think, muft prove* too much ; *fince the writers I have in view feem capable enough of recommending any metre they fhall choofe ; though it muft be owned alfo, that the choice* they make *of any, is at the fame time the ftrongeft prefumption in its favour.*

Perhaps it may be no great difficulty to compromife *the difpute. There is no one kind of metre that is diftinguifhed by rhimes, but is liable to fome objection or other. Heroic verfe, where every fecond line is terminated by a rhime, (with which the judgment requires that the* fenfe *fhould* *in some measure also terminate) is apt to render the expression either scanty or constrained. And this is sometimes observable in the writings of a poet lately deceased; though I believe no one ever threw so much sense together with so much ease into a couplet as Mr. POPE. But as an air of con-*straint *too often accompanies this metre, it seems by no means proper for a writer of* elegy.

The previous *rhime in* MILTON's LYCIDAS *is very frequently placed at such a distance from the following, that it is often dropt by the memory (much better employed in attending to the senti-ment) before it be brought to join its partner: and this seems to be the greatest objection to that kind of versification. But then the peculiar* ease *and* variety *it admits of, are no doubt sufficient to overbalance the objection, and to give it the pre-ference to any other, in an elegy of* length.

The chief exception to which stanza *of all kinds is liable, is, that it breaks the sense too* regularly, *when it is continued through a long poem. And this may be perhaps the fault of Mr.* WALLER's *excellent panegyric. But if this fault be less dis-*

3   *cernible*

cernible in smaller compositions, as I suppose it is, I flatter myself, that the advantages I have before mentioned resulting from alternate rhime (with which stanza is, I think, connected) may, at least in shorter elegies, be allowed to outweigh its imperfections.

I shall say but little of the different kinds of elegy. The melancholy of a lover is different, no doubt, from what we feel on other mixed occasions. The mind in which love and grief at once predominate is softened to an excess. Love-elegy therefore is more negligent of order and design, and, being addressed chiefly to the ladies, requires little more than tenderness. and perspicuity. Elegies, that are formed upon promiscuous incidents, and addressed to the world in general, inculcate some sort of moral, and admit a different degree of reasoning, thought, and order.

The author of the following elegies entered on his subjects occasionally, as particular incidents in life suggested, or dispositions of mind recommended them to his choice. If he describes a rural landskip, or unfolds the train of senti-

ments

ments it inspired, he fairly drew his picture from the spot; and felt very sensibly the affection he communicates. If he speaks of his humble shed, his flocks and his fleeces, he does not counterfeit the scene; who having (whether through choice or necessity, is not material) retired betimes to country solitudes, and sought his happiness in rural employments, has a right to consider himself as a real shepherd. The flocks, the meadows, and the grottos, are his own, and the embellishment of his farm his sole amusement. As the sentiments therefore were inspired by nature, and that in the earlier part of his life, he hopes they will retain a natural appearance; diffusing at least some part of that amusement, which he freely acknowledges he received from the composition of them.

There will appear perhaps a real inconsistency in the moral tenour of the several elegies; and the subsequent ones may sometimes seem a recantation of the preceding. The reader will scarcely impute this to oversight; but will allow, that men's opinions as well as tempers vary; that neither public nor private, active nor speculative life, are un-
exceptionably

exceptionably happy, and confequently that any change of opinion concerning them may afford an additional beauty to poetry, as it gives us a more ftriking reprefentation of life.

If the author has hazarded, throughout, the ufe of Englifh or modern allufions, he hopes it will not be imputed to an intire ignorance, or to the leaft *difefteem of the ancient learning. He has kept the ancient* plan *and* method *in his eye, though he builds his edifice with the materials of his own nation. In other words, through a fond-nefs for his native country, he has made ufe of the flowers it produced, though in order to exhibit them to the greater advantage, he has endeavoured to weave his garland by the beft model he could find: with what fuccefs, beyond his own amufement, muft be left to judges lefs partial to him than either his acquaintance or his friends.—If any of thofe fhould be fo candid, as to approve the variety of fubjects he has chofen, and the tendernefs of fentiment he has endeavoured to imprefs, he begs the* metre *alfo may not be too fuddenly condemned. The public ear, habituated of late to a quicker meafure, may perhaps confi-*

der

der this *as heavy and languid; but an objection of that kind may gradually lose its force, if this measure should be allowed to suit the nature of elegy.*

If it should happen to be considered as an objection with others, *that there is too much of a moral cast diffused through the whole; it is replied, that he* endeavoured *to animate the poetry so far as not to render this objection too obvious; or to* risque excluding *the fashionable reader: at the same time never deviating from a fixed principle, that poetry without morality is but the* bloſſom of a fruit-tree. *Poetry is indeed like that species of plants, which may bear at once both fruits and bloſſoms, and the tree is by no means in perfection without the* former, *however it may be embellished by the flowers which surround it.*

ELEGIES,

ELEGIES,

WRITTEN ON

Many different Occasions.

Tantùm inter denſas, umbroſa cacumina, fagos
Aſſiduè veniebat; ibi hæc incondita, ſolus,
Montibus et ſilvis ſtudio jaſtabat inani !   Virg.

IMITATION.

The ſpreading beech alone he would explore
With frequent ſtep; beneath it's ſhady top,
(Ah! profitleſs employ!) to hills and groves
Theſe indigeſted lays he wont repeat.

different Occasions

ELEGY I.

He arrives at his retirement in the country, and
takes occasion to expatiate in praise of simplicity. To a FRIEND.

FOR rural virtues, and for native skies,
    I bade AUGUSTA's venal sons farewel;
Now, 'mid the trees, I see my smoke arise;
    Now hear the fountains bubbling round my cell.

O may that Genius, which secures my rest,
    Preserve this villa for a friend that's dear!
Ne'er may my vintage glad the sordid breast;
    Ne'er tinge the lip that dares be unsincere!

                                      Far

Far from thefe paths, ye faithlefs friends, depart!
 Fly my plain board, abhor my hoftile name!
Hence! the faint verfe that flows not from the heart,
 But mourns in labour'd ftrains, the price of fame!

O lov'd fimplicity! be thine the prize!
 Affiduous art correct her page in vain!
His be the palm who, guiltlefs of difguife,
 Contemns the pow'r, the dull refource to feign!

Still may the mourner, lavifh of his tears
 For lucre's venal meed, invite my fcorn!
Still may the bard diffembling doubts and fears,
 For praife, for flatt'ry fighing, figh forlorn!

Soft as the line of love-fick HAMMOND flows,
 'Twas his fond heart effus'd the melting theme;
Ah! never could AONIA's hill difclofe
 So fair a fountain, or fo lov'd a ftream.

Ye lovelefs bards! intent with artful pains
 To form a figh, or to contrive a tear!
Forego your Pindus, and on —— plains
 Survey CAMILLA's charms, and grow fincere.

But thou, my friend! while in thy youthful foul
 Love's gentle tyrant feats his awful throne,
Write from thy bofom——let not art controul
 The ready pen, that makes his edicts known.

Pleafing

Pleasing when youth is long expir'd, to trace
  The forms our pencil, or our pen design'd!
" Such was our youthful air and shape and face!
  " Such the soft image of our youthful mind!"

Soft whilst we sleep beneath the rural bow'rs,
  The loves and graces steal unseen away;
And where the turf diffus'd its pomp of flow'rs,
  We wake to wintry scenes of chill decay!

Curse the sad fortune that detains thy fair;
  Praise the soft hours that gave thee to her arms;
Paint thy proud scorn of ev'ry vulgar care,
  When hope exalts thee, or when doubt alarms.

Where with Œnone thou hast worn the day,
  Near fount or stream, in meditation, rove;
If in the grove Œnone lov'd to stray,
  The faithful muse shall meet thee in the grove.

✦✦✦✦✦✦✦✦✦✦✦✦✦✦✦✦✦✦✦✦✦✦✦✦✦✦✦✦✦✦✦✦✦✦

ELEGY II.

On posthumous reputation.   To a FRIEND.

O GRIEF of griefs! that envy's frantic ire
  Should rob the living virtue of its praise;
O foolish muses! that with zeal aspire
  To deck the cold insensate shrine with bays!

When

When the free spirit quits her humble frame,
   To tread the skies with radiant garlands crown'd,
Say, will she hear the distant voice of fame?
   Or hearing, fancy sweetness in the sound?

Perhaps ev'n genius pours a slighted lay;
   Perhaps ev'n friendship sheds a fruitless tear;
Ev'n LYTTELTON but vainly trims the bay,
   And fondly graces HAMMOND's mournful bier.

Tho' weeping virgins haunt his favour'd urn,
   Renew their chaplets, and repeat their sighs;
Tho' near his tomb, Sabæan odours burn,
   The loit'ring fragrance will it reach the skies?

No, should his DELIA votive wreaths prepare,
   DELIA might place the votive wreaths in vain:
Yet the dear hope of DELIA's future care
   Once crown'd his pleasures, and dispell'd his pain.

Yes—the fair prospect of surviving praise
   Can ev'ry sense of present joys excel:
For this, great HADRIAN chose laborious days;
   Thro' this, expiring, bade a gay farewel.

Shall then our youths, who fame's bright fabric raise,
   To life's precarious date confine their care?
O teach them you, to spread the sacred base,
   To plan a work, thro' latest ages fair!

It is fmall tranfport, as with curious eye
  You trace the ftory of each attic fage,
To think your blooming praife fhall time defy?
  Shall waft like odóurs thro' the pleafing page?

To mark the day when through the bulky tome,
  Around your name the varying ftyle refines?
And readers call their loft attention home,
  Led by that index where true genius fhines?

Ah let not BRITONS doubt their focial aim,
  Whofe ardent bofoms catch this ancient fire!
Cold intereft melts before the vivid flame,
  And patriot ardours, but with life, expire!

ELEGY III.

On the untimely death of a certain learned
acquaintance.

IF proud PYGMALION quit his cumbrous frame,
  Funereal pomp the fcanty tear fupplies;
Whilft heralds loud with venal voice proclaim,
  Lo! here the brave and the puiffant lies.

When humbler ALCON leaves his drooping friends,
  Pageant nor plume diftinguifh ALCON's bier;
The faithful mufe with votive fong attends,
  And blots the mournful numbers with a tear.

He little knew the fly penurious art;
   That odious art which fortune's favourites know;
Form'd to beftow, he felt the warmeft heart,
   But envious fate forbade him to beftow.

He little knew to ward the fecret wound;
   He little knew that mortals could enfnare;
Virtue he knew; the nobleft joy he found,
   To fing her glories, and to paint her fair!

Ill was he fkill'd to guide his wand'ring fheep;
   And unforefeen difafter thin'd his fold;
Yet, at another's lofs, the fwain would weep;
   And, for his friend, his very crook were fold.

Ye fons of wealth! protect the mufe's train;
   From winds protect them, and with food fupply;
Ah! helplefs they, to ward the threaten'd pain,
   The meagre famine, and the wintry fky!

He lov'd a nymph: amidft his flender ftore,
   He dar'd to love; and CYNTHIA was his theme;
He breath'd his plaints along the rocky fhore,
   They only echo'd o'er the winding ftream.

His nymph was fair! the fweeteft bud that blows,
   Revives lefs lovely from the recent fhow'r;
So PHILOMEL enamour'd eyes the rofe;
   Sweet bird! enamour'd of the fweeteft flow'r!

He lov'd the mufe; fhe taught him to complain;
　　He faw his tim'rous loves on her depend;
He lov'd the mufe, altho' fhe taught in vain;
　　He lov'd the mufe, for fhe was virtue's friend.

She guides the foot that treads on Parian floors;
　　She wins the ear when formal pleas are vain;
She tempts patricians from the fatal doors
　　Of vice's brothel, forth to virtue's fane.

He wifh'd for wealth, for much he wifh'd to give;
　　He griev'd that virtue might not wealth obtain;
Piteous of woes, and hopelefs to relieve,
　　The penfive profpeft fadden'd all his ftrain.

I faw him faint! I faw him fink to reft!
　　Like one ordain'd to fwell the vulgar throng;
As tho' the virtues had not warm'd his breaft,
　　As tho' the mufes not infpir'd his tongue.

I faw his bier ignobly crofs the plain;
　　Saw peafant hands the pious rite fupply:
The generous ruftics mourn'd the friendly fwain,
　　But pow'r and wealth's unvarying cheek was dry!

Such ALCON fell; in meagre want forlorn!
　　Where were ye then, ye powerful patrons, where?
Wou'd ye the purple fhou'd your limbs adorn,
　　Go wafh the confcious blemifh with a tear.

　　　　　　　ELEGY

ELEGY IV.

Ophelia's urn. To Mr. G——.

THRO' the dim veil of ev'ning's dusky shade,
    Near some lone fane, or yew's funereal green,
What dreary forms has magic fear survey'd!
What shrouded spectres superstition seen!

But you secure shall pour your sad complaint,
    Nor dread the meagre phantom's wan array;
What none but fear's officious hand can paint,
    What none, but superstition's eye, survey.

The glim'ring twilight and the doubtful dawn
    Shall see your step to these sad scenes return:
Conftant, as cryftal dews impearl the lawn,
    Shall STREPHON's tear bedew OPHELIA's urn!

Sure nought unhallow'd shall presume to stray
    Where sleep the reliques of that virtuous maid;
Nor aught unlovely bend its devious way,
    Where soft OPHELIA's dear remains are laid.

Haply thy muse, as with unceasing sighs
    She keeps late vigils on her urn reclin'd,
May see light groups of pleasing visions rise;
    And phantoms glide, but of celestial kind.

Then

Then fame, her clarion pendant at her fide,
   Shall feek forgivenefs of OPHELIA's fhade;
" Why has fuch worth, without diftinction, dy'd,
   Why, like the defert's lilly, bloom'd to fade?"

Then young fimplicity, averfe to feign,
   Shall unmolefted breathe her foftest figh:
And candour with unwonted warmth complain,
   And innocence indulge a wailful cry.

Then elegance with coy judicious hand,
   Shall cull frefh flow'rets for OPHELIA's tomb:
And beauty chide the fates' fevere command,
   That fhew'd the frailty of fo fair a bloom!

And fancy then with wild ungovern'd woe,
   Shall her lov'd pupil's native tafte explain:
For mournful fable all her hues forego,
   And afk fweet folace of the mufe in vain!

Ah, gentle forms, expect no fond relief;
   Too much the facred Nine their lofs deplore:
Well may ye grieve, nor find an end of grief—
   Your beft, your brighteft fav'rite is no more.

ELEGY

ELEGY V.

He compares the turbulence of love with the
tranquillity of friendſhip.

To MELISSA his Friend.

FROM love, from angry love's inclement reign
I paſs awhile to friendſhip's equal ſkies;
Thou, gen'rous maid, reliev'ſt my partial pain,
And chear'ſt the victim of another's eyes.

'Tis thou, MELISSA, thou deſerv'ſt my care:
How can my will and reaſon diſagree?
How can my paſſion live beneath deſpair?
How can my boſom ſigh for aught but thee?

Ah dear MELISSA! pleas'd with thee to rove,
My ſoul has yet ſurviv'd its drearieſt time;
Ill can I bear the various clime of love!
Love is a pleaſing, but a various clime!

So ſmiles immortal MARO's fav'rite ſhore,
PARTHENOPE, with ev'ry verdure crown'd!
When ſtrait VESUVIO's horrid cauldrons roar,
And the dry vapour blaſts the regions round.

Oh

Oh blifsful regions! oh unrival'd plains!
   When MARO to thefe fragrant haunts retir'd!
O fatal realms! and oh accurft domains!
   When PLINY, 'mid fulphureous clouds, expir'd!

So fmiles the furface of the treacherous main,
   As o'er its wayes the peaceful halcyons play;
When foon rude winds their wonted rule regain,
   And fky and ocean mingle in the fray.

But let or air contend, or ocean rave;
   Ev'n hope fubfide amid the billows toft;
Hope, ftill emergent, ftill contemns the wave,
   And not a feature's wonted fmile is loft.

✦✦✦✦✦✦✦✦✦✦✦✦✦✦✦✦✦✦✦✦✦✦✦✦✦✦✦✦✦✦✦✦✦✦

ELEGY VI.

To a lady on the language of birds.

COME then DIONE, let us range the grove,
   The fcience of the feather'd choirs explore:
Hear linnets argue, larks defcant of love,
   And blame the gloom of folitude no more.

My doubt fubfides—'tis no Italian fong,
   Nor fenfelefs ditty chears the vernal tree:
Ah! who, that hears DIONE's tuneful tongue,
   Shall doubt that mufic may with fenfe agree?

C 4   And

And come, my mufe! that lov'ft the filvan fhade;
    Evolve the mazes, and the mift difpel:
Tranflate the fong; convince my doubting maid,
    No folemn dervife can explain fo well.—

Penfive beneath the twilight fhades I fate,
    The flave of hopelefs vows and cold difdain!
When PHILOMEL addrefs'd his mournful mate,
    And thus I conftru'd the mellifluent ftrain,

" Sing on, my bird—the liquid notes prolong,
    At ev'ry note a lover fheds his tear;
Sing on, my bird—'tis DAMON hears thy fong;
    Nor doubt to gain applaufe when lovers hear,

He the fad fource of our complaining knows;
    A foe to TEREUS and to lawlefs love!
He mourns the ftory of our ancient woes;
    Ah could our mufic his complaint remove!

Yon' plains are govern'd by a peerlefs maid;
    And fee pale CYNTHIA mounts the vaulted fky,
A train of lovers court the chequer'd fhade;
    Sing on, my bird, and hear thy mate's reply.

Ere while no fhepherd to thefe woods retir'd;
    No lover bleft the glow-worm's pallid ray:
But ill-ftar'd birds, that lift'ning not admir'd,
    Or lift'ning envy'd our fuperior lay.

Chear'd

Chear'd by the fun, the vaffals of his pow'r,
　Let fuch by day unite their jarring ftrains!
But let us chufe the calm, the filent hour,
　Nor want fit audience while DIONE reigns."

ELEGY VII.

He defcribes his vifion to an acquaintance,

Cætera per terras omnes animalia, &c.　VIRG.

IMITATION.

All animals befide, o'er all the earth, &c.

ON diftant heaths, beneath autumnal fkies,
　Penfive I faw the circling fhade defcend;
Weary and faint I heard the ftorm arife,
　While the fun vanifh'd like a faithlefs friend,

No kind companion led my fteps aright;
　No friendly planet lent its glim'ring ray;
Ev'n the lone cot refus'd its wonted light,
　Where toil in peaceful flumber clos'd the day.

Then the dull bell had giv'n a pleafing found;
　The village cur 'twere tranfport then to hear;
In dreadful filence all was hufh'd around,
　While the rude ftorm alone diftrefs'd mine ear.

A3

As led by ORWELL's winding banks I ſtray'd,
   Where tow'ring WOLSEY breath'd his native air;
A ſudden luſtre chas'd the flitting ſhade,
   The ſounding winds were huſh'd, and all was fair.

Inſtant a grateful form appear'd confeſt;
   White were his locks with awful ſcarlet crown'd,
And livelier far than Tyrian ſeem'd his veſt,
   That with the glowing purple ting'd the ground.

 " Stranger, he ſaid, amid this pealing rain,
   Benighted, loneſome, wither wou'dſt thou ſtray ?
Does wealth or pow'r thy weary ſtep conſtrain ?
   Reveal thy wiſh, and let me point the way.

For know I trod the trophy'd paths of pow'r;
   Felt every joy that fair ambition brings;
And left the lonely roof of yonder bow'r
   To ſtand beneath the canopies of kings.

I bade low hinds the tow'ring ardour ſhare;
   Nor meanly roſe, to bleſs myſelf alone :
I ſnatch'd the ſhepherd from his fleecy care,
   And bade his wholeſome dictate guard the throne.

Low at my feet the ſuppliant peer I ſaw;
   I ſaw proud empires my deciſion wait;
My will was duty, and my word was law,
   My ſmile was tranſport, and my frown was fate."

Ah

Ah me! faid I, nor pow'r I feek, nor gain;
 Nor urg'd by hope of fame thefe toils endure;
A fimple youth, that feels a lover's pain,
 And, from his friend's condolance, hopes a cure.

He, the dear youth, to whofe abodes I roam,
 Nor can mine honours, nor my fields extend;
Yet for his fake I leave my diftant home,
 Which oaks embofom, and which hills defend.

Beneath that home I fcorn the wintry wind;
 The fpring, to fhade me, robes her faireft tree;
And if a friend my grafs-grown threfhold find,
 O how my lonely cot refounds with glee!

Yet, tho' averfe to gold in heaps amafs'd,
 I wifh to blefs, I languifh to beftow;
And tho' no friend to fame's obftreperous blaft,
 Still, to her dulcet murmurs not a foe.

Too proud with fervile tone to deign addrefs;
 Too mean to think that honours are my due;
Yet fhou'd fome patron yield my ftores to blefs,
 I fure fhou'd deem my boundlefs thanks were few.

But tell me, thou! that, like a meteor's fire,
 Shot'ft blazing forth; difdaining dull degrees;
Shou'd I to wealth, to fame, to pow'r afpire,
 Muft I not pafs more rugged paths than thefe?

Muft

Muſt I not groan beneath a guilty load,
    Praiſe him I ſcorn, and him I love betray?
Does not felonious envy bar the road?
    Or falſchood's treach'rous foot beſet the way?

Say ſhou'd I paſs thro' favour's crowded gate,
    Muſt not fair truth inglorious wait behind?
Whilſt I approach the glitt'ring ſcenes of ſtate,
    My beſt companion no admittance find?

*Nurs'd in the ſhades by freedom's lenient care,
    Shall I the rigid ſway of fortune own?
Taught by the voice of pious truth, prepare
    To ſpurn an altar and adore a throne?

And when proud fortune's ebbing tide recedes,
    And when it leaves me no unſhaken friend,
Shall I not weep that e'er I left the meads,
    Which oaks emboſom, and which hills defend?

Oh! if theſe ills the price of pow'r advance,
    Check not my ſpeed where ſocial joys invite!
The troubled viſion caſt a mournful glance,
    And ſighing vaniſh'd in the ſhades of night.

ELEGY

ELEGY VIII.

He defcribes his early love of poetry, and its
confequences.   To Mr. G——. *1745.

AH me! what envious magic thins my fold?
   What mutter'd fpell retards their late increafe?
Such lefs'ning fleeces muft the fwain behold,
   That e'er with Doric pipe effays to pleafe.

I faw my friends in ev'ning circles meet;
   I took my vocal reed, and tun'd my lay;
I heard them fay my vocal reed was fweet:
   Ah fool! to credit what I heard them fay!

Ill-fated bard! that feeks his fkill to fhow,
   Then courts the judgment of a friendly ear!
Not the poor veteran, that permits his foe
   To guide his doubtful ftep, has more to fear.

Nor cou'd my G—— miftake the critic's laws,
   'Till pious friendfhip mark'd the pleafing way:
Welcome fuch error! ever bleft the caufe!
   Ev'n tho' it led me boundlefs leagues aftray!

Couldft

* N. B. Written after the death of Mr. P o p e.

Couldſt thou reprove me, when I nurs'd the flame
    On liſt'ning CHERWELL's oſier banks reclin'd?
While foe to fortune, unſeduc'd by fame,
    I ſooth'd the bias of a careleſs mind.

Youth's gentle kindred, health and love were met;
    What though in ALMA's guardian arms I play'd?
How ſhall the muſe thoſe vacant hours forget?
    Or deem that bliſs by ſolid cares repaid?

Thou know'ſt how tranſport thrills the tender breaſt,
    Where love and fancy fix their op'ning reign;
How nature ſhines in livelier colours dreſt,
    To bleſs their union, and to grace their train.

So firſt when PHOEBUS met the Cyprian queen,
    And favour'd RHODES beheld their paſſion crown'd,
Unuſual flow'rs enrich'd the painted green;
    And ſwift ſpontaneous roſes bluſh'd around.

Now ſadly lorn, from TWITNAM's widow'd bow'r,
    The drooping muſes take their caſual way;
And where they ſtop, a flood of tears they pour;
    And where they weep, no more the fields are gay.

Where is the dappled pink, the ſprightly roſe?
    The cowſlip's golden cup no more I ſee:
Dark and diſcolour'd ev'ry flow'r that blows,
    To form the garland, Elegy! for thee!—

                    Enough

Enough of tears has wept the virtuous dead;
   Ah might we now the pious rage controul!
Hufh'd be my grief ere ev'ry fmile be fled,
   Ere the deep fwelling figh fubvert the foul!

If near fome trophy fpring a ftripling bay,
   Pleas'd we behold the graceful umbrage rife;
But foon too deep it works its baneful way,
   And, low on earth, the proftrate * ruin lies.

⁕⁕⁂⁕⁕⁕⁕⁕⁕⁕⁕⁕⁕⁕⁕⁕⁕⁕⁕⁕⁕⁕⁕⁕⁕⁕⁕⁕⁕⁕⁕⁕⁕⁕⁕⁕

ELEGY IX.

He defcribes his difintereftednefs to a friend.

I NE'ER muft tinge my lip with Celtic wines;
   The pomp of India muft I ne'er difplay;
Nor boaft the produce of Peruvian mines,
   Nor, with Italian founds, deceive the day.

Down yonder brook my cryftal bev'rage flows;
   My grateful fheep their annual fleeces bring;
Fair in my garden buds the damafk rofe,
   And, from my grove, I hear the throftle fing.

                           My

⁕ Alludes to what is reported of the bay tree, that if it is planted
too near the walls of an edifice, its roots will work their way un-
derneath, till they deftroy the foundation.

My fellow fwains! avert your dazzled eyes;
   In vain allur'd by glittering fpoils they rove;
The fates ne'er meant them for the fhepherd's prize,
   Yet gave them ample recompence in love.

They gave you vigour from your parent's veins;
   They gave you toils; but toils your finews brace;
They gave you nymphs, that own their amorous pains,
   And fhades, the refuge of the gentle race.

To carve your loves, to paint your mutual flames,
   See! polifh'd fair, the beech's friendly rind!
To fing foft carrols to your lovely dames,
   See vocal grotts, and echoing vales affign'd!

Would'ft thou, my STREPHON, love's delighted flave!
   Tho' fure the wreaths of chivalry to fhare,
Forego the ribbon thy MATILDA gave,
   And giving, bade thee in remembrance wear?

Ill fare my peace, but ev'ry idle toy,
   If to my mind my DELIA's form it brings,
Has truer worth, imparts fincerer joy,
   Than all that bears the radiant ftamp of kings.

O my foul weeps, my breaft with anguifh bleeds,
   When love deplores the tyrant pow'r of gain!
Difdaining riches as the futile weeds,
   I rife fuperior, and the rich difdain.

Of

Oft from the ftream, flow-wandering down the glade,
　　Penfive I hear the nuptial peal rebound;
" Some mifer weds, I try, the captive maid,
　　" And fome fond lover fickens at the found."

Not SOMERVILLE, the mufe's friend of old,
　　Tho' now exalted to yon ambient fky,
So fhun'd a foul diftain'd with earth and gold,
　　So lov'd the pure, the generous breaft, as I.

Scorn'd be the wretch that quits his genial bowl,
　　His loves, his friendfhips, ev'n his felf, refigns;
Perverts the facred inftinct of his foul,
　　And to a ducate's dirty fphere confines.

But come, my friend, with tafte, with fcience bleft,
　　Ere age impair me, and ere gold allure;
Reftore thy dear idea to my breaft,
　　The rich depofit fhall the fhrine fecure.

Let others toil to gain the fordid ore,
　　The charms of independence let us fing;
Bleft with thy friendfhip can I wifh for more?
　　I'll fpurn the boafted wealth of * LYDIA's king.

* Crœfus.

ELEGY X.

To Fortune, fuggefting his motive for re-pining at her difpenfations.

ASK not the caufe, why this rebellious tongue
  Loads with frefh curfes thy detefted fway!
Afk not, thus branded in my fofteft fong,
  Why ftands the flatter'd name, which all obey?

'Tis not, that in my fhed I lurk forlorn,
  Nor fee my roof on Parian columns rife;
That, on this breaft, no mimic ftar is borne,
  Rever'd, ah! more than thofe that light the fkies.

'Tis not, that on the turf fupinely laid,
  I fing or pipe, but to the flocks that graze;
And, all inglorious, in the lonefome fhade,
  My finger ftiffens, and my voice decays.

Not, that my fancy mourns thy ftern command,
  When many an embrio dome is loft in air;
While guardian prudence checks my eager hand,
  And, ere the turf is broken, cries, "Forbear.

" Forbear, vain youth! be cautious, weigh thy gold;
  " Nor let yon rifing column more afpire;
" Ah! better dwell in ruins, than behold
  " Thy fortunes mould'ring, and thy domes entire.

" HONORIO

" Honorio built, but dar'd my laws defy;
  " He planted, foornful of my fage.commands;
" The peach's vernal bud regal'd his eye;
  " The fruitage ripen'd for more frugal hands."

See the fmall ftream that pours its murm'ring tide
  O'er fome rough rock that wou'd its wealth difplay,
Difplays it aught but penury and pride?
  Ah! conftrue wifely what fuch murmurs fay.

How wou'd fome flood, with ampler treafures bleft,
  Difdainful view the fcantling drops diftil!
How muft † Velino fhake his reedy creft!
  How ev'ry cygnet mock the boaftive rill!

Fortune, I yield! and fee, I give the fign;
  At noon the poor mechanic wanders home;
Collects the fquare, the level, and the line,
  And, with retorted eye, forfakes the dome.

Yes, I can patient view the fhadelefs plains;
  Can unrepining leave the rifing wall:
Check the fond love of art that fir'd my veins,
  And my warm hopes, in full purfuit, recall.

D 2

Defcend,

---

† A river in Italy, that falls an hundred yards perpendicular.

Defcend, ye ftorms! deftroy my rifing pile;
   Loos'd be the whirlwind's unremitting fway;
Contented I, altho' the gazer fmile
    To fee it fcarce furvive a winter's day.

Let fome dull dotard bafk in thy gay fhrine,
   As in the fun regales his wanton herd;
Guiltlefs of envy, why fhou'd I repine,
    That his rude voice, his grating reed's prefer'd?

Let him exult, with boundlefs wealth fupply'd,
   Mine and the fwain's reluctant homage fhare;
But ah! his tawdry fhepherdefs's pride,
    Gods! muft my DELIA, muft my DELIA bear?

Muft DELIA's foftnefs, elegance, and eafe
   Submit to MARIAN's drefs? to MARIAN's gold?
Muft MARIAN's robe from diftant INDIA pleafe?
    The fimple fleece my DELIA's limbs enfold?

" Yet fure on DELIA feems the ruffet fair;
   " Ye glitt'ring daughters of difguife, adieu!"
So talk the wife, who judge of fhape and air,
    But will the rural thane decide fo true?

Ah! what is native worth efteem'd of clowns?
   'Tis thy falfe glare, O fortune! thine they fee:
'Tis for my DELIA's fake I dread thy frowns,
    And my laft gafp fhall curfes breathe on thee.

ELEGY

ELEGY XI.

He complains how foon the pleafing novelty
of life is over.   To Mr. J————.

AH me, my friend ! it will not, will not laft !
　　This fairy fcene, that cheats our youthful eyes !
The charm diffolves ; th' aerial mufic's paft ;
　　The banquet ceafes, and the vifion flies.

Where are the fplendid forms, the rich perfumes,
　　Where the gay tapers, where the fpacious dome ?
Vanifh'd the coftly pearls, the crimfon plumes,
　　And we, delightlefs, left to wander home !

Vain now are books, the fage's wifdom vain !
　　What has the world to bribe our fteps aftray ?
Ere reafon learns by ftudy'd laws to reign,
　　The weaken'd paffions, felf-fubdued, obey.

Scarce has the fun fev'n annual courfes roll'd,
　　Scarce fhewn the whole that fortune can fupply ;
Since, not the mifer fo carefs'd his gold,
　　As I, for what it gave, was heard to figh.

On the world's ftage I wifh'd fome fprightly part ;
　　To deck my native fleece with tawdry lace !
'Twas life, 'twas tafte, and—oh my foolifh heart !
　　Subftantial joy was fix'd in pow'r and place.

And

And you, ye works of art! allur'd mine eye,
  The breathing picture, and the living stone :
" Tho', gold, tho' splendour, heav'n and fate deny,
  " Yet might I call one Titian stroke my own !"

Smit with the charms of fame, whose lovely spoil,
  : The wreath, the garland, fire the poet's pride,
I trim'd my lamp, consum'd the midnight oil—
  But soon the paths of health and fame divide !

Oft too I pray'd, 'twas nature form'd the pray'r,
  To grace my native scenes, my rural home ;
To see my trees express their planter's care,
  And gay, on Attic models, raise my dome.

But now 'tis o'er, the dear delusion's o'er !
  A stagnant breezeless air becalms my soul :
A fond aspiring candidate no more,
  I scorn the palm, before I reach the goal.

O youth ! enchanting stage, profusely blest !
  Bliss ev'n obtrusive courts the frolic mind ;
Of health neglectful, yet by health carest ;
  Careless of favour, yet secure to find.

Then glows the breast, as op'ning roses fair ;
  More free, more vivid than the linnet's wing ;
Honest as light, transparent ev'n as air,
  Tender as buds, and lavish as the spring.

Not

Not all the force of manhood's active might,
  Not all the craft to subtle age assign'd,
Not science shall extort that dear delight,
  Which gay delusion gave the tender mind.

Adieu soft raptures! transports void of care!
  Parent of raptures, dear deceit, adieu!
And you, her daughters, pining with despair,
  Why, why so soon her fleeting steps pursue!

Tedious again to curse the drizling day!
  Again to trace the wint'ry tracts of snow!
Or, sooth'd by vernal airs, again survey
  The self-same hawthorns bud, and cowslips blow!

O life! how soon of ev'ry bliss forlorn!
  We start false joys, and urge the devious race:
A tender prey; that cheers our youthful morn,
  Then sinks untimely, and defrauds the chace.

<hr>

ELEGY XII.

His recantation.

NO more the muse obtrudes her thin difguise!
  No more with awkward fallacy complains,
How ev'ry fervour from my bosom flies,
  And reafon in her lonesome palace reigns.

Ere

Ere the chill winter of our days arrive,
    No more fhe paints the breaft from paffion free ;
I feel, I feel one loitering wifh furvive—
    Ah need I, FLORIO, name that wifh to thee ?

The ftar of VENUS ufhers in the day,
    The firft, the lovelieft of the train that fhine !
The ftar of VENUS lends her brighteft ray,
    When other ftars their friendly beams refign.

Still in my breaft one foft defire remains,
    Pure as that ftar, from guilt, from int'reft free ;
Has gentle DELIA trip'd acrofs the plains,
    And need I, FLORIO, name that wifh to thee ?

While, cloy'd to find the fcenes of life the fame,
    I tune with carelefs hand my languid lays ;
Some fecret impulfe wakes my former flame,
    And fires my ftrain with hopes of brighter days.

I flept not long beneath yon rural bow'rs ;
    And lo ! my crook with flow'rs adorn'd I fee :
Has gentle DELIA bound my crook with flow'rs,
    And need I, FLORIO, name my hopes to thee ?

ELEGY

ELEGY XIII.

To a friend, on some slight occasion estranged
from him.

HEALTH to my friend, and many a chearful day
 Around his seat may peaceful shades abide !
Smooth flow the minutes, fraught with smiles, away;
 And, till they crown our union, gently glide !

Ah me ! too swiftly fleets our vernal bloom !
 Lost to our wonted friendship, lost to joy !
Soon may thy breast the cordial wish resume,
 Ere wintry doubt its tender warmth destroy !

Say, were it ours, by fortune's wild command,
 By chance to meet beneath the torrid zone ;
Would'st thou reject thy DAMON's plighted hand ?
 Would'st thou with scorn thy once lov'd friend disown

Life is that stranger land, that alien clime :
 Shall kindred souls forego their social claim ?
Launch'd in the vast abyss of space and time,
 Shall dark suspicion quench the gen'rous flame ?

Myriads of souls, that knew one parent mold,
 See sadly sever'd by the laws of chance !
Myriads, in time's perennial list enroll'd,
 Forbid by fate to change one transient glance !

But

But we have met—where ills of every form,
    Where paſſions rage, and hurricanes deſcend :
Say, ſhall we nurſe the rage, aſſiſt the ſtorm ?
    And guide them to the boſom—of a friend !

Yes, we have met—thro' rapine, fraud, and wrong :
    Might our joint aid the paths of peace explore !
Why leave thy friend amid the boiſt'rous throng,
    Ere death divide us, and we part no more ?

For oh ! pale ſickneſs warns thy friend away ;
    For me no more the vernal roſes bloom !
I ſee ſtern Fate his ebon wand diſplay ;
    And point the wither'd regions of the tomb.

Then the keen anguiſh from thine eye ſhall ſtart,
    Sad as thou follow'ſt my untimely bier ;
" Fool that I was—if friends ſo ſoon muſt part,
    " To let ſuſpicion intermix a fear."

ELEGY

ELEGY XIV.

Declining an invitation to vifit foreign countries, he takes occafion to intimate the advantages of his own.

To Lord TEMPLE.

WHILE others loft to friendfhip, loft to love,
    Wafte their beft minutes on a foreign ftrand,
Be mine, with Britifh nymph or fwain to rove,
    And court the genius of my native land.

Deluded youth ! that quits thefe verdant plains,
    To catch the follies of an alien foil !
To win the vice his genuine foul difdains,
    Return exultant, and import the fpoil !

In vain he boafts of his detefted prize ;
    No more it blooms to Britifh climes convey'd,
Cramp'd by the impulfe of ungenial fkies,
    See its frefh vigour, in a moment, fade !

Th' exotic folly knows its native clime ;
    An awkward ftranger, if we waft it o'er ;
Why then thefe toils, this coftly wafte of time,
    To fpread foft poifon on our happy fhore ?

I covet

I covet not the pride of foreign looms ;
   In search of foreign modes I scorn to rove
Nor, for the worthless bird of brighter plumes,
   Wou'd change the meanest warbler of my grove.

No distant clime shall servile airs impart,
   Or form these limbs with pliant ease to play;
Trembling I view the GAUL's illusive art,
   That steals my lov'd rusticity away.

'Tis long since freedom fled th' Hesperian clime ;
   Her citron groves, her flow'r-embroider'd shore ;
She saw the British oak aspire sublime,
   And soft CAMPANIA's olive charms no more.

Let partial suns mature the western mine,
   To shed its lustre o'er th' Iberian maid ;
Mien, beauty, shape, O native soil, are thine ;
   Thy peerless daughters ask no foreign aid.

Let * CEYLON's envy'd plant perfume the seas,
   'Till torn to season the Batavian bowl ;
Ours is the breast whose genuine ardours please,
   Nor need a drug to meliorate the soul.

Let the proud Soldan wound th' Arcadian groves,
   Or with rude lips th' Aonian fount profane ;
The muse no more by flow'ry LADON roves,
   She seeks her THOMSON, on the British plain.

Tell

* The cinnamon.

'Tell not of realms by ruthlefs war difmay'd;
   Ah! haplefs realms that war's opprcffioh feel!
In vain may AUSTRIA boaft her Noric blade,
   If AuŝTRIA bleed beneath her boafted fteel.

Beneath her palm IDUME vents her moan;
   Raptur'd fhe once beheld its friendly fhade!
And hoary MEMPHIS boafts her tombs alone,
   The mournful types of mighty pow'r decay'd!

No crefcent here difplays its baneful horns;
   No turban'd hoft the voice of truth reproves;
Learning's free fource the fage's breaft adorns,
   And poets, not inglorious, chaunt their loves.

Boaft, favour'd MEDIA, boaft thy flow'ry ftores;
   Thy thoufand hues by chymic funs refin'd;
'Tis not the drefs or mien my foul adores,
   'Tis the rich beauties of BRITANNIA's mind.

While * GREENVILLE's breaft cou'd virtue's ftores afford,
   What envy'd flota bore fo fair a freight?
The mine compar'd in vain its latent hoard,
   The gem its luftre, and the gold its weight.

Thee, GREENVILLE, thee with calmeft courage fraught,
   Thee the lov'd image of thy native fhore!
Thee by the Virtues arm'd, the Graces taught,
   When fhall we ceafe to boaft, or to deplore?

                          Pre-

* Written about the time of captain GREENVILLE's death.

Prefumptuous war, which could thy life deftroy,
  What fhall it now in recompence decree ?
While friends that merit every earthly joy,
  Feel every anguifh ; feel—the lofs of thee !

Bid me no more a fervile realm compare,
  No more the mufe of partial praife arraign ;
BRITANNIA fees no foreign breaft fo fair,
  And if fhe glory, glories not in vain.

+++

ELEGY XV.

In memory of a * private family in WORCESTERSHIRE.

FROM a lone tow'r with rev'rend ivy crown'd,
    The pealing bell awak'd a tender figh ;
Still, as the village caught the waving found,
  A fwelling tear diftream'd from ev'ry eye.

So droop'd, I ween, each BRITON's breaft of old,
  When the dull curfew fpoke their freedom fled ;
For fighing as the mournful accent roll'd,
  Our hope, they cry'd, our kind fupport, is dead !

'Twas

* The Penns of HARBOROUGH ; a place whofe name in the SAXON language, alludes to an army. And there is a tradition that there was a battle fought, on the Downs adjoining, betwixt the BRITONS and the ROMANS.

'Twas good PALEMON—near a fhaded pool,
  A group of ancient elms umbrageous rofe;
'The flocking rooks, by inftinct's native rule,
  This peaceful fcene, for their asylum, chofe.

A few fmall fpires, to Gothic fancy fair,
  Amid the fhades emerging ftruck the view;
'Twas here his youth refpir'd its earlieft air;
  'Twas here his age breath'd out its laft adieu.

One favour'd fon engag'd his tendereft care;
  One pious youth his whole affection crown'd:
In his young breaft the virtues fprung fo fair,
  Such charms difplay'd, fuch fweets diffus'd around.

But whilft gay tranfport in his face appears,
  A noxious vapour clogs the poifon'd fky;
Blafts the fair crop—the fire is drown'd in tears,
  And, fcarce furviving, fees his CYNTHIO die!

O'er the pale corfe we faw him gently bend;
  Heart-chill'd with grief—" My thread, he cry'd, is fpun!
If Heav'n had meant I fhou'd my life extend,
  Heav'n had preferv'd my life's fupport, my fon.

Snatch'd in thy prime! alas the ftroke were mild,
  Had my frail form obey'd the fates' decree!
Bleft were my lot, O CYNTHIO! O my child!
  Had Heav'n fo pleas'd, and I had dy'd for thee."

Five

Five fleeplefs nights he ftem'd this tide of woes;
Five irkfome funs he faw, thro' tears, forlorn!
On his pale corfe the fixth fad morning rofe;
From yonder dome the mournful bier was borne.

'Twas on thofe * downs, by Roman hofts annoy'd,
Fought our bold fathers; ruftic, unrefin'd!
Freedom's plain fons, in martial cares employ'd!
They ting'd their bodies, but unmafk'd their mind.

'Twas there, in happier times, this virtuous race,
Of milder merit, fix'd their calm retreat;
War's deadly crimfon had forfook the place,
And freedom fondly lov'd the chofen feat.

No wild ambition fir'd their tranquil breaft,
To fwell with empty founds a fpotlefs name;
If foft'ring fkies, the fun, the fhow'r were bleft,
Their bounty fpread; their field's extent the fame.

Thofe fields, profufe of raiment, food, and fire,
They fcorn'd to leffen, carelefs to extend;
Bade luxury, to lavifh courts afpire,
And avarice, to city-breafts defcend.

None, to a virgin's mind, prefer'd her dow'r;
To fire with vicious hopes a modeft heir:
The fire, in place of titles, wealth, or pow'r,
Affign'd him virtue; and his lot was fair.

They

* HARBOROUGH Downs.

They ſpoke of fortune, as ſome doubtful dame,
　　That ſway'd the natives of a diſtant ſphere;
From lucre's vagrant ſons had learnt her fame,
　　But never wiſh'd to place her banners here.

Here youth's free ſpirit, innocently gay,
　　Enjoy'd the moſt that innocence can give;
Thoſe wholeſome ſweets that border virtue's way;
　　Thoſe cooling fruits, that we may taſte and live.

Their board no ſtrange ambiguous viand bore;
　　From their own ſtreams their choicer fare they drew,
To lure the ſcaly glutton to the ſhore,
　　The ſole deceit their artleſs boſom knew!

Sincere themſelves, ah too ſecure to find
　　The common boſom, like their own, ſincere!
'Tis its own guilt alarms the jealous mind;
　　'Tis her own poiſon bids the viper fear.

Sketch'd on the lattice of the adjacent fane,
　　Their ſuppliant buſts implore the reader's pray'r:
Ah gentle ſouls! enjoy your bliſsful reign,
　　And let frail mortals claim your guardian care.

For ſure, to bliſsful realms the ſouls are flown,
　　That never flatter'd, injur'd, cenſur'd, ſtrove;
The friends of ſcience! muſic all their own;
　　Muſic, the voice of virtue and of love!

The journeying peasant, thro' the secret shade,
  Heard their soft lyres engage his list'ning ear;
And haply deem'd some courteous angel play'd;
  No angel play'd—but might with transport hear.

For these the sounds that chase unholy strife!
  Solve envy's charm, ambition's wretch release!
Raise him to spurn the radiant ills of life:
  To pity pomp, to be content with peace.

Farewel, pure spirits! vain the praise we give,
  The praise you sought from lips angelic flows;
Farewel! the virtues which deserve to live,
  Deserve an ampler bliss than life bestows.

Last of his race, PALEMON, now no more
  The modest merit of his line display'd;
Then pious HOUGH VIGORNIA's mitre wore—
  Soft sleep the dust of each deserving shade.

+++

E L E G Y XVI.

He suggests the advantages of birth to a per-
son of merit, and the folly of a superci-
liousness that is built upon that sole foundation.

WHEN genius grac'd with lineal splendor glows,
  When title shines with ambient virtues crown'd,
Like some fair almond's flow'ry pomp it shews;
  The pride, the perfume of the regions round.

Then

Then learn, ye fair! to soften splendor's ray;
  Endure the swain, the youth of low degree;
Let meekness join'd its temperate beam display:
  'Tis the mild verdure that endears the tree.

Pity the sandal'd swain, the shepherd's boy;
  He sighs to brighten a neglected name;
Foe to the dull appulse of vulgar joy,
  He mourns his lot; he wishes, merits fame.

In vain to groves and pathless vales we fly;
  Ambition there the bow'ry haunt invades;
Fame's awful rays fatigue the courtier's eye,
  But gleam still lovely thro' the chequer'd shades.

Vainly, to guard from love's unequal chain,
  Has fortune rear'd us in the rural grove;
Should ****'s eyes illume the desart plain,
  Ev'n I may wonder, and ev'n I must love.

Nor unregarded sighs the lowly hind;
  Tho' you contemn, the gods respect his vows;
Vindictive rage awaits the scornful mind,
  And vengeance, too severe! the gods allow.

On SARUM's plain I met a wand'ring fair;
  The look of sorrow, lovely still she bore:
Loose flow'd the soft redundance of her hair,
  And, on her brow, a flow'ry wreath she wore.

Oft

Oft ſtooping as ſhe ſtray'd, ſhe cull'd the pride
   Of ev'ry plain ; ſhe pillag'd ev'ry grove !
The fading chaplet daily ſhe ſupply'd,
   And ſtill her hand ſome various garland wove. -

Erroneous fancy ſhap'd her wild attire ;
   From BETHLEM's walls the poor lympatic ſtray'd ;
Seem'd with her air her accent to conſpire,
   When as wild fancy taught her, thus ſhe ſaid ;

" Hear me, dear youth ! oh hear an hapleſs maid,
   Sprung from the ſcepter'd line of ancient kings !
Scorn'd by the world, I aſk thy tender aid ;
   Thy gentle voice ſhall whiſper kinder things.

The world is frantic—fly the race profane—
   Nor I, nor you, ſhall its compaſſion move ;
Come friendly let us wander, and complain,
   And tell me, ſhepherd ! haſt thou ſeen my love ?

My love is young—but other loves are young ;
   And other loves are fair, and ſo is mine ;
An air divine diſcloſes whence he ſprung ;
   He is my love, who boaſts that air divine.

No vulgar DAMON robs me of my reſt,
   IANTHE liſtens to no vulgar vow ;
A prince, from gods deſcended, fires her breaſt ;
   A brilliant crown diſtinguiſhes his brow.

What,

What, fhall I ftain the glories of my race !
   More clear, more lovely bright than Hesper's beam ?
The porc'lain pure with vulgar dirt debafe ?
   Or mix with puddle the pellucid ftream ?

See thro' thefe veins the faphire current fhine !
   'Twas Jove's own nectar gave th' etherial hue :
Can bafe plebeian forms contend with mine !
   Difplay the lovely white, or match the blue ?

The painter ftrove to trace its azure ray;
   He chang'd his colours, and in vain he ftrove;
He frown'd—I fmiling view'd the faint effay ;
   Poor youth ! he little knew it flow'd from Jove.

Pitying his toil, the wond'rous truth I told;
   How am'rous Jove trepann'd a mortal fair ;
How thro' the race the generous current roll'd,
   And mocks the poet's art, and painter's care.

Yes, from the gods, from earlieft Saturn, fprung
   Our facred race ; thro' demigods, convey'd ;
And he, ally'd to Phoebus, ever young,
   My god-like boy, muft wed their duteous maid.

Oft, when a mortal vow profanes my ear,
   My fire's dread fury murmurs thro' the fky;
And fhould I yield—his inftant rage appears,
   He darts th' uplifted vengeance—and I die.

Have

Have you not heard unwonted thunders roll?
    Have you not feen more horrid light'nings glare?
'Twas then a vulgar love enfnar'd my foul:
    'Twas then—I hardly fcap'd the fatal fnare.

'Twas then a peafant pour'd his amorous vow,
    All as I liften'd to his vulgar ftrain;—
Yet fuch his beauty—wou'd my birth allow,
    Dear were the youth, and blifsful were the plain,

But oh! I faint! why waftes my vernal bloom,
    In fruitlefs fearches ever doom'd to rove?
My nightly dreams the toilfome path refume,
    And fhall I die—before I find my love,

When laft I flept, methought, my ravifh'd eye
    On diftant heaths his radiant form furvey'd;
Tho' night's thick clouds encompafs'd all the fky,
    The gems that bound his brow, difpell'd the fhade.

O how this bofom kindled at the fight!
    Led by their beams I urg'd the pleafing chace;
'Till, on a fudden, thefe with-held their light—
    All, all things envy the fublime embrace.

But now no more—behind the diftant grove,
    Wanders my deftin'd youth, and chides my ftay:
See, fee, he grafps the fteel—forbear, my love—
    IANTHE comes; thy princefs haftes away."

                       Scornful

Scornful she spoke, and heedless of reply
  The lovely maniac bounded o'er the plain;
The piteous victim of an angry sky!
  Ah me! the victim of her proud disdain!

+++

E L E G Y XVII.

He indulges the suggestions of spleen:
an elegy to the winds.

Æole, namque tibi divum pater atque hominum rex
Et mulcere dedit mentes *et tollere vento.*

I M I T A T I O N.

O! Æolus, to thee, the Sire supreme
Of gods and men, the mighty pow'r bequeath'd
To rouse or to assuage the *human mind.*

STERN monarch of the winds, admit my pray'r!
  Awhile thy fury check, thy storms confine!
No trivial blast impels the passive air,
  But brews a tempest in a breast like mine.

What bands of black ideas spread their wings!
  The peaceful regions of content invade!
With deadly poison taint the crystal springs!
  With noisome vapour blast the verdant shade!

E 4   I know

I know their leader, SPLEEN ; and dread the fway
    Of rigid EURUS, his detefted fire ;
Thro' one my bloffoms and my fruits decay ;
    Thro' one my pleafures and my hopes expire.

Like fome pale ftripling, when his icy way
    Relenting yields beneath the noontide beam,
I ftand aghaft ; and chill'd with fear furvey
    How far I've tempted life's deceitful ftream !

Where by remorfe impell'd, repuls'd by fears,
    Shall wretched fancy a retreat explore ?
She flies the fad prefage of coming years,
    And forr'wing dwells on pleafures now no more !

Again with patrons, and with friends fhe roves ;
    But friends and patrons never to return !
She fees the nymphs, the graces, and the loves,
    But fees them, weeping o'er LUCINDA's urn.

She vifits, ISIS ! thy forfaken ftream,
    Oh ill forfaken for Bœotian air !
She deems no flood reflects fo bright a beam,
    No reed fo verdant, and no flow'rs fo fair.

She deems beneath thy facred fhades were peace,
    Thy bays might ev'n the civil ftorm repel ;
Reviews thy focial blifs, thy learned eafe,
    And with no chearful accent cries, farewel !

                        Farewel,

Farewel, with whom to thefe retreats I ſtray'd !
   By youthful ſports, by youthful toils ally'd !
Joyous we ſojourn'd in thy circling ſhade,
   And wept to find the paths of life divide.

She paints the progreſs of my rival's vow ;
   Sees ev'ry muſe a partial ear incline ;
Binds with luxuriant bays his favour'd brow,
   Nor yields the refuſe of his wreath to mine.

She bids the flatt'ring mirror, form'd to pleaſe,
   Now blaſt my hope, now vindicate deſpair ;
Bids my fond verſe the love-ſick parley ceaſe ;
   Accuſe my rigid fate, acquit my fair.

Where circling rocks defend ſome pathleſs vale,
   Superfluous mortal, let me ever roye !
Alas ! there echo will repeat the tale——
   Where ſhall I find the ſilent ſcenes I love ?

Fain would I mourn my luckleſs fate alone ;
   Forbid to pleaſe, yet fated to admire ;
Away, my friends ! my ſorrows are my own !
   Why ſhould I breathe around my ſick deſire ?

Bear me, ye winds, indulgent to my pains,
   Near ſome ſad ruin's ghaſtly ſhade to dwell !
There let me fondly eye the rude remains,
   And from the mould'ring refuſe, build my cell !

Genius

Genius of ROME! thy proſtrate pomp diſplay!
  Trace ev'ry diſmal proof of fortune's pow'r;
Let me the wreck of theatres ſurvey,
  Or penſive ſit beneath ſome nodding tow'r.

Or where ſome duſt, by rolling ſeaſons worn,
  Convey'd pure ſtreams to ROME's imperial wall,
Near the wide breach in ſilence let me mourn;
  Or tune my dirges to the water's fall.

Genius of CARTHAGE! paint thy ruin'd pride;
  Tow'rs, arches, fanes in wild confuſion ſtrewn;
Let baniſh'd * MARIUS, low'ring by thy ſide,
  Compare thy fickle fortunes with his own.

Ah no! thou monarch of the ſtorms! forbear;
  My trembling nerves abhor thy rude controul;
And ſcarce a pleaſing twilight ſoothes my care,
  Ere one vaſt death-like darkneſs ſhocks my ſoul.

Forbear

:

* *Incepemque vitam in tugurio ruinarum Carthaginenſium toleravit, cum Marius inſpiciens Carthaginem, illa intuens Marium, alter alteri poſſent eſſe ſolatio.*   LIV.

EXPLANATION.

Marius endured a life of poverty, under ſhelter of the Carthaginian ruins; and while he contemplated Carthage, and Carthage beheld him, they might be ſaid mutually to reſemble and account for each other.

Forbear thy rage—on no perennial base
　Is built frail fear, or hope's deceitful pile;
My pains are fled—my joy resumes its place,
　Shou'd the sky brighten, or MELISSA smile.

+++

E L E G Y   XVIII.

He repeats the song of COLLIN, a discerning
　shepherd; lamenting the state of the wool-
　len manufactory.

Ergo omni studio glaciem ventosque nivales,
Quo minus est illis curæ mortalis egestas,
Avertes: victumque feres.　　　VIRGIL.

IMITATION.

Thou therefore, in proportion to their lack
Of human aid, with all thy care defend
From frozen seasons, and inclement blasts,
And give them timely food.

NEAR AVON's bank, on ARDEN's flow'ry plain,
　　A * tuneful shepherd charm'd the list'ning wave;
And sunny COTSOL' fondly lov'd the strain;
　Yet not a garland crowns the shepherd's grave!
　　　　　　　　　　　　　　　　Oh

* Mr. SOMERVILLE.

Oh loſt OPHELIA ! ſmoothly flow'd the day,
   To feel his muſic with my flames agree !
To taſte the beauties of his melting lay,
   To taſte, and fancy it was dear to thee.

When, for his tomb, with each revolving year,
   I ſteal the muſk-roſe from the ſcented brake,
I ſtrew my cowſlips, and I pay my tear,
   I'll add the myrtle for OPHELIA's ſake.

Shiv'ring beneath a leafleſs thorn he lay,
   When death's chill rigour ſeiz'd his flowing tongue;
The more I found his fault'ring notes decay,
   The more prophetic truth ſublim'd the ſong.

" Adieu my flocks, he ſaid ! my wonted care,
   By ſunny mountain, or by verdant ſhore !
May ſome more happy hand your fold prepare,
   And may you need your COLLIN's crook no more,

And you, ye ſhepherds ! lead my gentle ſheep;
   To breezy hills, or leafy ſhelters lead ;
But if the ſky with ſhow'rs inceſſant weep,
   Avoid the putrid moiſture of the mead,

Where the wild thyme perfumes the purpled heath,
   Long loit'ring there your fleecy tribes extend——
But what avail the maxims I bequeath ?
   The fruitleſs gift of an officious friend !

                             Ah !

Ah ! what avails the tim'rous lambs to guard,
  Tho' nightly cares, with daily labours, join ?
If foreign floth obtain the rich reward,
  If GALLIA's craft the pond'rous fleece purloin !

Was it for this, by conftant vigils worn,
  I met the terrors of an early grave ?
For this, I led them from the pointed thorn ?
  For this, I bath'd 'em in the lucid wave ?

Ah heedlefs ALBION ! too benignly prone
  Thy blood to lavifh, and thy wealth refign !
Shall ev'ry other virtue grace thy throne,
  But quick-ey'd prudence never yet be thine ?

From the fair natives of this peerlefs hill
  Thou gav'ft the fheep that browze Iberian plains :
Their plaintive cries the faithlefs region fill,
  Their fleece adorns an haughty foe's domains.

Ill-fated flocks ! from cliff to cliff they ftray ;
  Far from their dams, their native guardians, far !
Where the foft fhepherd, all the livelong day,
  Chaunts his proud miftrefs to his hoarfe guittar.

But ALBION's youth her native fleece defpife ;
  Unmov'd they hear the pining fhepherd's moan ;
In filky folds each nervous limb difguife,
  Allur'd by ev'ry treafure, but their own.

Oft

Oft have I hurry'd down the rocky steep,
　　Anxious, to see the wintry tempest drive;
Preserve, said I, preserve your fleece, my sheep!
　　Ere long will PHILLIS, will my love arrive.

Ere long she came: ah! woe is me, she came!
　　Rob'd in the Gallic loom's extraneous twine:
For gifts like these they give their spotless fame,
　　Resign their bloom, their innocence resign.

Will no bright maid, by worth, by titles known,
　　Give the rich growth of British hills to fame?
And let her charms, and her example, own
　　That virtue's dress, and beauty's are the same?

Will no fam'd chief support this gen'rous maid?
　　Once more the patriot's arduous path resume?
And, comely from his native plains array'd,
　　Speak future glory to the British loom?

What pow'r unseen my ravish'd fancy fires?
　　I pierce the dreary shade of future days;
Sure 'tis the genius of the land inspires,
　　To breathe my latest breath in * * * praise.

O might my breath for * * * praise suffice,
　　How gently shou'd my dying limbs repose!
O might his future glory bless mine eyes,
　　My ravish'd eyes! how calmly would they close!

* * * was

* * * was born to fpread the gen'ral joy;
   By virtue rapt, by party uncontroul'd,
BRITONS for BRITAIN fhall the crook employ;
   BRITONS for BRITAIN's glory fhear the fold."

ELEGY XIX.

Written in fpring 1743.

AGAIN the lab'ring hind inverts the foil;
   Again the merchant ploughs the tumid wave;
Another fpring renews the foldier's toil,
   And finds me vacant in the rural cave.

As the foft lyre difplay'd my wonted loves,
   The penfive pleafure and the tender pain,
The fordid ALPHEUS hurry'd thro' my groves;
   Yet ftop'd to vent the dictates of difdain.

He glanc'd contemptuous o'er my ruin'd fold;
   He blam'd the graces of my fav'rite bow'r;
My breaft, unfully'd by the luft of gold;
   My time unlavifh'd in purfuit of pow'r.

Yes, ALPHEUS! fly the purer paths of fate;
   Abjure thefe fcenes from venal paffions free;
Know, in this grove, I vow'd perpetual hate,
   War, endlefs war, with lucre and with thee.

                  Here

Here nobly zealous, in my youthful hours,
    I dreſt an altar to THALIA's name :
Here, as I crown'd the verdant ſhrine with flow'rs,
    Sóft on my labours ſtole the ſmiling dame.

DAMON, ſhe cry'd, if pleas'd with honeſt praiſe,
    Thou court ſucceſs by virtue or by ſong,
Fly the falſe dictates of the venal race ;
    Fly the groſs accents of the venal tongue.

Swear that no lucre ſhall thy zeal betray ;
    · Swerve not thy foot with fortune's vot'ries more ;
Brand thou their lives, and brand their lifeleſs day——
    The winning phantom urg'd me, and I ſwore.

Forth from the ruſtic altar ſwift I ſtray'd,
    " Aid my firm purpoſe, ye celeſtial pow'rs !
Aid me to quell the ſordid breaſt," I ſaid ;
    And * threw my jav'lin tow'rds their hoſtile tow'rs.

Think not regretful I ſurvey the deed ;
    Or added years no more the zeal allow ;
Still, ſtill obſervant to the grove I ſpeed,
    The ſhrine embelliſh, and repeat the vow.

Sworn from his cradle ROME's relentleſs foe,
    Such gen'rous hate the † Punic champion bore ;
Thy lake, O THRASIMENE ! beheld it glow,
    And CANNÆ's walls, and TREBIA's crimſon ſhore.

                               But

* The Roman ceremony in declaring war.   † HANNIBAL.

But let grave annals paint the warrior's fame;
 Fair shine his arms in history enroll'd;
Whilst humbler lyres his civil worth proclaim,
 His nobler hate of avarice and gold.—

Now Punic pride its final eve survey'd;
 Its hosts exhausted, and its fleets on fire;
Patient the victors' lurid frown obey'd,
 And saw th' unwilling elephants retire.

But when their gold deprefs'd the yielding scale,
 Their gold in pyramidic plenty pil'd,
He saw th' unutterable grief prevail;
 He saw their tears, and, in his fury, smil'd.

Think not, he cry'd, ye view the smiles of ease,
 Or this firm breast disclaims a patriot's pain;
I smile, but from a soul estrang'd to peace,
 Frantic with grief, delirious with disdain!

But were it cordial, this detested smile,
 Seems it less timely than the grief ye show?
O sons of CARTHAGE! grant me to revile
 The sordid source of your indecent woe!

Why weep ye now! ye saw with tearless eye
 When your fleet perish'd on the Punic wave;
Where lurk'd the coward tear, the lazy sigh,
 When TYRE's imperial state commenc'd a slave?

'Tis paſt—O CARTHAGE! vanquiſh'd! honour'd ſhade!
　Go, the mean ſorrows of thy ſons deplore;
Had freedom ſhar'd the vow to fortune paid,
　She ne'er, like fortune, had forſook thy ſhore."

He ceas'd—abaſh'd the conſcious audience hear;
　Their pallid cheeks a crimſon bluſh unfold;
Yet o'er that virtuous bluſh diſtreams a tear,
　And falling moiſtens their abandon'd gold. *

✦✦✦✦✦✦✦✦✦✦✦✦✦✦✦✦✦✦✦✦✦✦✦✦✦✦✦✦✦✦

ELEGY XX.

He compares his humble fortune with the diſ-
treſs of others; and his ſubjection to DELIA,
with the miſerable ſervitude of an *African*
ſlave.

WHY droops this heart with fancy'd woes forlorn?
　Why ſinks my ſoul beneath each wint'ry ſky?
What penſive crowds, by ceaſeleſs labours worn,
　What myriads, wiſh to be as bleſt as I!

　　　　　　　　　　　　　　　　What

* By the terms forced upon the CARTHAGINIANS by SCIPIO,
they were to deliver up all the elephants, and to pay near two
millions ſterling.

What tho' my roofs devoid of pomp arife,
  Nor tempt the proud to quit his deftin'd way?
Nor coftly art my flow'ry dales difguife,
  Where only fimple friendfhip deigns to ftray?

See the wild fons of LAPLAND's chill domain,
  That fcoop their couch beneath the drifted fnows!
How void of hope they ken the frozen plain,
  Where the fharp eaft for ever, ever blows!

Slave tho' I be, to DELIA's eyes a flave,
  My DELIA's eyes endear the bands I wear;
The figh fhe caufes well becomes the brave,
  The pang fhe caufes, 'tis ev'n blifs to bear.

See the poor native quit the Lybian fhores,
  Ah! not in love's delightful fetters bound!
No radiant fmile his dying peace reftores,
  Nor love, nor fame, nor friendfhip heals his wound.

Let vacant bards difplay their boafted woes,
  Shall I the mockery of grief difplay?
No, let the mufe his piercing pangs difclofe,
  Who bleeds and weeps his fum of life away!

On the wild beach in mournful guife he ftood,
  Ere the fhrill boatfwain gave the hated fign;
He dropt a tear unfeen into the flood;
  He ftole one fecret moment, to repine.

F 2

Yet

Yet the mufe liften'd to the plaints he made;
  Such moving plaints as nature could infpire;
To me the mufe his tender plea convey'd,
  But fmooth'd and fuited to the founding lyre.

" Why am I ravifh'd from my native ftrand?
  What favage race protects this impious gain?
Shall foreign plagues infeft this teeming land,
  And more than fea-born monfters plough the main?

Here the dire locufts horrid fwarms prevail;
  Here the blue afps with livid poifon fwell;
Here the dry dipfa writhes his finuous mail;
  Can we not here, fecure from envy, dwell?

When the grim lion urg'd his cruel chace,
  When the ftern panther fought his midnight prey,
What fate referv'd me for this * chriftian race?
  O race more polifh'd, more fevere than they!

Ye prouling wolves, purfue my lateft cries!
  Thou hungry tyger, leave thy reeking den!
Ye fandy waftes, in rapid eddies rife!
  O tear me from the whips and fcorns of men!

Yet in their face fuperior beauty glows;
  Are fmiles the mien of rapine and of wrong?
Yet from their lip the voice of mercy flows,
  And ev'n religion dwells upon their tongue.

Of

* Spoke by a favage.

Of blifsful haunts they tell, and brighter climes,
    Where gentle minds convey'd by death repair;
But ftain'd with blood, and crimfon'd o'er with crimes,
- Say, fhall they merit what they paint fo fair?

No, carelefs, hopelefs of thofe fertile plains,
    Rich by our toils, and by our forrows gay,
They ply our labours, and enhance our pains,
    And feign thefe diftant regions to repay.

For them our tufky elephant expires;
    For them we drain the mine's embowel'd gold;
Where rove the brutal nations' wild defires?—
    Our limbs are purchas'd, and our life is fold!

Yet fhores there are, bleft fhores for us remain,
    And favour'd ifles with golden fruitage crown'd,
Where tufted flow'rets paint the verdant plain,
    Where ev'ry breeze fhall med'cine ev'ry wound.

There the ftern tyrant that embitters life,
    Shall, vainly fuppliant, fpread his afking hand;
There fhall we view the billows' raging ftrife,
    Aid the kind breaft, and waft his boat to land,".

ELEGY

ELEGY XXI.

Taking a view of the country from his retirement, he is led to meditate on the character of the ancient BRITONS. Written
at the time of a rumoured tax upon
luxury, 1746.

THUS DAMON sung—What tho' unknown to praise
  Umbrageous coverts hide my muse and me;
Or 'mid the rural shepherds, flow my days,
  Amid the rural shepherds, I am free.

To view sleek vassals crowd a stately hall,
  Say, should I grow myself a solemn slave?
To find thy tints, O TITIAN! grace my wall,
  Forego the flow'ry fields my fortune gave?

Lord of my time, my devious path I bend,
  Thro' fringy woodland, or smooth-shaven lawn;
Or pensile grove, or airy cliff ascend,
  And hail the scene by nature's pencil drawn.

Thanks be to fate—tho' nor the racy vine,
  Nor fatt'ning olive cloath the fields I rove,
Sequester'd shades, and gurgling founts are mine,
  And ev'ry silvan grott the muses love.

Here

Here if my vista point the mould'ring pile,
    Where hood and cowl devotion's aspect wore,
I trace the tott'ring reliques with a smile,
    To think the mental bondage is no more!

Pleas'd, if the glowing landscape wave with corn;
    Or the tall oaks, my country's bulwark, rise;
Pleas'd if mine eye, o'er thousand vallies borne,
    Discern the Cambrian hills support the skies.

And see PLINLIMMON ! ev'n the youthful sight
    Scales the proud hill's etherial cliffs with pain !
Such, CAER-CARADOC ! thy stupendous height,
    Whose ample shade obscures th' Iernian main.

Bleak, joyless regions ! where, by science fir'd,
    Some prying sage his lonely step may bend;
There, by the love of novel plants inspir'd,
    Inviduous view the clamb'ring goats ascend.

Yet for those mountains, clad with lasting snow,
    The freeborn BRITON left his greenest mead;
Receding sullen from his mightier foe,
    For here he saw fair liberty recede.

Then if a chief perform'd a patriot's part,
    Sustain'd her drooping sons, repell'd her foes,
Above or Persian luxe, or Attic art,
    The rude majestic monument arose.

F 4   · Progressive

Progreffive ages carol'd forth his fame;
  Sires, to his praife, attun'd their children's tongue;
The hoary druid fed the gen'rous flame,
  While, in fuch ftrains, the rev'rend wizard fung.

" Go forth, my fons !—for what is vital breath,
  Your gods expell'd, your liberty refign'd?
Go forth, my fons !—for what is inftant death
  To fouls fecure perennial joys to find?

For fcenes there are, unknown to war or pain,
  Where drops the balm that heals a tyrant's wound;
Where patriots, bleft with boundlefs freedom, reign,
  With mifletoe's myfterious garlands crown'd.

Such are the names that grace your myftic fongs;
  Your folemn woods refound their martial fire;
To you, my fons, the ritual meed belongs,
  If in the caufe you vanquifh, or expire.

Hark! from the facred oak that crowns the groves,
  What aweful voice my raptur'd bofom warms;
This is the favour'd moment heav'n approves,
  Sound the fhrill trump; this inftant, found, to arms."

Theirs was the fcience of a martial race,
  To fhape the lance, or decorate the fhield;
Ev'n the fair virgin ftain'd her native grace,
  To give new horrors to the tented field.

Now,

Now, for some cheek where guilty blushes glow,
   For some false FLORIMEL's impure disguise,
The lifted youth, nor war's loud signal know,
   Nor virtue's call, nor fame's imperial prize.

. Then if soft concord lull'd their fears to sleep,
   Inert and silent slept the manly car;
But rush'd horrific o'er the fearful steep,
   If freedom's aweful clarion breath'd to war.

Now the sleek courtier, indolent and vain,
   Thron'd in the splendid carriage glides supine;
To taint his virtue with a foreign strain,
   Or at a fav'rite's board, his faith resign.

Leave then, O luxury! this happy soil!
   Chase her, BRITANNIA, to some hostile shore!
Or * fleece the baneful pest with annual spoil,
   And let thy virtuous offspring weep no more!

E L E G Y XXII.

Written in the year —— when the rights of
sepulture were so frequently violated.

SAY, gentle Sleep, that lov'st the gloom of night,
   Parent of dreams! thou great magician, say,
Whence my late vision thus endures the light;
   Thus haunts my fancy thro' the glare of day.

The

* Alludes to a tax upon Luxury, then in debate.

The silent moon had scal'd the vaulted skies,
 And anxious care resign'd my limbs to rest;
A sudden lustre struck my wond'ring eyes,
 And SILVIA stood before my couch confest.

Ah! not the nymph so blooming and so gay,
 That led the dance beneath the festive shade!
But she that, in the morning of her day,
 Intomb'd beneath the grass-green sod was laid.

No more her eyes their wonted radiance cast;
 No more her breast inspir'd the lover's flame;
No more her cheek the Pæstan rose surpast;
 Yet seem'd her lip's etherial smile the same.

Nor such her hair as deck'd her living face;
 Nor such her voice as charm'd the list'ning crowd;
Nor such her dress as heighten'd ev'ry grace;
 Alas! all vanish'd for the mournful shroud!

Yet seem'd her lip's etherial charm the same;
 That dear distinction every doubt remov'd;
Perish the lover, whose imperfect flame
 Forgets one feature of the nymph he lov'd.

"DAMON, she said, mine hour allotted flies;
 Oh do not waste it with a fruitless tear!
Tho' griev'd to see thy SILVIA's pale disguise,
 Suspend thy sorrow, and attentive hear.

So

So may thy mufe with virtuous fame be bleft!
 So be thy love with mutual love repaid!
So may thy bones in facred filence reft,
 Faft by the reliques of fome happier maid!

Thou know'ft, how ling'ring on a diftant fhore
 Difeafe invidious nipt my flow'ry prime;
And oh! what pangs my tender bofom tore,
 To think I ne'er muft view my native clime!

No friend was near to raife my drooping head!
 No dear companion wept to fee me die;
Lodge me within my native foil, I faid;
 There my fond parents' honour'd reliques lie.

Tho' now debarr'd of each domeftic tear,
 Unknown, forgot, I meet the fatal blow;
There many a friend fhall grace my woeful bier,
 And many a figh fhall rife, and tear fhall flow.

I fpoke, nor fate forbore his trembling fpoil;
 Some venal mourner lent his carelefs aid;
And foon they bore me to my native foil,
 Where my fond parents' dear remains were laid.

'Twas then the youths from ev'ry plain and grove,
 Adorn'd with mournful verfe thy SILVIA's bier;
'Twas then the nymphs their votive garlands wove,
 And ftrew'd the fragrance of the youthful year.

But

But why alas ! the tender scene display !
 Cou'd DAMON's foot the pious path decline ?
Ah no ! 'twas DAMON first attun'd his lay,
 And sure no sonnet was so dear as thine.

Thus was I bosom'd in the peaceful grave ;
 My placid ghost no longer wept its doom ;
When savage robbers every sanction brave,
 And with outrageous guilt defraud the tomb !

Shall my poor corse, from hostile realms convey'd,
 Lose the cheap portion of my native sands ?
Or, in my kindred's dear embraces laid,
 Mourn the vile ravage of barbarian hands ?

Say, wou'd thy breast no death-like torture feel,
 To see my limbs the felon's gripe obey ?
To see them gash'd beneath the daring steel ?
 To crowds a spectre, and to dogs a prey ?

If PÆAN's sons these horrid rites require,
 If health's fair science be by these refin'd,
Let guilty convicts, for their use, expire ;
 And let their breathless corse avail mankind.

Yet hard it seems, when guilt's last fine is paid,
 To see the victim's corse deny'd repose !
Now, more severe ! the poor offenceless maid
 Dreads the dire outrage of inhuman foes.

Where

Where is the faith of ancient pagans fled?
  Where the fond care the wand'ring manes claim?
Nature, inftinctive, cries, Protect the dead,
  And facred be their afhes, and their fame!

Arife, dear youth! ev'n now the danger calls;
  Ev'n now the villain fnuffs his wonted prey;
See! fee! I lead thee to yon' facred walls——
  Oh! fly to chafe thefe human wolves away."

++

ELEGY XXIII.

Reflections fuggefted by his fituation.

BORN near the fcene for * KENELM's fate renown'd,
  I take my plaintive reed, and range the grove,
And raife my lay, and bid the rocks refound
  The favage force of empire, and of love.

' Faſt

---

* KENELM in the Saxon heptarchy was heir to the kingdom
of MERCIA; but being very young at his father's death, was, by
the artifices of his fifter and her lover, depriv'd of his crown and
life together. The body was found in a piece of ground near
the top of Clent Hill, exactly facing Mr. SHENSTONE's houfe:
near which place a church was afterwards erected to his memory,
ftill ufed for divine worfhip, and called St. KENELM's. See
PLOT's Hiftory of Staffordfhire.

Fast by the centre of yon' various wild,
   Where spreading oaks embow'r a gothic fane;
KENDRIDA's arts a brother's youth beguil'd;
   There nature urg'd her tend'rest pleas in vain.

Soft o'er his birth, and o'er his infant hours,
   Th' ambitious maid cou'd every care employ;
Then with assiduous fondness cropt the flow'rs,
   To deck the cradle of the princely boy !

But soon the bosom's pleasing calm is flown;
   Love fires her breast; the sultry passions rise;
A favour'd lover seeks the Mercian throne,
   And views her KENELM with a rival's eyes.

How kind were fortune, ah ! how just were fate,
   Wou'd fate or fortune MERCIA's heir remove !
How sweet to revel on the couch of state !
   To crown at once her lover and her love !

See, garnish'd for the chace, the fraudful maid
   To these lone hills direct his devious way;
The youth, all prone, the sister guide obey'd,
   Ill-fated youth ! himself the destin'd prey.

But now, nor shaggy hill, nor pathless plain,
   Forms the lone refuge of the silvan game;
Since LYTTELTON has crown'd the sweet domain,
   With softer pleasures, and with fairer fame.

Where

Where the rough bowman urg'd his headlong steed,
   Immortal bards, a polish'd race, retire ;
And where hoarse scream'd the strepent horn, succeed
   The melting graces of no vulgar lyre.

See Thomson, loit'ring near some limpid well,
   For Britain's friend the verdant wreath prepare !
Or, studious of revolving seasons, tell,
   How peerless Lucia made all seasons fair !

See ****** from civic garlands fly,
   And in these groves indulge his tuneful vein !
Or from yon' summit, with a guardian's eye,
   Observe how freedom's hand attires the plain !

Here Pope !——ah never must that tow'ring mind
   To his lov'd haunts, or dearer friend, return !
What art, what friendships ! oh ! what fame resign'd !
   —In yonder glade I trace his mournful urn.

Where is the breast can rage or hate retain,
   And these glad streams and smiling lawns behold ?
Where is the breast can hear the woodland strain,
   And think fair freedom well exchang'd for gold ?

Thro' these soft shades delighted let me stray,
   While o'er my head forgotten suns descend !
Thro' these dear valleys bend my casual way,
   'Till setting life a total shade extend !

Here

Here far from courts, and void of pompous cares,
   I'll mufe how much I owe mine humbler fate:
Or fhrink to find, how much ambition dares,
   To fhine in anguifh, and to grieve in ftate !

Canft thou, O fun ! that fpotlefs throne difclofe,
   Where her bold arm has left no fanguine ftain ?
Where, fhew me whcre, the lineal fcepter glows,
   Pure, as the fimple crook that rules the plain ?

Tremendous pomp ! where hate, diftruft, and fear,
   In kindred bofoms folve the focial tie;
There not the parent's fmile is half fincere;
   Nor void of art the confort's melting eye.

There with the friendly wifh, the kindly flame,
   No face is brighten'd, and no bofoms beat;
Youth, manhood, age, avow one fordid aim,
   And ev'n the beardlefs lip effays deceit.

There coward rumours walk their murd'rous round;
   The glance, that more than rural blame inftills;
Whifpers, that ting'd with friendfhip doubly wound,
   Pity that injures, and concern that kills.

There anger whets, but love can ne'er engage;
   Careffing brothers part but to revile;
There all men fmile, and prudence warns the wife
   To dread the fatal ftroke of all that fmile.

There

There all are rivals ! fifter, fon, and fire,
   With horrid purpofe hug deftructive arms;
There foft-ey'd maids in murd'rous plots confpire,
   And fcorn the gentler mifchief of their charms.

Let fervile minds one endlefs watch endure;
   Day, night, nor hour, their anxious guard refign;
But lay me, fate ! on flow'ry banks, fecure,
   Tho' my whole foul be, like my limbs, fupine.

Yes, may my tongue difdain a vaffal's care;
   My lyre refound no proftituted lays;
More warm to merit, more elate to wear
   The cap of freedom, than the crown of bays.

Sooth'd by the murmurs of my pebbled flood,
   I wifh it not o'er golden fands to flow;
Chear'd by the verdure of my fpiral wood,
   I fcorn the quarry, where no fhrub can grow.

No midnight pangs the fhepherd's peace purfue;
   His tongue, his hand, attempts no fecret wound;
He fings his DELIA, and if fhe be true,
   His love at once, and his ambition's crown'd.

ELEGY XXIV.

He takes occafion from the fate of ELEANOR
of BRETAGNE *, to fuggeft the imperfect
pleafures of a folitary life.

WHEN beauty mourns, by fate's injurious doom,
 Hid from the chearful glance of human eye;
When nature's pride inglorious waits the tomb,
 Hard is that heart which checks the rifing figh.

Fair ELEONORA! wou'd no gallant mind
 The caufe of love, the caufe of juftice own?
Matchlefs thy charms, and was no life refign'd
 To fee them fparkle from their native throne?

Or had fair freedom's hand unveil'd thy charms,
 Well might fuch brows the regal gem refign;
Thy radiant mien might fcorn the guilt of arms,
 Yet ALBION's aweful empire yield to thine.

O fhame of BRITONS! in one fullen tow'r
 She wet with royal tears her daily cell;
She found keen anguifh ev'ry rofe devour;
 They fprung, they fhone, they faded, and they fell.

Thro'

---

* ELEANOR of BRETAGNE, the lawful heirefs of the Englifh
crown, upon the death of ARTHUR, in the reign of king JOHN.
She was efteemed the beauty of her time; was imprifoned forty
years (till the time of her death) in Briftol caftle.

'Thro' one dim lattice fring'd with ivy round,
    Succeffive funs a languid radiance threw;
To paint how fierce her angry guardian frown'd,
    To mark how faft her waning beauty flew.

This, age might bear; then fated fancy palls,
    Nor warmly hopes what fplendor can fupply;
Fond youth inceffant mourns, if rigid walls
    Reftrain its lift'ning ear, its curious eye.

Believe me * * * * the pretence is vain!
    This boafted calm that fmooths our early days;
For never yet could youthful mind reftrain
    Th' alternate pant for pleafure and for praife.

Ev'n me, by fhady oak or limpid fpring,
    Ev'n me, the fcenes of polifh'd life allure;
Some genius whifpers " Life is on the wing,
    And hard his lot that languifhes obfcure.

What tho' thy riper mind admire no more—
    The fhining cincture, and the broider'd fold
Can pierce like lightning thro' the figur'd ore,
    And melt to drofs the radiant forms of gold.

Furs, ermins, rods may well attract thy fcorn;
    The futile prefents of capricious pow'r!
But wit, but worth, the public fphere adorn,
    And who but envies then the focial hour?

Can

Can virtue, careless of her pupil's meed,
   Forget how * * * suſtains the ſhepherd's cauſe ?
Content in ſhades to tune a lonely reed,
   Nor join the ſounding pæan of applauſe ?

For public haunts, impell'd by BRITAIN's weal,
   See GRENVILLE quit the muſe's fav'rite eaſe ;
And ſhall not ſwains admire his noble zeal ?
   Admiring praiſe, admiring ſtrive to pleaſe ?

Life, ſays the ſage, affords no bliſs ſincere ;
   And courts, and cells in vain our hopes renew :
But ah ! where GRENVILLE charms the liſt'ning ear,
   'Tis hard to think the chearleſs maxim true.

The groves may ſmile ; the rivers gently glide ;
   Soft thro' the vale reſound the loneſome lay ;
Ev'n thickets yield delight, if taſte preſide,
   But can they pleaſe, when LYTTELTON's away ?

Pure as the ſwain's the breaſt of * * * glows,
   Ah ! were the ſhepherd's phraſe, like his, refin'd !
But, how improv'd the generous dictate flows
   Thro' the clear medium of a poliſh'd mind !

Happy the youths who warm with BRITAIN's love,
   Her inmoſt wiſh in * * * periods hear !
Happy that in the radiant circle move,
   Attendant orbs, where LONSDALE gilds the ſphere !

While

While rural faith, and ev'ry polifh'd art,
    Each friendly charm, in * * * confpire,
From public fcenes all penfive muft you part;
    All joylefs to the greeneft fields retire!

Go, plaintive youth! no more by fount or ftream,
    Like fome lone halcyon, focial pleafure fhun;
Go dare the light, enjoy its chearful beam,
    And hail the bright proceffion of the fun.

Then cover'd by thy ripen'd fhades, refume
    The filent walk; no more by paffion toft:
Then feek thy ruftic haunts; the dreary gloom,
    Where ev'ry art that colours life, is loft."——

In vain! the lift'ning mufe attends in vain!
    Reftraints in hoftile bands her motions wait——
——Yet will I grieve, and fadden all my ftrain,
    When injur'd beauty mourns the mufe's fate.

+++

ELEGY XXV,

To DELIA, with fome flowers; complaining
how much his benevolence fuffers on account of his humble fortune.

WHate'er could fculpture's curious art employ,
    Whate'er the lavifh hand of wealth can fhow'r,
Thefe would I give——and every gift enjoy,
    That pleas'd my fair—but fate denies my pow'r.

Bleft

Bleft were my lot to feed the focial fires !
  To learn the latent wifhes of a friend !
To give the boon his native tafte admires,
  And, for my tranfport, on his fmile depend !

Bleft too is he, whofe ev'ning ramble ftrays
  Where droop the fons of indigence and care !
His little gifts their gladden'd eyes amaze,
  And win, at fmall expence, their fondeft pray'r !

And oh the joy ! to fhun the confcious light,
  To fpare the modeft blufh ; to give unfeen !
Like fhow'rs that fall behind the veil of night,
  Yet deeply tinge the fmiling vales with green.

But happieft they, who drooping realms relieve !
  Whofe virtues in our cultur'd vales appear !
For whofe fad fate a thoufand fhepherds grieve,
  And fading fields allow the grief fincere.

To call loft worth from its oppreffive fhade ;
  To fix its equal fphere, and fee it fhine ;
To hear it grateful own the gen'rous aid;
  This, this is tranfport—but muft ne'er be mine.

Faint is my bounded blifs ; nor I refufe
  To range where daifies open, rivers roll ;
While profe or fong the languid hours amufe,
  And foothe the fond impatience of my foul.

Awhile

Awhile I'll weave the roofs of jafmin bow'rs,
   And urge with trivial cares the loit'ring year;
Awhile I'll prune my grove, protect my flow'rs,
   Then, unlamented, prefs an early bier!

Of thofe lov'd flowers the lifelefs corfe may fhare,
   Some hireling hand a fading wreath beftow;
The reft will breathe as fweet, will glow as fair,
   As when their mafter fmil'd to fee them glow.

The feqùent morn fhall wake the filvan quire;
   The kid again fhall wanton ere 'tis noon;
Nature will fmile, will wear her beft attire;
   O! let not gentle Delia fmile fo foon!

While the rude hearfe conveys me flow away,
   And carelefs eyes my vulgar fate proclaim,
Let thy kind tear my utmoft worth o'erpay;
   And, foftly fighing, vindicate my fame.—

O Delia! chear'd by thy fuperior praife,
   I blefs the filent path the fates decree;
Pleas'd, from the lift of my inglorious days,
   To raze the moments crown'd with blifs, and thee.

      ELEGY

ELEGY XXVI.

Defcribing the forrow of an ingenuous mind,
on the melancholy event of a licentious
amour.

WHY mourns my friend! why weeps his downcaft eye?
 That eye where mirth, where fancy us'd to fhine;
Thy chearful meads reprove that fwelling figh;
 Spring ne'er enamell'd fairer meads than thine.

Art thou not lodg'd in fortune's warm embrace?
 Wert thou not form'd by nature's partial care?
Bleft in thy fong, and bleft in ev'ry grace
 That wins the friend, or that enchants the fair!

DAMON, faid he, thy partial praife reftrain!
 Not DAMON's friendfhip can my peace reftore;
Alas! his very praife awakes my pain,
 And my poor wounded bofom bleeds the more.

For oh! that nature on my birth had frown'd,
 Or fortune fix'd me to fome lowly cell!
Then had my bofom 'fcap'd this fatal wound,
 Nor had I bid thefe vernal fweets farewel.

But led by fortune's hand, her darling child,
 My youth her vain licentious blifs admir'd;
In fortune's train the fyren flatt'ry fmil'd,
 And rafhly hallow'd all her queen infpir'd.

         Of

Of folly ftudious, ev'n of vices vain,
 Ah vices ! gilded by the rich and gay !
I chas'd the guilelefs daughters of the plain,
 Nor dropt the chace, till JESSY was my prey.

Poor artlefs maid ! to ftain thy fpotlefs uame,
 Expence, and art, and toil, united ftrove;
To lure a breaft that felt the pureft flame,
 Suftain'd by virtue, but betray'd by love.

School'd in the fcience of love's mazy wiles,
 I cloath'd each feature with affected fcorn;
I fpoke of jealous doubts, and fickle fmiles,
 And, feigning, left her anxious and forlorn.

Then, while the fancy'd rage alarm'd her care,
 Warm to deny, and zealous to difprove;
I bade my words the wonted foftnefs wear,
 And feiz'd the minute of returning love.

To thee, my DAMON, dare I paint the reft?
 Will yet thy love a candid ear incline?
Affur'd that virtue, by misfortune preft,
 Feels not the fharpnefs of a pang like mine.

Nine envious moons matur'd her growing fhame;
 Ere while to flaunt it in the face of day;
When fcorn'd of virtue, ftigmatiz'd by fame,
 Low at my feet defponding JESSY lay.

5   "HENRY,

" Henry, she said, by thy dear form subdu'd,
    See the sad reliques of a nymph undone!
I find, I find this rising sob renew'd:
    I sigh in shades, and sicken at the sun.

Amid the dreary gloom of night, I cry,
    When will the morn's once pleasing scenes return?
Yet what can morn's returning ray supply,
    But foes that triumph, or but friends that mourn?

Alas! no more that joyous morn appears
    That led the tranquil hours of spotless fame;
For I have steep'd a father's couch in tears,
    And ting'd a mother's glowing cheek with shame.

The vocal birds that raise their matin strain,
    The sportive lambs, increase my pensive moan;
All seem to chase me from the chearful plain,
    And talk of truth and innocence alone.

If thro' the garden's flow'ry tribes I stray,
    Where bloom the jasmins that could once allure,
Hope not to find delight in us, they say,
    For we are spotless, Jessy; we are pure.

Ye flow'rs! that well reproach a nymph so frail,
    Say, could ye with my virgin fame compare?
The brightest bud that scents the vernal gale
    Was not so fragant, and was not so fair.

Now

Now the grave old alarm the gentler young,
 And all my fame's abhorr'd contagion flee;
Trembles each lip, and faulters ev'ry tongue,
 That bids the morn propitious smile on me.

Thus for your sake I shun each human eye;
 I bid the sweets of blooming youth adieu;
To die I languish, but I dread to die,
 Lest my sad fate shou'd nourish pangs for you.

Raise me from earth; the pains of want remove,
 And let me silent seek some friendly shore;
There only, banish'd from the form I love,
 My weeping virtue shall relapse no more.

Be but my friend; I ask no dearer name;
 Be such the meed of some more artful fair;
Nor could it heal my peace, or chase my shame,
 That pity gave, what love refus'd to share.

Force not my tongue to ask its scanty bread;
 Nor hurl thy JESSY to the vulgar crew;
Not such the parent's board at which I fed!
 Not such the precept from his lips I drew!

Haply, when age has silver'd o'er my hair,
 Malice may learn to scorn so mean a spoil;
Envy may slight a face no longer fair;
 And pity welcome to my native soil."

She fpoke—nor was I born of favage race;
  Nor could thefe hands a niggard boon affign;
Grateful fhe clafp'd me in a laft embrace,
  And vow'd to wafte her life in pray'rs for mine.

I faw her foot the lofty bark afcend;
  I faw her breaft with ev'ry paffion heave;
I left her—torn from ev'ry earthly friend;
  Oh! my hard bofom, which could bear to leave!

Brief let me be; the fatal ftorm arofe;
  The billows rag'd, the pilot's art was vain;
O'er the tall maft the circling furges clofe;
  My JESSY—floats upon the wat'ry plain!

And—fee my youth's impetuous fires decay;
  Seek not to ftop reflection's bitter tear;
But warm the frolic, and inftruct the gay,
  From JESSY floating on her wat'ry bier!

ODES,

O D E S,

S O N G S,

B A L L A D S, &c.

&c.

RURAL ELEGANCE.

An ODE to the late Dutchefs of SOMERSET.
Written 1750.

WHILE orient fkies reftore the day,
　　And drew-drops catch the lucid ray;
Amid the fprightly fcenes of morn,
　Will aught the mufe infpire!
Oh! peace to yonder clam'rous horn
　That drowns the facred lyre!

Ye rural thanes that o'er the moffy down
　　Some panting, timorous hare purfue;
Does nature mean your joys alone to crown?
　　Say, does fhe fmooth her lawns for you?
For you does echo bid the rocks reply,
And urg'd by rude conftraint refound the jovial cry?

See

See from the neighbouring hill, forlorn
   The wretched fwain your fport furvey;
He finds his faithful fences torn,
   He finds his labour'd crops a prey;
He fees his flock—no more in circles feed;
Haply beneath your ravage bleed,
And with no random curfes loads the deed.

  Nor yet, ye fwains, conclude
  'That nature fmiles for you alone;
Your bounded fouls, and your conceptions crude,
   The proud, the felfifh boaft difown:
   Yours be the produce of the foil:
   O may it ftill reward your toil!
   Nor ever the defencelefs train
Of clinging infants, afk fupport in vain!

But tho' the various harveft gild your plains,
   Does the mere landfcape feaft your eye?
Or the warm hope of diftant gains
   Far other caufe of glee fupply?
Is not the red-ftreak's future juice
   The fource of your delight profound,
Where Ariconium pours her gems profufe,
   Purpling a whole horizon round?
Athirft ye praife the limpid ftream, 'tis true:
   But tho', the pebbled fhores among,
   It mimic no unpleafing fong,
The limpid fountain murmurs not for you.

                        Unpleas'd

Unpleas'd ye fee the thickets bloom,
Unpleas'd the fpring her flowery robe refume ;
Unmov'd the mountain's airy pile,
The dappled mead without a fmile.
O let a rural confcious mufe,
For well fhe knows, your froward fenfe accufe :
Forth to the folemn oak you bring the fquare,
And fpan the maffy trunk, before you cry, 'tis fair.

Nor yet ye learn'd, nor yet ye courtly train,
If haply from your haunts ye ftray
To wafte with us a fummer's day,
Exclude the tafte of every fwain,
Nor our untutor'd fenfe difdain :
'Tis nature only gives exclufive right
To relifh her fupreme delight ;
She, where fhe pleafes kind or coy,
Who furnifhes the fcene, and forms us to enjoy.

Then hither bring the fair ingenuous mind,
By her aufpicious aid refin'd ;
Lo ! not an hedge-row hawthorn blows,
Or humble hare-bell paints the plain,
Or valley winds, or fountain flows,
Or purple heath is ting'd in vain :
For fuch the rivers dafh the foaming tides,
The mountain fwells, the dale fubfides ;
Ev'n thriftlefs furze detains their wandering fight,
And the rough barren rock grows pregnant with delight.

With what fufpicious fearful care
   The fordid wretch fecures his claim,
If haply fome luxurious heir
   Should alienate the fields that wear his name!
What fcruples left fome future birth
   Should litigate a fpan of earth!
Bonds, contracts, feoffments, names unmeet for profe,
The towering mufe endures not to difclofe;
   Alas! her unrevers'd decree,
   More comprehenfive and more free,
Her lavifh charter, tafte, appropriates all we fee.

   Let gondolas their painted flags unfold,
   And be the folemn day enroll'd,
   When to confirm his lofty plea,
     In nuptial fort, with bridal gold,
   The grave Venetian weds the fea:
Each laughing mufe derides the vow;
   Ev'n ADRIA fcorns the mock embrace,
To fome lone hermit on the mountain's brow,
   Allotted, from his natal hour,
   With all her myrtle fhores in dow'r.
His breaft to admiration prone
   Enjoys the fmile upon her face,
   Enjoys triumphant every grace,
And finds her more his own.

Fatigu'd with form's oppreffive laws,
   When SOMERSET avoids the great;

                    When

When cloy'd with merited applauſe,
  She ſeeks the rural calm retreat;
Does ſhe not praiſe each moſſy cell,
And feel the truth my numbers tell?
When deafen'd by the loud acclaim,
  Which genius grac'd with rank obtains,
Could ſhe not more delighted hear
Yon throſtle chaunt the riſing year?
Could ſhe not ſpurn the wreaths of fame,
  To crop the primroſe of the plains?
Does ſhe not ſweets in each fair valley find,
Loſt to the ſons of pow'r, unknown to half mankind?

Ah can ſhe covet there to ſee
The ſplendid ſlaves, the reptile race,
  That oil the tongue, and bow the knee,
That ſlight her merit, but adore her place?
  Far happier, if aright I deem,
When from gay throngs, and gilded ſpires,
  To where the lonely halcyons play,
Her philoſophic ſtep retires:
While ſtudious of the moral theme,
She, to ſome ſmooth ſequeſter'd ſtream
  Likens the ſwain's inglorious day;
Pleas'd from the flowery margin to ſurvey,
How cool, ſerene, and clear the current glides away.

O blind to truth, to virtue blind,
Who ſlight the ſweetly-penſive mind!
On whoſe fair birth the graces mild,
And every muſe prophetic ſmil'd.

Not

Not that the poet's boasted fire
   Should fame's wide-echoing trumpet swell;
Or, on the music of his lyre
   Each future age with rapture dwell;
The vaunted sweets of praise remove,
   Yet shall such bosoms claim a part
   In all that glads the human heart;
Yet these the spirits, form'd to judge and prove
All nature's charms immense, and heaven's unbounded
                                            [love.

And oh; the transport, most ally'd to song,
   In some fair villa's peaceful bound,
To catch soft hints from nature's tongue,
   And bid ARCADIA bloom around:
Whether we fringe the sloping hill,
   Or smoothe below the verdant mead;
Whether we break the falling rill,
   Or thro' meandering mazes lead;
Or in the horrid bramble's room
Bid careless groups of roses bloom;
Or let some shelter'd lake serene
Reflect flow'rs, woods and spires, and brighten all the scene.

O sweet disposal of the rural hour;
   O beauties never known to cloy!
While worth and genius haunt the favour'd bow'r,
   And every gentle breast partakes the joy!
While charity at eve surveys the swain,
   Enabled by these toils to chear
   A train of helpless infants dear,
Speed whistling home across the plain;

See vagrant luxury, her hand-maid grown,
 For half her gracelefs deeds atone,
And hails the bounteous work, and ranks it with her own.

 Why brand thefe pleafures with the name
Of foft, unfocial toils, of indolence and fhame?
 Search but the garden, or the wood,
  Let yon admir'd carnation own,
 Not all was meant for raiment or for food,
  Not all for needful ufe alone;
 There while the feeds of future bloffoms dwell,
'Tis colour'd for the fight, perfum'd to pleafe the fmell.

  Why knows the nightingale to fing?
  Why flows the pine's nectareous juice?
 Why fhines with paint the linnet's wing?
  For fuftenance alone? For ufe?
 For prefervation? Every fphere
Shall bid fair pleafure's rightful claim appear.
 And fure there feem, of human kind,
  Some born to fhun the folemn ftrife;
 Some for amufive tafks defign'd,
  To foothe the certain ills of life;
 Grace its lone vales with many a budding rofe,
  New founts of blifs difclofe,
Call forth refrefhing fhades, and decorate repofe.
 From plains and woodlands; from the view
  Of rural nature's blooming face,
  Smit with the glare of rank and place,
 To courts the fons of fancy flew;

There

There long had art ordain'd a rival feat,
  There had fhe lavifh'd all her care
  To form a fcene more dazzling fair,
And call'd them from their green retreat
    To fhare her proud controul;
  Had given the robe with grace to flow,
  Had taught extotic gems to glow;
    And emulous of nature's pow'r,
    Mimick'd the plume, the leaf, the flow'r;
  Chang'd the complexion's native hue,
  Moulded each ruftic limb anew,
    And warp'd the very foul.

Awhile her magic ftrikes the novel eye,
  Awhile the fairy forms delight;
  And now aloof we feem to fly
On purple pinions thro' a purer fky,
  Where all is wonderous, all is bright:
  Now landed on fome fpangled fhore
    Awhile each dazzled maniac roves
    By faphire lakes, thro' em'rald groves.
  Paternal acres pleafe no more;
Adieu the fimple, the fincere delight—
  Th' habitual fcene of hill and dale,
  The rural herds, the vernal gale,
  The tangled vetch's purple bloom,
  The fragrance of the bean's perfume,
Be theirs alone who cultivate the foil,
And drink the cup of thirft, and eat the bread of toil.
                                        But

But foon the pageant fades away !
'Tis nature only bears perpetual fway.
 We pierce the counterfeit delight,
 Fatigu'd with fplendor's irkfome beams.
 Fancy again demands the fight
 Of native groves, and wonted ftreams,
Pants for the fcenes that charm'd her youthful eyes,
Where truth maintains her court, and banifhes difguife.

Then hither oft ye fenators retire,
 With nature here high converfe hold ;
For who like STAMFORD her delights admire,
 Like STAMFORD fhall with fcorn behold
Th' unequal bribes of pageantry and gold ;
Beneath the Britifh oak's majeftic fhade,
 Shall fee fair truth, immortal maid,
 Friendfhip in artlefs guife array'd,
 Honour, and moral beauty fhine
With more attractive charms, with radiance more divine.

Yes, here alone did higheft heav'n ordain
 The lafting magazine of charms,
 Whatever wins, whatever warms,
 Whatever fancy feeks to fhare,
 The great, the various, and the fair,
  For ever fhould remain !

Her impulfe nothing may reftrain—
Or whence the joy 'mid columns, tow'rs,
 'Midft all the city's artful trim,
 To rear fome breathlefs vapid flow'rs,

Or

Or fhrubs fuliginoufly grim:
From rooms of filken foliage vain,
To trace the dun far diftant grove,
Where fmit with undiffembled pain,
The wood-lark mourns her abfent love,
Borne to the dufty town from native air,
To mimic rural life, and foothe fome vapour'd fair?

But how muft faithlefs art prevail,
Should all who tafte our joy fincere,
To virtue, truth, or fcience dear,
Forego a court's alluring pale,
For dimpled brook and leafy grove,
For that rich luxury of thought they love!
Ah no, from thefe the public fphere requires
Example for its giddy bands;
From thefe impartial heav'n demands
To fpread the flame itfelf infpires;
To fift opinion's mingled mafs,
Imprefs a nation's tafte, and bid the fterling pafs.

Happy, thrice happy they,
Whofe graceful deeds have exemplary fhone
Round the gay precincts of a throne,
With mild effective beams!
Who bands of fair ideas bring,
By folemn grott, or fhady fpring,
To join their pleafing dreams!
Theirs is the rural blifs without alloy,
They only that deferve, enjoy.

What

What tho' nor fabled dryad haunt their grove,
 Nor naiad near their fountains rove,
Yet all embody'd to the mental fight,
 A train of fmiling virtues bright
 Shall there the wife retreat allow,
Shall twine triumphant palms to deck the wanderer's brow.

 And though by faithlefs friends alarm'd,
Art have with nature wag'd prefumptuous war;
 By SEYMOUR's winning influence charm'd,
 In whom their gifts united fhine,
  No longer fhall their counfels jar.
'Tis hers to mediate the peace;
  Near PERCY-lodge, with awe-ftruck mien,
 The rebel feeks her lawful queen,
And havock and contention ceafe.
  I fee the rival pow'rs combine,
  And aid each other's fair defign;
Nature exalt the mound where art fhall build;
Art fhape the gay alcove, while nature paints the field.

 Begin, ye fongfters of the grove!
 O warble forth your nobleft lay;
 Where SOMERSET vouchfafes to rove
 Ye leverets freely fport and play.
  —Peace to the ftrepent horn!
Let no harfh diffonance difturb the morn,
 No founds inelegant and rude
 Her facred folitudes profane,

Unlefs

Unlefs her candour not exclude
The lowly fhepherd's votive ftrain,
Who tunes his reed amidft his rural chear,
Fearful, yet not averfe, that SOMERSET fhould hear.

ODE to MEMORY. 1748.

O Memory! celeftial maid!
    Who glean'ft the flow'rets cropt by time;
And, fuffering not a leaf to fade,
    Preferv'ft the bloffoms of our prime;
Bring, bring thofe moments to my mind
When life was new, and LESBIA kind.

And bring that garland to my fight,
    With which my favor'd crook fhe bound;
And bring that wreath of rofes bright,
    Which then my feftive temples crown'd.
And to my raptur'd ear convey
The gentle things fhe deign'd to fay.

And fketch with care the mufe's bow'r,
    Where ISIS rolls her filver tide;
Nor yet omit one reed or flow'r
    That fhines on CHERWELL's verdant fide;
If fo thou may'ft thofe hours prolong,
When polifh'd LYCON join'd my fong.

The

The fong it 'vails not to recite————
 But fure, to foothe our youthful dreams,
Thofe banks and ftreams appear'd more bright
 Than other banks, than other ftreams:
Or by thy foftening pencil fhewn,
Affume they beauties not their own?

And paint that fweetly vacant fcene,
 When, all beneath the poplar bough,
My fpirits light, my foul ferene,
 I breath'd in verfe one cordial vow:
That nothing fhould my foul infpire,
But friendfhip warm, and love entire.

Dull to the fenfe of new delight,
 On thee the drooping mufe attends;
As fome fond lover, robb'd of fight,
 On thy expreffive pow'r depends;
Nor would exchange thy glowing lines,
To live the lord of all that fhines.

But let me chafe thofe vows away
 Which at ambition's fhrine I made;
Nor ever let thy fkill difplay
 Thofe anxious moments, ill repaid:
Oh! from my breaft that feafon rafe,
And bring my childhood in its place.

Bring me the bells, the rattle bring,
 And bring the hobby I beftrode;

When

When pleas'd, in many a fportive ring,
   Around the room I jovial rode:
Ev'n let me bid my lyre adieu,
And bring the whiftle that I blew.

Then will I mufe, and penfive fay,
   Why did not thefe enjoyments laft;
How fweetly wafted I the day,
   While innocence allow'd to wafte?
Ambition's toils alike are vain,
But ah! for pleafure yield us pain.

✛✛✛✛✛✛✛✛✛✛✛✛✛✛✛✛✛✛✛✛✛✛✛✛✛✛✛✛✛✛✛✛✛

The Princess ELIZABETH:
A Ballad alluding to a ftory recorded of her,
when fhe was prifoner at WOODSTOCK, 1554.

WILL you hear how once repining
   Great ELIZA captive lay?
Each ambitious thought refigning,
   Foe to riches, pomp, and fway?

While the nymphs and fwains delighted
   Tript around in all their pride;
Envying joys by others flighted,
   Thus the royal maiden cry'd.

" Bred on plains, or born in vallies,
   Who would bid thofe fcenes adieu?
Stranger to the arts of malice,
   Who would ever courts purfue?

Malice

Malice never taught to treasure,
   Censure never taught to bear:
Love is all the shepherd's pleasure;
   Love is all the damsel's care.

How can they of humble station
   Vainly blame the powers above?
Or accuse the dispensation
   Which allows them all to love?

Love like air is widely given;
   Pow'r nor chance can these restrain;
Truest, noblest gifts of heaven!
   Only purest on the plain!

Peers can no such charms discover,
   All in stars and garters drest,
As, on Sundays, does the lover
   With his nosegay on his breast.

Pinks and roses in profusion,
   Said to fade when CHLOE's near;
Fops may use the same allusion;
   But the shepherd is sincere.

Hark to yonder milk-maid singing
   Chearly o'er the brimming pail;
Cowslips all around her springing
   Sweetly paint the golden vale.

                              Never

Never yet did courtly maiden
  Move fo fprightly, look fo fair;
Never breaft with jewels laden
  Pour a fong fo void of care.

Would indulgent heav'n had granted
  Me fome rural damfel's part!
All the empire I had wanted
  Then had been my fhepherd's heart.

Then, with him, o'er hills and mountains,
  Free from fetters, might I rove:
Fearlefs tafte the cryftal fountains;
  Peaceful fleep beneath the grove.

Ruftics had been more forgiving;
  Partial to my virgin bloom:
None had envy'd me when living;
  None had triumph'd o'er my tomb."

ODE to a young LADY,

Somewhat too folicitous about her manner of
expreffion.

SURVEY, my fair! that lucid ftream
  Adown the fmiling valley ftray;
Would art attempt, or fancy dream,
  To regulate its winding way?

So

So pleas'd I view thy shining hair
   In loose dishevel'd ringlets flow:
Not all thy art, not all thy care
   Can there one single grace bestow.

Survey again that verdant hill,
   With native plants enamel'd o'er;
Say, can the painter's utmost skill
   Instruct one flow'r to please us more?

As vain it were, with artful dye,
   To change the bloom thy cheeks disclose;
And oh may LAURA, ere she try,
   With fresh vermilion paint the rose.

Hark, how the wood-lark's tuneful throat
   Can every study'd grace excel;
Let art constrain the rambling note,
   And will she, LAURA, please so well?

Oh ever keep thy native ease,
   By no pedantic law confin'd!
For LAURA's voice is form'd to please,
   So LAURA's words be not unkind.

NANCY

NANCY of the VALE. A BALLAD.

Nerine Galatea! thymo mibi dulcior Hyblæ!
Candidior cygnis! bederâ formosior alba!

IMITATION.

O Galatea, Nereus' blooming child,
More fweet than thyme by * Hybla bees exhal'd,
Fairer than fwans, more beauteous to behold
Than ivy's pureft white.

THE weftern fky was purpled o'er
 With every pleafing ray:
And flocks reviving felt no more
 The fultry heats of day:

When from an hazle's artlefs bower
 Soft warbled STREPHON's tongue;
He bleft the fcene, he bleft the hour,
 While NANCY's praife he fung.

" Let fops with fickle falfhood range
 The paths of wanton love,
While weeping maids lament their change,
 And fadden every grove:

But endlefs bleffings crown the day
 I faw fair ESHAM's dale !
And every bleffing find its way
 To NANCY of the Vale.

'Twas

* HYBLA—a mountain in Sicily, famous for producing the fineft
honey.

'Twas from Avon a's banks the maid
  Diffus'd her lovely beams;
And every shining glance display'd
  The naiad of the streams.

Soft as the wild-duck's tender young,
  That float on Avon's tide;
Bright as the water-lily, sprung,
  And glittering near its side.

Fresh as the bordering flowers, her bloom;
  Her eye, all mild to view;
The little halcyon's azure plume.
  Was never half so blue.

Her shape was like the reed so sleek,
  So taper, strait, and fair;
Her dimpled smile, her blushing cheek,
  How charming sweet they were!

Far in the winding Vale retir'd,
  This peerless bud I found;
And shadowing rocks, and woods conspir'd
  To fence her beauties round.

That nature in so lone a dell
  Should form a nymph so sweet!
Or fortune to her secret cell
  Conduct my wandering feet!

VOL. I.   I   Gay

Gay lordlings fought her for their bride,
　　But she would ne'er incline:
" Prove to your equals true, she cry'd,
　　As I will prove to mine.

'Tis STREPHON, on the mountain's brow,
　　Has won my right good-will;
To him I gave my plighted vow,
　　With him I'll climb the hill."

Struck with her charms and gentle truth,
　　I clasp'd the constant fair;
To her alone I gave my youth,
　　And vow my future care:

And when this vow shall faithless prove,
　　Or I those charms forego;
The stream that saw our tender love,
　　That stream shall cease to flow.

✤✤✤✤✤✤✤✤✤✤✤✤✤✤✤✤✤✤✤✤✤✤✤✤✤✤✤✤✤✤✤✤✤✤✤

ODE to INDOLENCE. 1750.

AH! why for ever on the wing
　　Persists my weary'd soul to roam?
Why, ever cheated, strives to bring
　　Or pleasure or contentment home?

Thus

Thus the poor bird, that draws his name
   From Paradife's honour'd groves,
Carelefs fatigues his little frame;
   Nor finds the refting-place he loves.

Lo! on the rural moffy bed
   My limbs with carelefs eafe reclin'd;
Ah, gentle floth! indulgent fpread
   The fame foft bandage o'er my mind.

For why fhould ling'ring thought invade,
   Yet ev'ry worldly profpect cloy?
Lend me, foft floth, thy friendly aid,
   And give me peace, debarr'd of joy.

Lov'ft thou yon calm and filent flood,
   That never ebbs, that never flows;
Protected by the circling wood
   From each tempeftuous wind that blows?

An altar on its bank fhall rife,
   Where oft thy votary fhall be found;
What time pale autumn lulls the fkies,
   And fickening verdure fades around.

Ye bufy race, ye factions train,
   That haunt ambition's guilty fhrine;
No more perplex the world in vain,
   But offer here your vows with mine.

And

And thou, puiſſant queen ! be kind :
  If e'er I ſhar'd thy balmy pow'r ;
If e'er I ſway'd my active mind,
  To weave for thee the rural bow'r ;

Diſſolve in ſleep each anxious care ;
  Each unavailing ſigh remove ;
And only let me wake to ſhare,
  The ſweets of friendſhip and of love.

+

ODE to HEALTH. 1730.

O HEALTH, capricious maid !
  Why doſt thou ſhun my peaceful bow'r,
Where I had hope to ſhare thy pow'r,
  And bleſs thy laſting aid ?

  Since thou, alas ! art flown,
It 'vails not whether muſe or grace,
With tempting ſmile, frequent the place ;
  I ſigh for thee alone.

  Age not forbids thy ſtay ;
Thou yet might'ſt act the friendly part ;
Thou yet might'ſt raiſe this languid heart ;
  Why ſpeed ſo ſwift away ?

Thou

Thou fcorn'ft the city-air;
I breathe freſh gales o'er furrow'd ground,
Yet haft not thou my wiſhes crown'd,
 O falfe! O partial fair!

 I plunge into the wave;
And tho' with pureft hands I raife
A rural altar to thy praife,
 Thou wilt not deign to fave.

 Amid my well-known grove,
Where mineral fountains vainly bear
Thy boafted name, and titles fair,
 Why fcorns thy foot to rove?

 Thou hear'ft the fportfman's claim;
Enabling him, with idle noife,
To drown the mufe's melting voice,
 And fright the timorous game.

 Is thought thy foe? adieu
Ye midnight lamps! ye curious tomes!
Mine eye o'er hills and valleys roams,
 And deals no more with you.

 Is it the clime you flee?
Yet 'midft his unremitting fnows,
The poor LAPONIAN's bofom glows,
 And ſhares bright rays from thee.

    There

There was, there was a time,
When tho' I fcorn'd thy guardian care,
Nor made a vow, nor faid a pray'r,
   I did not rue the crime.

Who then more bleft than I ?
When the glad fchool-boy's tafk was done,
And forth, with jocund-fprite, I run
   To freedom, and to joy ?

How jovial then the day !
What fince have all my labours found,
Thus climbing life to gaze around,
   That can thy lofs repay ?

Wert thou, alas ! but kind,
Methinks no frown that fortune wears,
Nor leffen'd hopes, nor growing cares,
   Could fink my chearful mind.

Whate'er my ftars include ;
What other breafts convert to pain,
My tow'ring mind fhould foon difdain,
   Should fcorn—Ingratitude !

Repair this mouldering cell,
And bleft with objects found at home,
And envying none their fairer dome,
   How pleas'd my foul fhould dwell !

Tem-

Temperance fhould guard the doors ;
From room to room fhould memory ftray,
And, ranging all in neat array,
    Enjoy her pleafing ftores.——

  There let them reft unknown,
The types of many a pleafing fcene ;
But to preferve them bright, or clean,
    Is thine, fair queen! alone.

✦✦✦✦✦✦✦✦✦✦✦✦✦✦✦✦✦✦✦✦✦✦✦✦✦✦✦✦✦✦✦✦✦

To a LADY of QUALITY,

Fitting up her LIBRARY. 1738.

AH! what is fcience, what is art,
    Or what the pleafure, thefe impart?
Ye trophies which the learn'd purfue
Through endlefs fruitlefs toils, adieu!

What can the tedious tomes beftow,
To foothe the miferies they fhew?
What, like the blifs for him decreed,
Who tends his flock, and tunes his reed!

Say, wretched fancy! thus refin'd
From all that glads the fimpleft hind,
How rare that object, which fupplies
A charm for too difcerning eyes!

The polifh'd bard, of genius vain,
Endures a deeper fenfe of pain:
As each invading blaft devours
The richeft fruits, the faireft flow'rs.

Sages, with irkfome wafte of time,
The fteep afcent of knowledge climb;
Then, from the tow'ring heights they fcale,
Behold contentment range—the vale.

Yet why, ASTERIA, tell us why
We fcorn the crowd, when you are nigh;
Why then does reafon feem fo fair,
Why learning then, deferve our care?

Who can unpleas'd your fhelves behold,
While you fo fair a proof unfold
What force the brighteft genius draws
From polifh'd wifdom's written laws?

Where are our humbler tenets flown?
What ftrange perfection bids us own
That blifs with toilfome fcience dwells,
And happieft he, who moft excels?

UPON

UPON A

VISIT to the fame in WINTER. 1748.

ON fair ASTERIA's blifsful plains,
  Where ever-blooming fancy reigns,
How pleas'd we pafs the winter's day;
And charm the dull-ey'd fpleen away!

No linnet, from the leaflefs bough,
Pours forth her note melodious now;
But all admire ASTERIA's tongue,
Nor wifh the linnet's vernal fong.

No flow'rs emit their tranfient rays:
Yet fure ASTERIA's wit difplays
More various tints, more glowing lines,
And with perennial beauty fhines.

Tho' rifled groves and fetter'd ftreams
But ill befriend a poet's dreams:
ASTERIA's prefence wakes the lyre;
And well fupplies poetic fire.

The fields have loft their lovely dye;
No chearful azure decks the fky;
Yet ftill we blefs the louring day;
ASTERIA fmiles—and all is gay.

Hence

Hence let the muse no more presume
To blame the winter's dreary gloom;
Accuse his loit'ring hours no more;
But ah! their envious haste deplore!

For soon, from wit and friendship's reign,
The social hearth, the sprightly vein,
I go—to meet the coming year,
On savage plains, and deserts drear!

I go—to feed on pleasures flown,
Nor find the spring my loss atone!
But 'mid the flow'ry sweets of May
With pride recal this winter's day.

❖❖❖❖❖❖❖❖❖❖❖❖❖❖❖❖❖❖❖❖❖❖❖❖❖❖❖❖❖❖❖❖❖❖❖

AN
Irregular ODE after Sickness. 1749.

——— *Melius, cum venerit ipsa, canemus.*

IMITATION.

His wish'd-for presence will improve the song.

TOO long a stranger to repose,
    At length from pain's abhorred couch I rose,
    And wander'd forth alone;
To court once more the balmy breeze,
And catch the verdure of the trees,
    Ere yet their charms were flown.

'Twas

'Twas from a bank with panfies gay
I hail'd once more the chearful day,
   The fun's forgotten beams :
O fun! how pleafing were thy rays,
Reflected from the polifh'd face
   Of yon refulgent ftreams!

Rais'd by the fcene my feeble tongue
Effay'd again the fweets of fong :
And thus in feeble ftrains and flow
The loitering numbers 'gan to flow.

" Come, gentle air! my languid limbs reftore,
And bid me welcome from the Stygian fhore :
   For fure I heard the tender fighs,
   I feem'd to join the plaintive cries
Of haplefs youths, who thro' the myrtle grove
Bewail for ever their unfinifh'd love :
     To that unjoyous clime,
Torn from the fight of thefe etherial fkies ;
Debarr'd the luftre of their DELIA's eyes ;
     And banifh'd in their prime.

Come, gentle air! and, while the thickets bloom,
   Convey the jafmin's breath divine,
   Convey the woodbine's rich perfume,
    Nor fpare the fweet-leaft eglantine.
   And may'ft thou fhun the rugged ftorm
    'Till health her wonted charms explain,
    With rural pleafure in her train,
  To greet me in her faireft form.

While

While from this lofty mount I view
The sons of earth, the vulgar crew,
Anxious for futile gains, beneath me stray,
And seek with erring step contentment's obvious way.

Come, gentle air! and thou celestial muse,
  Thy genial flame infuse;
Enough to lend a pensive bosom aid,
  And gild retirement's gloomy shade;
  Enough to rear such rustic lays
As foes may slight, but partial friends will praise."

The gentle air allow'd my claim;
And more to chear my drooping frame,
She mix'd the balm of opening flowers;
Such as the bee, with chymic powers,
From HYBLA's fragrant hills inhales,
Or scents SABEA's blooming vales.
But ah! the nymphs that heal the pensive mind,
  By prescripts more refin'd,
  Neglect their votary's anxious moan:
Oh, how should they relieve?—the muses all were flown.

By flow'ry plain, or woodland shades,
I fondly sought the charming maids;
By woodland shades, or flow'ry plain,
I sought them, faithless maids! in vain!
  When lo! in happier hour,
  I leave behind my native mead,
  To range where zeal and friendship lead,
  To visit L * * * *'s honour'd bower.

Ah

Ah foolifh man ! to feek the tuneful maids
On other plains, or near lefs verdant fhades !

Scarce have my footfteps prefs'd the favour'd ground,
   When founds etherial ftrike my ear ;
   At once celeftial forms appear ;
     My fugitives are found !
The mufes here attune their lyres,
Ah partial ! with unwonted fires ;
Here, hand in hand, with carelefs mien,
The fportive graces trip the green.

But whilft I wander'd o'er a fcene fo fair,
   Too well at one furvey I trace,
   How every mufe, and every grace,
     Had long employ'd their care.
Lurks not a ftone enrich'd with lively ftain,
   Blooms not a flower amid the vernal ftore,
Falls not a plume on INDIA's diftant plain,
   Glows not a fhell on ADRIA's rocky fhore,
But torn methought from native lands or feas,
From their arrangement, gain frefh pow'r to pleafe.

And fome had bent the wildering maze,
   Bedeckt with every fhrub that blows ;
And fome entwin'd the willing fprays,
   To fhield th' illuftrious dame's repofe :
Others had grac'd the fprightly dome,
   And taught the portrait where to glow ;
Others arrang'd the curious tome ;

                     Or

Or 'mid the decorated fpace,
Affign'd the laurel'd buft a place,
And given to learning all the pomp of fhow.
And now from every tafk withdrawn,
They met and frifk'd it o'er the lawn.

Ah! woe is me, faid I,
And * * *'s hilly circuit heard my cry;
Have I for this, with labour ftrove,
And lavifh'd all my little ftore .
To fence for you my fhady grove,
And fcollop every winding fhore;
And fringe with every purple rofe
The faphire ftream that down my valley flows?

Ah! lovely treacherous maids!
To quit unfeen my votive fhades,
When pale difeafe, and torturing pain
Had torn me from the breezy plain,
And to a reftlefs couch confin'd,
Who ne'er your wonted tafks declin'd.
She needs not your officious aid
To fwell the fong, or plan the fhade;
By genuine fancy fir'd,
Her native genius guides her hand,
And while fhe marks the fage command,
More lovely fcenes her fkill fhall raife,
Her lyre refound with nobler lays
Than ever you infpir'd.

Thus

Thus I my rage and grief diſplay;
But vainly blame, and vainly mourn,
Nor will a grace or muſe return
    'Till LUXBOROUGH lead the way.

✦✦✦✦✦✦✦✦✦✦✦✦✦✦✦✦✦✦✦✦✦✦✦✦✦✦✦✦✦✦✦✦✦✦✦✦✦✦✦

Written in a FLOWER BOOK of my own Colouring, deſigned, for Lady PLIMOUTH. 1753-4.

Debitæ nymphis opifex coronæ.   HOR.

IMITATION.

Conſtructor of the tributary wreath
For rural maids.

BRING, FLORA, bring thy treaſures here;
    The pride of all the blooming year;
And let me, thence, a garland frame,
To crown this fair, this peerleſs dame!

  But ah! ſince envious winter lours,
And HEWELL meads reſign their flow'rs,
Let art and friendſhip's joint eſſay
Diffuſe their flow'rets in her way.

  Not nature can, herſelf, prepare
A worthy wreath for LESBIA's hair,
Whoſe temper, like her forehead, ſmooth,
Whoſe thoughts and accents form'd to ſoothe,
Whoſe pleaſing mien, and make refin'd,
Whoſe artleſs breaſt, and poliſh'd mind,
From all the nymphs of plain or grove,
Deſerv'd and won my PLIMOUTH's love!

                ANA-

ANACREONTIC. 1738.

'TWAS in a cool Aonian glade,
  The wanton CUPID, fpent with toil,
Had fought refrefhment from the fhade;
  And ftretch'd him on the moffy foil.

A vagrant mufe drew nigh, and found
  The fubtle traitor faft afleep;
And is it thine to fnore profound,
  She faid, yet leave the world to weep?

But hufh——from this aufpicioqs hour,
  The world, I ween, may reft in peace;
And robb'd of darts, and ftript of pow'r,
  Thy peevifh petulance decreafe.

Sleep on, poor child! whilft I withdraw,
  And this thy vile artillery hide——
When the Caftalian fount fhe faw,
  And plung'd his arrows in the tide.

That magic fount—ill-judging maid!
  Shall caufe you foon to curfe the day
You dar'd the fhafts of love invade;
  And gave his arms redoubled fway.

For

For in a ftream fo wonderous clear,
　　When angry CUPID fearches round,
Will not the radiant points appear?
　　Will not the furtive fpoils be found?

Too foon they were; and every dart,
　　Dipt in the mufe's myftic fpring,
Acquir'd new force to wound the heart;
　　And taught at once to love and fing.

Then farewell ye Pierian quire;
　　For who will now your altars throng?
From love we learn to fwell the lyre;
　　And echo afks no fweeter fong.

✦✦✦✦✦✦✦✦✦✦✦✦✦✦✦✦✦✦✦✦✦✦✦✦✦✦✦✦✦✦✦✦✦

ODE. Written 1739.

Urit *fpes animi credula mutui.*   HOR.

IMITATION.
Fond hope of a reciprocal defire
Inflames the breaft.

'TWAS not by beauty's aid alone,
　　That love ufurp'd his airy throne,
His boafted pow'r difplay'd:
'Tis kindnefs that fecures his aim,
'Tis hope that feeds the kindling flame,
　　Which beauty firft convey'd.

In CLARA's eyes, the lightnings view;
Her lips with all the rofe's hue
　　Have all its fweets combin'd;

VOL. I.   K   Yet

Yet vain the blush, and faint the fire,
'Till lips at once, and eyes conspire
  To prove the charmer kind——

Tho' wit might gild the tempting snare,
With softest accent, sweetest air,
  By envy's self admir'd;
If LESBIA's wit betray'd her scorn,
In vain might every grace adorn
  What every muse inspir'd.

Thus airy STREPHON tun'd his lyre——
He scorn'd the pangs of wild desire,
  Which love-sick swains endure:
Resolv'd to brave the keenest dart;
Since frowns could never wound his heart,
  And smiles—must ever cure.

But ah! how false these maxims prove,
How frail security from love,
  Experience hourly shows!
Love can imagin'd smiles supply,
On every charming lip and eye
  Eternal sweets bestows.

In vain we trust the fair-one's eyes;
In vain the sage explores the skies,
  To learn from stars his fate:
'Till led by fancy wide astray,
He finds no planet mark his way;
  Convinc'd and wise—too late.

As partial to their words we prove;
Then boldly join the lifts of love,
   With towering hopes fupply'd :
So heroes, taught by doubtful fhrines,
Miftook their deity's defigns ;
   Then took the field—and dy'd.

+++

The DYING KID.

Optima quæque dies miferis mortalibus ævi
Prima fugit——   Virg.

IMITATION.

Ah ! wretched mortals we !—our brighteft days
On fleeteft pinion fly.

A Tear bedews my DELIA's eye,
   To think yon playful kid muft die;
From cryftal fpring, and flow'ry mead,
Muft, in his prime of life, recede !

Erewhile, in fportive circles round
She faw him wheel, and frifk, and bound;
From rock to rock purfue his way,
And, on the fearful margin, play.

Pleas'd on his various freaks to dwell,
She faw him climb my ruftic cell;
Thence eye my lawns with verdure bright,
And feem all ravifh'd at the fight.

K 2   She

She tells, with what delight he ſtood,
To trace his features in the flood:
Then ſkip'd aloof with quaint amaze;
And then drew near again to gaze.

She tells me how with eager ſpeed
He flew, to hear my vocal reed;
And how with critic face profound,
And ſtedfaſt ear, devour'd the ſound.

His every frolic, light as air,
Deſerves the gentle DELIA's care;
And tears bedew her tender eye,
To think the playful kid muſt die.—

But knows my DELIA, timely wiſe,
How ſoon this blameleſs æra flies?
While violence and craft ſucceed;
Unfair deſign, and ruthleſs deed!

Soon would the vine his wounds deplore,
And yield her purple gifts no more;
Ah ſoon, eras'd from every grove
Were DELIA's name, and STREPHON's love.

No more thoſe bow'rs might STREPHON ſee,
Where firſt he fondly gaz'd on thee;
No more thoſe beds of flow'rets find,
Which for thy charming brows he twin'd.

Each

Each wayward paſſion ſoon would tear
His boſom, now ſo void of care;
And, when they left his ebbing vein,
What, but inſiped age, remain?

Then mourn not the decrees of fate,
That gave his life ſo ſhort a date;
And I will join my tendereſt ſighs,
To think that youth ſo ſwiftly flies!

✦✦✦

SONGS, written chiefly between the Year 1737 and 1742.

SONG I.

I Told my nymph, I told her true,
My fields were ſmall, my flocks were few;
While faultering accents ſpoke my fear,
That FLAVIA might not prove ſincere.

Of crops deſtroy'd by vernal cold,
And vagrant ſheep that left my fold:
Of theſe ſhe heard, yet bore to hear;
And is not FLAVIA then ſincere?

How chang'd by fortune's fickle wind,
The friends I lov'd became unkind,
She heard, and ſhed a generous tear;
And is not FLAVIA then ſincere?

How

How, if fhe deign'd my love to blefs,
My FLAVIA muft not hope for drefs;
This too fhe heard, and fmil'd to hear;
And FLAVIA fure muft be fincere.

Go fhear your flocks, ye jovial fwains,
Go reap the plenty of your plains;
Defpoil'd of all which you revere,
I know my FLAVIA's love fincere.

＋＋＋＋＋＋＋＋＋＋＋＋＋＋＋＋＋＋＋＋＋＋＋＋＋＋＋＋＋＋＋＋＋＋＋＋＋

SONG II. The LANDSKIP.

HOW pleas'd within my native bowers
  Ere while I pafs'd the day!
Was ever fcene fo deck'd with flowers?
  Were ever flowers fo gay?

How fweetly fmil'd the hill, the vale,
  And all the landfkip round!
The river gliding down the dale!
  The hill with beeches crown'd!

But now, when urg'd by tender woes
  I fpeed to meet my dear,
That hill and ftream my zeal oppofe,
  And check my fond career.

No

No more, since DAPHNE was my theme,
 Their wonted charms I see:
That verdant hill, and silver stream,
 Divide my love and me.

++

SONG III.

YE gentle nymphs and generous dames,
 That rule o'er every British mind ;
Be sure ye soothe their amorous flames,
 Be sure your laws are not unkind,

For hard it is to wear their bloom
 In unremitting sighs away :
To mourn the night's oppressive gloom,
 And faintly bless the rising day.

And cruel 'twere a free-born swain,
 A British youth should vainly moan ;
Who, scornful of a tyrant's chain,
 Submits to yours, and yours alone.

Nor pointed spear, nor links of steel,
 Could e'er those gallant minds subdue,
Who beauty's wounds with pleasure feel,
 And boast the fetters wrought by you.

SONG IV. The SKY-LARK,

G O, tuneful bird, that glad'ft the fkies,
   To DAPHNE's window fpeed thy way;
And there on quiv'ring pinions rife,
   And there thy vocal art difplay.

And if fhe deign thy notes to hear,
   And if fhe praife thy matin fong,
Tell her the founds that foothe her ear,
   To DAMON's native plains belong.

Tell her, in livelier plumes array'd,
   The bird from Indian groves may fhine;
But afk the lovely partial maid,
   What are his notes compar'd to thine?

Then bid her treat yon witlefs beau,
   And all his flaunting race with fcorn;
And lend an ear to DAMON's woe,
   Who fings her praife, and fings forlorn.

SONG V.

Ah! ego non aliter tristes evincere morbos
Optarem, quam te sic quoque velle putem.

IMITATION.

Why should I wish to banish sore disease,
Unless returning health my DELIA please?

ON every tree, in every plain,
  I trace the jovial spring in vain!
A sickly langour veils mine eyes,
And fast my waning vigor flies.

Nor flow'ry plain, nor budding tree,
That smile on others, smile on me;
Mine eyes from death shall court repose,
Nor shed a tear before they close.

What bliss to me can seasons bring?
Or, what the needless pride of spring?
The cypress bough, that suits the bier,
Retains its verdure all the year.

'Tis true, my vine so fresh and fair
Might claim awhile my wonted care;
My rural store some pleasure yield;
So white a flock, so green a field!

My friends, that each in kindness vie,
Might well expect one parting sigh;
Might well demand one tender tear;
For when was DAMON unsincere?

But

But ere I aſk once more to. view
Yon ſetting ſun his race renew,
Inform me, ſwains; my friends, declare,
Will pitying DELIA join the prayer?

+++

SONG VI.

The Attribute of VENUS.

YES; FULVIA is like VENUS fair;
    Has all her bloom, and ſhape, and air :
But ſtill, to perfect ev'ry grace,
She wants—the ſmile upon her face.

The crown majeſtic JUNO wore;
And CYNTHIA's brow the creſcent bore,
An helmet mark'd MINERVA's mien,
But ſmiles diſtinguiſh'd beauty's queen.

Her train was form'd of ſmiles and loves,
Her chariot drawn by gentleſt doves !
And from her zone, the nymph may find,
'Tis beauty's province to be kind.

Then ſmile, my fair; and all whoſe aim
Aſpires to. paint the Cyprian dame,
Or bid her breathe in living ſtone,
Shall take their forms from you alone.

SONG

SONG VII. 1744.

THE lovely DELIA smiles again !
 That killing frown has left her brow:
Can she forgive my jealous pain,
 And give me back my angry vow ?

Love is an April's doubtful day : ·
 Awhile we see the tempest low'r ;
Anon the radiant heav'n survey,
 And quite forget the flitting show'r.

The flow'rs, that hung their languid head,
 Are burnish'd by the transient rains ;
The vines their wonted tendrils spread,
 And double verdure gilds the plains.

The sprightly birds, that droop'd no less,
 Beneath the pow'r of rain and wind,
In every raptur'd note, express
 The joy I feel—when thou art kind.

SONG VIII. 1742.

WHEN bright ROXANA treads the green,
 In all the pride of dress and mien;
Averse to freedom, love and play,
The dazzling rival of the day :

None other beauty ſtrikes mine eye,
The lilies droop, the roſes die.

But when, diſclaiming art, the fair
Aſſumes a ſoft engaging air ;
Mild as the opening morn of May,
Familiar, friendly, free and gay :
The ſcene improves, where'er ſhe goes,
More ſweetly ſmile the pink and roſe.

O lovely maid ! propitious hear,
Nor deem thy ſhepherd inſincere ;
Pity a wild illuſive flame,
That varies objects ſtill the ſame :
And let their very changes prove
The never-vary'd force of love.

+++

SONG IX. 1743. VALENTINE'S DAY.

'TIS ſaid that under diſtant ſkies,
  Nor you the fact deny ;
What firſt attracts an Indian's eyes
  Becomes his deity.

Perhaps a lily, or a roſe,
  That ſhares the morning's ray,
May to the waking ſwain diſcloſe
  The regent of the day.

Perhaps

Perhaps a plant in yonder grove,
   Enrich'd with fragrant pow'r,
May tempt his vagrant eyes to rove,
   Where blooms the fov'reign flow'r.

Perch'd on the cedar's topmoft bough,
   And gay with gilded wings,
Perchance, the patron of his vow,
   Some artlefs linnet fings.

The fwain furveys her pleas'd, afraid,
   Then low to earth he bends ;
And owns upon her friendly aid
   His health, his life depends.

Vain futile idols, bird or flow'r,
   To tempt a votary's pray'r !——
How would his humble homage tow'r
   Should he behold my Fair !

Yes—might the pagan's waking eyes,
   O'er FLAVIA's beauty range,
He there would fix his lafting choice,
   Nor dare, nor wifh to change.

SONG

SONG X. 1743.

THE fatal hours are wonderous near,
   That, from thefe fountains, bear my dear;
A little fpace, is giv'n; in vain:
She robs my fight, and fhuns the plain.

A little fpace, for me to prove
My boundlefs flame, my endlefs love;
And like the train of vulgar hours,
Invidious time that fpace devours.

Near yonder beech is DELIA's way,
On that I gaze the livelong day;
No eaftern monarch's dazzling pride
Should draw my longing eyes afide.

The chief, that knows of fuccours nigh,
And fees his mangled legions die,
Cafts not a more impatient glance,
To fee the loitering aids advance.

Not more, the fchool-boy that expires
Far from his native home, requires
To fee fome friend's familiar face,
Or meet a parent's laft embrace——

She comes—but ah! what crowds of beaux
In radiant bands my fair enclose;
Oh! better hadst thou shun'd the green,
Oh DELIA! better far unseen.

Methinks, by all my tender fears,
By all my sighs, by all my tears,
I might from torture now be free—
'Tis more than death to part from thee!

SONG XI. 1744.

PERHAPS it is not love, said I,
That melts my soul when FLAVIA's nigh;
Where wit and sense like her's agree,
One may be pleas'd, and yet be free.

The beauties of her polish'd mind,
It needs no lover's eye to find;
The hermit freezing in his cell
Might wish the gentle FLAVIA well.

It is not love—averse to bear
The servile chain that lovers wear;
Let, let me all my fears remove,
My doubts dispel—it is not love—

Oh!

Oh! when did wit fo brightly fhine
In any form lefs fair than thine?
It is——it is love's fubtle fire,
And under friendfhip lurks defire.

✦✦

SONG XII. 1744.

O'ER defert plains, and rufhy meers,
   And wither'd heaths I rove;
Where tree, nor fpire, nor cot appears,
   I pafs to meet my love.

But tho' my path were damafk'd o'er
   With beauties e'er fo fine;
My bufy thoughts would fly before
   To fix alone—on thine.

No fir-crown'd hills cou'd give delight,
   No palace pleafe mine eye:
No pyramid's aerial height,
   Where mouldering monarchs lie.

Unmov'd, fhould Eaftern kings advance,
   Could I the pageant fee:
Splendour might catch one fcornful glance,
   Not fteal one thought from thee.

SONG

SONG XIII. The Scholar's Relapse.

BY the fide of a grove, at the foot of a hill,
Where whifper'd the beech, and where murmur'd
I vow'd to the mufes my time and my care,   [the rill;
Since neither could win me the fmiles of my fair.

Free I rang'd like the birds, like the birds free I fung,
And DELIA's lov'd name fcarce efcap'd from my tongue:
But if once a fmooth accent delighted my ear,
I fhould wifh, unawares, that my DELIA might hear.

With faireft ideas my bofom I ftor'd,
Allufive to none but the nymph I ador'd!
And the more I with ftudy my fancy refin'd,
The deeper impreffion fhe made on my mind.

So long as of nature the charms I purfue,
I ftill muft my DELIA's dear image renew:
The graces have yielded with DELIA to rove,
And the mufes are all in alliance with love.

SONG XIV. The ROSE-BUD.

SEE, DAPHNE, fee, FLORELIO cry'd,
And learn the fad effects of pride;
Yon fhelter'd rofe, how fafe conceal'd!
How quickly blafted, when reveal'd!

The fun with warm attractive rays
Tempts it to wanton in the blaze:
A gale fucceeds from Eaftern fkies,
And all its blufhing radiance dies.

So you, my fair, of charms divine,
Will quit the plains, too fond to fhine
Where fame's tranfporting rays allure,
Tho' here more happy, more fecure.

The breath of fome neglected maid
Shall make you figh you left the fhade;
A breath to beauty's bloom unkind,
As, to the rofe, an Eaftern wind.

The nymyh reply'd—You firft, my fwain,
Confine your fonnets to the plain;
One envious tongue alike difarms,
You, of your wit, me, of my charms.

What

What is, unknown, the poet's ſkill ?
Or what, unheard, the tuneful thrill ?
What, unadmir'd, a charming mien,
Or what the roſe's bluſh, unſeen ?

✦✦

SONG XV. WINTER. 1746.

NO more, ye warbling birds, rejoice :
   Of all that chear'd the plain,
Echo alone preſerves her voice,
   And ſhe—repeats my pain.

Where'er my love-ſick limbs I lay,
   To ſhun the ruſhing wind,
Its buſy murmur ſeems to ſay,
   " She never will be kind ! "

The naiads, o'er their frozen urns,
   In icy chains repine ;
And each in ſullen ſilence mourns
   Her freedom loſt, like mine !

Soon will the ſun's returning rays
   The chearleſs froſt controul ;
When will relenting DELIA chaſe
   The winter of my ſoul ?

SONG

SONG XVI. Daphne's Visit.

YE birds ! for whom I rear'd the grove,
   With melting lay salute my love :
My DAPHNE with your notes detain :
Or I have rear'd my grove in vain.

Ye flow'rs ! before her footsteps rise ;
Display at once your brightest dyes ;
That she your opening charms may see :
Or what were all your charms to me ?

Kind Zephyr ! brush each fragrant flow'r,
And shed its odours round my bow'r :
Or never more, O gentle wind,
Shall I, from thee, refreshment find.

Ye streams ! if e'er your banks I lov'd,
If e'er your native sounds improv'd,
May each soft murmur soothe my fair :
Or oh ! 'twill deepen my despair.

And thou, my grot ! whose lonely bounds
The melancholy pine surrounds,
May DAPHNE praise thy peaceful gloom ;
Or thou shalt prove her DAMON's tomb.

SONG XVII. Written in a Collection
of BACCHANALIAN SONGS.

ADieu, ye jovial youths, who join
To plunge old care in floods of wine;
And, as your dazzled eye-balls roll,
Difcern him ftruggling in the bowl.

Nor yet is hope fo wholly flown,
Nor yet is thought fo tedious grown,
But limpid ftream and fhady tree
Retain, as yet, fome fweets for me.

And fee, thro' yonder filent grove,
See yonder does my DAPHNE rove:
With pride her footfteps I purfue,
And bid your frantic joys adieu.

The fole confufion I admire,
Is that my DAPHNE's eyes infpire:
I fcorn the madnefs you approve,
And value reafon next to love.

SONG XVIII. Imitated from the FRENCH.

YES, thefe are the fcenes where with Iris I ftray'd,
 But fhort was her fway for fo lovely a maid !
In the bloom of her youth to a cloyfter fhe run ;
In the bloom of her graces, too fair for a nun !
Ill-grounded, no doubt, a devotion muft prove,
So fatal to beauty, fo killing to love !

Yes, thefe are the meadows, the fhrubs and the plains,
Once the fcene of my pleafures, the fcene of my pains ;
How many foft moments I fpent in this grove !
How fair was my nymph ! and how fervent my love !
Be ftill tho', my heart ! thine emotion give o'er ;
Remember, the feafon of love is no more.

With her how I ftray'd amid fountains and bow'rs
Or loiter'd behind and collected the flow'rs !
Then breathlefs with ardor my fair-one purfu'd,
And to think with what kindnefs my garland fhe view'd !
But be ftill, my fond heart ! this emotion give o'er !
Fain wouldft thou forget thou muft love her no more.

‡‡‡‡‡‡‡‡‡‡‡‡‡‡‡‡‡‡‡‡‡‡‡‡‡‡‡‡‡‡‡‡‡‡‡‡‡

The HALCYON.

WHY o'er the verdant banks of ooze
 Does yonder halcyon fpeed fo faft ?
'Tis all becaufe fhe would not lofe
 Her fav'rite calm that will not laft.

The

The fun with azure paints the fkies,
 The ftream reflects each flow'ry fpray ;
And frugal of her time fhe flies
 To take her fill of love and play.

See her, when rugged Boreas blows,
 Warm in fome rocky cell remain ;
To feek for pleafure, well fhe knows,
 Would only then enhance the pain.

Defcend, fhe cries, thou hated fhow'r,
 Deform my limpid waves to-day,
For I have chofe a fairer hour
 To take my fill of love and play.

You too, my SILVIA fure will own
 Life's azure feafons fwiftly roll :
And when our youth, or health is flown,
 To think of love but fhocks the foul.

Could DAMON but deferve thy charms,
 As thou art DAMON's only theme ;
He'd fly as quick to DELIA's arms,
 As yonder halcyon fkims the ftream.

O D E.

O D E.

SO dear my LUCIO is to me,
   So well our minds and tempers blend;
That feafons may for ever flee,
   And ne'er divide me from my friend;
But let the favour'd boy forbear
To tempt with love my only fair.

O LYCON, born when every mufe,
   When every grace benignant fmil'd,
With all a parent's breaft could chufe
   To blefs her lov'd, her only child;
'Tis thine, fo richly grac'd, to prove
More noble cares, than cares of love.

Together we from early youth
   Have trod the flowery tracks of time,
Together mus'd in fearch of truth,
   O'er learned fage, or bard fublime;
And well thy cultur'd breaft I know,
What wonderous treafure it can fhow.

Come then, refume thy charming lyre,
   And fing fome patriot's worth fublime,
Whilft I in fields of foft defire,
   Confume my fair and fruitlefs prime;
Whofe reed afpires but to difplay
The flame that burns me night and day.

                      O come!

O come ! the dryads of the woods
   Shall daily foothe thy ftudious mind,
The blue-ey'd nymphs of yonder floods
   Shall meet and court thee to be kind ;
And fame fits liftening for thy lays
To fwell her trump with Lucio's praife.

Like me, the plover fondly tries
   To lure the fportfman from her neft,
And flutt'ring on with anxious cries,
   Too plainly fhews her tortur'd breaft;
O let him, confcious of her care,
Pity her pains, and learn to fpare.

+++

A PASTORAL ODE,

To the Honourable

Sir RICHARD LYTTELTON.

THE morn difpens'd a dubious light,
   A fullen mift had ftolen from fight
   Each pleafing vale and hill ;
When DAMON left his humble bowers
To guard his flocks, to fence his flowers,
   Or check his wandering rill.

Tho' fchool'd from fortune's paths to fly,
The fwain beneath each low'ring fky,
   Would oft his fate bemoan;

That

That he, in fylvan fhades, forlorn!
Muft wafte his chearlefs ev'n and morn,
   Nor prais'd, nor lov'd, nor known.

No friend to fame's obftreperous noife,
Yet to the whifpers of her voice,
   Soft murmuring, not a foe:
The pleafures he thro' choice declin'd,
When gloomy fogs deprefs'd his mind,
   It griev'd him to forego.

Griev'd him to lurk the lakes befide,
Where coots in rufhy dingles hide,
   And moorcocks fhun the day;
While caitiff bitterns, undifmay'd,
Remark the fwain's familiar fhade,
   And fcorn to quit their prey.

But fee, the radiant fun once more
The brightening face of heaven reftore,
   And raife the doubtful dawn;
And more to gild his rural fphere,
At once the brighteft train appear,
   That ever trod the lawn.

Amazement chill'd the fhepherd's frame,
To think * BRIDGEWATER's honour'd name
   Should grace his ruftic cell;

That

* The Duchefs of BRIDGEWATER, married to Sir RICHARD
LYTTELTON.

That she, on all whose motions wait
Distinction, titles, rank and state,
   Should rove where shepherds dwell.

But true it is, the generous mind,
By candour sway'd, by taste refin'd,
   Will nought but vice disdain;
Nor will the breast where fancy glows
Deem every flower a weed, that blows
   Amid the desart plain.

Beseems it such, with honour crown'd,
To deal its lucid beams around,
   Nor equal meed receive:
At most such garlands from the field,
As cowslips, pinks, and pansies yield,
   And rural hands can weave.

Yet strive, ye shepherds, strive to find,
And weave the fairest of the kind,
   The prime of all the spring;
If haply thus yon lovely fair
May round her temples deign to wear
   The trivial wreaths you bring.

O how the peaceful halcyons play'd,
Where'er the conscious lake betray'd
   ATHENIA's placid mien!
How did the sprightlier linnets throng,
Where PAPHIA's charms requir'd the song,
   'Mid hazel copses green!

                   Lo,

Lo, DARTMOUTH on thofe banks reclin'd,
While bufy fancy calls to mind
   The glories of his line !
Methinks my cottage rears its head,
The ruin'd walls of yonder fhed,
   As thro' enchantment, fhine.

But who the nymph that guides their way?
Could ever nymph defcend to ftray
   From HAGLEY's fam'd retreat ?
Elfe by the blooming features fair,
The faultlefs make, the matchlefs air,
   'Twere CYNTHIA's form compleat.

So would fome tuberofe delight,
That ftruck the pilgrim's wondering fight
   'Mid lonely defarts drear;
All as at eve, the fovereign flower
Difpenfes round its balmy power,
   And crowns the fragrant year,

Ah, now no more, the fhepherd cry'd,
Muft I ambition's charms deride,
   Her fubtle force difown ;
No more of fawns or fairies dream,
While fancy, near each cryftal ftream,
   Shall paint thefe forms alone.

By low-brow'd rock, or pathlefs mead,
I deem'd that fplendour ne'er fhould lead
   My dazzled eyes aftray ;

                              But

But who, alas ! will dare contend,
If beauty add, or merit blend
   Its more illuſtrious ray ?

Nor is it long——O plaintive ſwain !
Since GUERNSEY ſaw, without diſdain,
   Where, hid in woodlands green,
The * partner of his early days,
And once the rival of his praiſe,
   Had ſtol'n thro' life unſeen.

Scarce faded is the vernal flower,
Since STAMFORD left his honour'd bower
   To ſmile familiar here :
O form'd by nature to diſcloſe
How fair that courteſy which flows
   From ſocial warmth ſincere !

Nor yet have many moons decay'd,
Since POLLIO ſought this lonely ſhade,
   Admir'd this rural maze :
The nobleſt breaſt that virtue fires,
The graces love, the muſe inſpires,
   Might pant for POLLIO's praiſe.

Say THOMSON here was known to reſt;
For him yon vernal ſeat I dreſt,
   Ah, never to return !
In place of wit, and melting ſtrains,
And ſocial mirth, it now remains
   To weep beſide his urn.

                           Come

     * They were ſchool-fellows.

Come then, my LELIUS, come once more,
And fringe the melancholy fhore
   With rofes and with bays ;
While I each wayward fate accufe,
That envy'd his impartial mufe,
   To fing your early praife.

While PHILO, to whofe favour'd fight,
Antiquity, with full delight,
   Her inmoft wealth difplays,
Beneath yon ruin's moulder'd wall
Shall mufe, and with his friend recall
   The pomp of ancient days.

Here too fhall CONWAY's name appear;
He prais'd the ftream fo lovely clear,
   That fhone the reeds among ;
Yet clearnefs could it not difclofe,
To match the rhetoric that flows
   From CONWAY's polifh'd tongue.

Ev'n PITT, whofe fervent periods roll
Refiftlefs, thro' the kindling foul
   Of fenates, councils, kings !
Tho' form'd for courts, vouchfaf'd to rove
Inglorious, thro' the fhepherd's grove,
   And ope his bafhful fprings.

But what can courts difcover more,
Than thefe rude haunts have feen before,
   Each fount and fhady tree ?

Have

Have not thefe trees and fountains feen
The pride of courts, the winning mien
   Of peerlefs AYLESBURY?

And GRENVILLE, fhe whofe radiant eyes
Have mark'd by flow gradation rife
   The princely piles of STOW;
Yet prais'd thefe unembellifh'd woods,
And fmil'd to fee the babbling floods
   Thro' felf-worn mazes flow.

Say DARTMOUTH, who your banks admir'd,
Again beneath your caves retir'd,
   Shall grace the penfive fhade;
With all the bloom, with all the truth,
With all the fprightlinefs of youth,
   By cool reflection fway'd!

Brave, yet humane, fhall SMITH appear;
Ye failors, tho' his name be dear,
   Think him not yours alone:
Grant him in other fpheres to charm;
The fhepherds' breafts tho' mild are warm,
   And ours are all his own.

O LYTTELTON! my honour'd gueft,
Could I defcribe thy generous breaft,
   Thy firm, yet polifh'd mind;
How public love adorns thy name,
How fortune too confpires with fame;
   The fong fhould pleafe mankind.

                VERSES

VERSES written towards the clofe of the
Year 1748, to WILLIAM LYTTELTON, Efq.

HOW blithely pafs'd the fummer's day!
How bright was every flow'r!
While friends arriv'd, in circles gay,
To vifit DAMON's bow'r!

But now, with filent ftep, I range
Along fome lonely fhore;
And DAMON's bow'r, alas the change!
Is gay with friends no more.

Away to crowds and cities borne
In queft of joy they fteer;
Whilft I, alas! am left forlorn,
To weep the parting year!

O penfive Autumn! how I grieve
Thy forrowing face to fee!
When languid funs are taking leave
Of every drooping tree.

Ah let me not, with heavy eye,
This dying fcene furvey!
Hafte, Winter, hafte; ufurp the fky;
Compleat my bow'r's decay.

Ill can I bear the motley caſt
   Yon ſickening leaves retain ;
That ſpeak at once of pleaſure paſt,
   And bode approaching pain.

At home unbleſt, I gaze around,
   My diſtant ſcenes require ;
Where all in murky vapours drown'd
   Are hamlet, hill, and ſpire.

Tho' THOMSON, ſweet deſcriptive bard!
   Inſpiring Autumn ſung ;
Yet how ſhould we the months regard,
   That ſtopp'd his flowing tongue ?

Ah luckleſs months, of all the reſt,
   To whoſe hard ſhare it fell !
For ſure he was the gentleſt breaſt
   That ever ſung ſo well.

And ſee, the ſwallows now diſown
   The roofs they lov'd before ;
Each, like his tuneful genius, flown
   To glad ſome happier ſhore.

The wood-nymph eyes, with pale affright,
   The ſportſman's frantic deed ;
While hounds and horns and yells unite
   To drown the muſe's reed.

Ye fields with blighted herbage brown,
　　Ye fkies no longer blue !
Too much we feel from fortune's frown,
　　To bear thefe frowns from you.

Where is the mead's unfullied green ?
　　The zephyr's balmy gale ?
And where fweet friendfhip's cordial mien,
　　That brighten'd every vale ?

What tho' the vine difclofe her dyes,
　　And boaft her purple ftore ;
Not all the vineyard's rich fupplies
　　Can foothe our forrows more.

He ! he is gone, whofe moral ftrain
　　Could wit and mirth refine ;
He ! he is gone, whofe focial vein
　　Surpafs'd the pow'r of wine.

Faft by the ftreams he deign'd to praife,
　　In yon fequefter'd grove,
To him a votive urn I raife ;
　　To him, and friendly love.

Yes there, my friend ! forlorn and fad,
　　I grave your Thomson's name ;
And there, his lyre ; which fate forbad
　　To found your growing fame.

　　　　　　　　　　　　　　There

'There fhall my plaintive fong recount
  Dark themes of hopelefs woe;
And fafter than the dropping fount,
  I'll teach mine eyes to flow.

There leaves, in fpite of Autumn green,
  Shall fhade the hallow'd ground;
And Spring will there again be feen,
  To call forth flow'rs around.

But no kind funs will bid me fhare,
  Once more, his focial hour;
Ah Spring! thou never canft repair
  This lofs, to DAMON's bow'r.

JEMMY DAWSON.

A BALLAD; written about the Time of his Execution, in the Year 1745.

COME liften to my mournful tale,
    Ye tender hearts and lovers dear;
Nor will you fcorn to heave a figh,
  Nor need you blufh to fhed a tear.

And thou, dear KITTY, peerlefs maid,
  Do thou a penfive ear incline;
For thou canft weep at every woe;
  And pity every plaint—but mine.

M 2   Young

Young DAWSON was a gallant boy,
  A brighter never trod the plain;
And well he lov'd one charming maid,
  And dearly was he lov'd again.

One tender maid, she lov'd him dear,
  Of gentle blood the damsel came;
And faultless was her beauteous form,
  And spotless was her virgin fame.

But curse on party's hateful strife,
  That led the favour'd youth astray;
The day the rebel clans appear'd,
  O had he never seen that day!

Their colours, and their sash he wore,
  And in the fatal dress was found;
And now he must that death endure,
  Which gives the brave the keenest wound.

How pale was then his true-love's cheek,
  When JEMMY's sentence reach'd her ear!
For never yet did Alpine snows
  So pale, or yet so chill appear.

With faultering voice, she weeping said,
  O DAWSON, monarch of my heart;
Think not thy death shall end our loves,
  For thou and I will never part.

Yet

Yet might fweet mercy find a place,
  And bring relief to JEMMY's woes;
O GEORGE, without a pray'r for thee,
  My orifons fhould never clofe.

The gracious prince that gave him life,
  Would crown a never-dying flame;
And every tender babe I bore
  Should learn to lifp the giver's name.

But tho' he fhould be dragg'd in fcorn
  To yonder ignominious tree;
He fhall not want one conftant friend
  To fhare the cruel fates' decree.

O then her mourning coach was call'd,
  The fledge mov'd flowly on before;
Tho' borne in a triumphal car,
  She had not lov'd her fav'rite more.

She follow'd him, prepar'd to view
  The terrible behefts of law;
And the laft fcene of JEMMY's woes,
  With calm and ftedfaft eye fhe faw.

Diftorted was that blooming face,
  Which fhe had fondly lov'd fo long;
And ftifled was that tuneful breath,
  Which in her praife had fweetly fung.

And

And fever'd was that beauteous neck,
    Round which her arms had fondly clos'd;
And mangled was that beauteous breast,
    On which her love-sick head repos'd:

And ravish'd was that constant heart,
    She did to every heart prefer;
For tho' it could its king forget,
    'Twas true and loyal still to her.

Amid those unrelenting flames,
    She bore this constant heart to see;
But when 'twas moulder'd into dust,
    Yet, yet, she cry'd, I follow thee.

My death, my death alone can shew
    The pure, the lasting love I bore;
Accept, O heaven! of woes like ours,
    And let us, let us weep no more.

The dismal scene was o'er and past,
    The lover's mournful hearse retir'd;
The maid drew back her languid head,
    And sighing forth his name, expir'd.

Tho' justice ever must prevail,
    The tear my KITTY sheds, is due;
For seldom shall she hear a tale
    So sad, so tender, yet so true.

                                A Pastoral

A Pastoral BALLAD, in Four Parts.
Written 1743.

Arbusta humilesque myricæ.   VIRG.

EXPLANATION.
Groves and lowly shrubs.

I. ABSENCE.

YE shepherds so chearful and gay,
   Whose flocks never carelesly roam;
Should CORYDON's happen to stray,
   Oh! call the poor wanderers home.
Allow me to muse and to sigh,
   Nor talk of the change that ye find;
None once was so watchful as I;
   —I have left my dear PHILLIS behind.

Now I know what it is to have strove
   With the torture of doubt and desire;
What it is, to admire and to love,
   And to leave her we love and admire.
Ah lead forth my flock in the morn,
   And the damps of each ev'ning repel;
Alas! I am faint and forlorn:
   —I have bade my dear PHYLLIS farewel.

Since PHILLIS vouchsaf'd me a look,
   I never once dreamt of my vine;
May I lose both my pipe and my crook,
   If I knew of a kid that was mine.

M 4   I priz'd

I priz'd every hour that went by,
   Beyond all that had pleas'd me before;
But now they are paft, and I figh;
   And I grieve that I priz'd them no more.

But why do I languifh in vain?
   Why wander thus penfively here?
Oh! why did I come from the plain,
   Where I fed on the fmiles of my dear?
They tell me, my favorite maid,
   The pride of that valley, is flown;
Alas! where with her I have ftray'd,
   I could wander with pleafure, alone.

When forc'd the fair nymph to forego,
   What anguifh I felt at my heart!
Yet I thought—but it might not be fo—
   'Twas with pain that fhe faw me depart.
She gaz'd, as I flowly withdrew;
   My path I could hardly difcern;
So fweetly fhe bade me adieu,
   I thought that fhe bade me return.

The pilgrim that journeys all day
   To vifit fome far-diftant fhrine,
If he bear but a relique away,
   Is happy, nor heard to repine.
Thus widely remov'd from the fair,
   Where my vows, my devotion, I owe,
Soft hope is the relique I bear,
   And my folace wherever I go.

                       II. HOPE.

II. HOPE.

MY banks they are furnifh'd with bees,
   Whofe murmur invites one to fleep;
My grottos are fhaded with trees,
   And my hills are white-over with fheep.
I feldom have met with a lofs,
   Such health do my fountains beftow;
My fountains all border'd with mofs,
   Where the hare-bells and violets grow.

Not a pine in my grove is there feen,
   But with tendrils of woodbine is bound:
Not a beech's more beautiful green,
   But a fweet-briar entwines it around,
Not my fields, in the prime of the year,
   More charms than my cattle unfold;
Not a brook that is limped and clear,
   But it glitters with fifhes of gold.

One would think fhe might like to retire
   To the bow'r I have labour'd to rear:
Not a fhrub that I heard her admire,
   But I hafted and planted it there.
O how fudden the jeffamine ftrove
   With the lilac to render it gay!
Already it calls for my love,
   To prune the wild branches away.

From

From the plains, from the woodlands and groves,
 What strains of wild melody flow !
How the nightingales warble their loves
 From thickets of roses that blow !
And when her bright form shall appear,
 Each bird shall harmoniously join
In a concert so soft and so clear,
 As—she may not be fond to resign.

I have found out a gift for my fair;
 I have found where the wood-pigeons breed :
But let me that plunder forbear,
 She will say 'twas a barbarous deed.
For he ne'er could be true, she averr'd,
 Who could rob a poor bird of its young :
And I lov'd her the more, when I heard
 Such tenderness fall from her tongue.

I have heard her with sweetness unfold
 How that pity was due to—a dove ;
That it ever attended the bold ;
 And she call'd it the sister of love.
But her words such a pleasure convey,
 So much I her accents adore,
Let her speak, and whatever she say,
 Methinks I should love her the more.

Can

Can a bosom so gentle remain
 Unmov'd, when her CORYDON sighs!
Will a nymph that is fond of the plain,
 These plains and this valley despise?
Dear regions of silence and shade!
 Soft scenes of contentment and ease!
Where I could have pleasingly stray'd,
 If aught, in her absence, could please.

But where does my PHYLLIDA stray?
 And where are her grots and her bow'rs?
Are the groves and the valleys as gay,
 And the shepherds as gentle as ours?
The groves may perhaps be as fair,
 And the face of the valleys as fine;
The swains may in manners compare,
 But their love is not equal to mine.

III. SOLICITUDE.

WHY will you my passion reprove?
 Why term it a folly to grieve?
Ere I shew you the charms of my love,
 She is fairer than you can believe.
With her mien she enamours the brave;
 With her wit she engages the free;
With her modesty pleases the grave;
 She is ev'ry way pleasing to me.

O you

O you that have been of her train,
  Come and join in my amorous lays ;
I could lay down my life for the fwain,
  That will fing but a fong in her praife.
When he fings, may the nymphs of the town
  Come trooping, and liften the while ;
Nay on him let not PHYLLIDA frown ;
  —But I cannot allow her to fmile.

For when PARIDEL tries in the dance
  Any favour with Phyllis to find,
O how, with one trivial glance,
  Might fhe ruin the peace of my mind !
In ringlets he dreffes his hair,
  And his crook is be-ftudded around ;
And his pipe—oh may PHYLLIS beware
  Of a magic there is in the found !

'Tis his with mock paffion to glow ;
  'Tis his in fmooth tales to unfold,
" How her face is as bright as the fnow,
  And her bofom, be fure, is as cold.
How the nightingales labour the ftrain,
  With the notes of his charmer to vie ;
How they vary their accents in vain,
  Repine at her triumphs, and die."

To the grove or the garden he ſtrays,
   And pillages every ſweet;
Then, ſuiting the wreath to his lays,
   He throws it at PHYLLIS's feet.
" O PHYLLIS, he whiſpers, more fair,
   More ſweet than the jeſſamine's flow'r!
What are pinks, in a morn, to compare?
   What is eglantine, after a ſhow'r?

Then the lily no longer is white;
   Then the roſe is depriv'd of its bloom;
Then the violets die with deſpight,
   And the wood-bines give up their perfume."
Thus glide the ſoft numbers along,
   And he fancies no ſhepherd his peer;
——Yet I never ſhould envy the ſong,
   Were not PHYLLIS to lend it an ear.

Let his crook be with hyacinths bound,
   So PHYLLIS the trophy deſpiſe:
Let his forehead with laurels be crown'd,
   So they ſhine not in PHYLLIS's eyes.
The language that flows from the heart
   Is a ſtranger to PARIDEL's tongue;
——Yet may ſhe beware of his art,
   Or ſure I muſt envy the ſong.

IV. DIS-

IV. DISAPPOINTMENT.

YE fhepherds give ear to my lay,
 And take no more heed of my fheep :
They have nothing to do but to ftray ;
 I have nothing to do but to weep.
Yet do not my folly reprove ;
 She was fair—and my paffion begun ;
She fmil'd—and I could not but love ;
 She is faithlefs—and I am undone.

Perhaps I was void of all thought :
 Perhaps it was plain to forefee,
That a nymph fo compleat would be fought
 By a fwain more engaging than me.
Ah ! love ev'ry hope can infpire ;
 It banifhes wifdom the while ;
And the lip of the nymph we admire
 Seems for ever adorn'd with a fmile,

She is faithlefs, and I am undone ;
 Ye that witnefs the woes I endure,
Let reafon inftruct you to fhun
 What it cannot inftruct you to cure.
Beware how you loiter in vain
 Amid nymphs of an higher degree :
It is not for me to explain
 How fair, and how fickle they be.

        Alas !

Alas! from the day that we met,
　　What hope of an end to my woes?
When I cannot endure to forget
　　The glance that undid my repose.
Yet time may diminish the pain:
　　The flow'r, and the shrub, and the tree,
Which I rear'd for her pleasure in vain,
　　In time may have comfort for me.

The sweets of a dew-sprinkled rose,
　　The sound of a murmuring stream,
The peace which from solitude flows,
　　Henceforth shall be CORYDON's theme:
High transports are shewn to the sight,
　　But we are not to find them our own;
Fate never bestow'd such delight,
　　As I with my PHYLLIS had known.

O ye woods, spread your branches apace;
　　To your deepest recesses I fly;
I would hide with the beasts of the chace
　　I would vanish from every eye.
Yet my reed shall resound thro' the grove
　　With the same sad complaint it begun;
How she smil'd, and I could not but love;
　　Was faithless, and I am undone!

LEVITIES;

L E V I T I E S;

O R

PIECES of HUMOUR.

LEVITIES

OR

PIECES of HUMOUR.

FLIRT and PHIL;
A Decision for the LADIES.

A Wit, by learning well refin'd,
   A beau, but of the rural kind,
  To SILVIA made pretences;
They both profess'd an equal love:
Yet hop'd, by different means to move
  Her judgment, or her senses.

Young sprightly FLIRT, of blooming mien,
Watch'd the best minutes to be seen;
  Went—when his glass advis'd him:
While meagre PHIL of books enquir'd;
A wight for wit and parts admir'd;
  And witty ladies priz'd him.

SILVIA

SILVIA had wit, had spirits too;
To hear the one, the other view,
   Suspended held the scales:
Her wit, her youth too, claim'd its share,
Let none the preference declare,
   But turn up—heads or tails.

✦✦✦✦✦✦✦✦✦✦✦✦✦✦✦✦✦✦✦✦✦✦✦✦✦✦✦✦✦✦✦✦✦✦✦

STANZAS to the Memory of an agreeable LADY, buried in Marriage to a Person undeserving her.

'TWAS always held, and ever will,
   By sage mankind, discreeter,
T' anticipate a lesser ill,
   Than undergo a greater.

When mortals dread diseases, pain,
   And languishing conditions;
Who don't the lesser ills sustain
   Of physic—and physicians?

Rather than lose his whole estate,
   He that but little wise is,
Full gladly pays four parts in eight
   To taxes and excises.

Our merchants Spain has near undone
   For lost ships not requiting:
This bears our noble k—, to shun
   The loss of blood—in fighting!

With

With num'rous ills, in single life,
  The bachelor's attended:
Such to avoid, he takes a wife—
  And much the case is mended!

Poor GRATIA, in her twentieth year,
  Foreseeing future woe,
Chose to attend a monkey here,
  Before an ape below.

✦✦✦✦✦✦✦✦✦✦✦✦✦✦✦✦✦✦✦✦✦✦✦✦✦✦✦✦✦✦✦

COLEMIRA.
A Culinary ECLOGUE.

Nec tantum Veneris, quantum studiosa culinæ.
IMITATION.
Insensible of soft desire,
  Behold Colemira prove
More partial to the *kitchen fire*
  Than to the *fire of love.*

Night's sable clouds had half the globe o'erspread,
  And silence reign'd, and folks were gone to bed:
When love, which gentle sleep can ne'er inspire,
Had seated DAMON by the kitchen fire.

Pensive he lay, extended on the ground;
The little lares kept their vigils round;
The fawning cats compassionate his case,
And purr around, and gently lick his face:

To all his 'plaints the fleeping curs reply,
And with hoarfe fnorings imitate a figh.
Such gloomy fcenes with lovers' minds agree,
And folitude to them is beft fociety.

Could I (he cry'd) exprefs, how bright a grace
Adorns thy morning hands, and well-wafh'd face;
Thou would'ft, COLEMIRA, grant what I implore,
And yield me love, or wafh thy face no more.

Ah! who can fee, and feeing not admire,
Whene'er fhe fets the pot upon the fire!
Her hands out-fhine the fire, and redder things!
Her eyes are blacker than the pots fhe brings.

But fure no chamber-damfel can compare,
When in meridian luftre fhines my fair,
When warm'd with dinner's toil, in pearly rills,
Adown her goodly cheek the fweat diftills.

Oh! how I long, how ardently defire,
To view thofe rofy fingers ftrike the lyre!
For late, when bees to change their climes began,
How did I fee 'em thrum the frying-pan!

With her! I fhould not envy G— his queen,
Tho' fhe in royal grandeur deck'd be feen:
Whilft rags, juft fever'd from my fair-one's gown,
In ruffet pomp, and greafy pride hang down.

Ah!

Ah! how it does my drooping heart rejoice,
When in the hall I hear thy mellow voice!
How would that voice exceed the village bell;
Wou'dst thou but sing, "I like thee paffing well!"

When from the hearth she bade the pointers go,
How soft! how eafy, did her accents flow!
"Get out," she cry'd, "when ftrangers come to fup,
"One ne'er can raife those fnoring devils up."

Then, full of wrath, she kick'd each lazy brute,
Alas! I envy'd even that falute:
'Twas fure mifplac'd,—SHOCK faid, or feem'd to fay,
He had as lief, I had the kick, as they.

If she the myftic bellows take in hand,
Who like the fair can that machine command?
O may'ft thou ne'er by EOLUS be feen,
For he wou'd fure demand thee for his queen.

But shou'd the flame this rougher aid refufe,
And only gentler med'cines be of ufe;
With full-blown cheeks she ends the doubtful ftrife,
Foments the infant flame, and puffs it into life.

Such arts, as these, exalt the drooping fire,
But in my breaft a fiercer flame infpire:
I burn! I burn! O! give thy puffing o'er,
And fwell thy cheeks, and pout thy lips no more!

With

With all her haughty looks, the time I've feen,
When this proud damfel has more humble been,
When with nice airs fhe hoift the pancake round,
And dropt it, haplefs fair ! upon the ground.

Look, with what charming grace ! what winning tricks !
The artful charmer rubs the candlefticks !
So bright fhe makes the candlefticks fhe handles,
Oft have I faid,—there were no need of candles.

But thou, my fair ! who never would'ft approve,
Or hear the tender ftory of my love ;
Or mind, how burns my raging breaft,—a button—
Perhaps art dreaming of—a breaft of mutton.

Thus faid, and wept, the fad defponding fwain,
Revealing to the fable walls his pain :
But nymphs are free with thofe they fhou'd deny ;
To thofe, they love, more exquifitely coy !

Now chirping crickets raife their tinkling voice, ⎫
The lambent flames in languid ftreams arife,   ⎬
And fmoke in azure folds evaporates and dies.   ⎭

✠

The RAPE of the TRAP.
A BALLAD, 1737.

'TWAS in a land of learning,
       The mufes' fav'rite city,
Such pranks of late
Were play'd by a rat,
   As—tempt one to be witty.

All

All in a college ſtudy,
 Where books were in great plenty;
This rat would devour
More ſenſe in an hour,
 Than I cou'd write—in twenty.

Corporeal food, 'tis granted,
 Serves vermin leſs refin'd, Sir;
But this, a rat of taſte,
All other rats ſurpaſs'd;
 And he prey'd on the food of the mind, Sir.

His breakfaſt, half the morning,
 He conſtantly attended;
And when the bell rung
For ev'ning ſong,
 His dinner ſcarce was ended!

He ſpar'd not ev'n heroics,
 On which we poets pride us;
And wou'd make no more
Of king ARTHUR's *, by the ſcore,
 Than—all the world beſide does.

In books of geo-graphy,
 He made the maps to flutter:
A river or a ſea
Was to him a diſh of tea;
 And a kingdom, bread and butter.

But

* By BLACKMORE.

But if fome mawkifh potion
   Might chance to over-dofe him,
'To check its rage,
He took a page
   Of logic—to compofe him—

A trap, in hafte and anger,
   Was bought, you need not doubt on't;
And, fuch was the gin,
Were a lion once got in,
   He cou'd not, I think, get out on't.

With cheefe, not books, 'twas baited,
   The fact—I'll not belye it—
Since none—I tell you that—
Whether fcholar or rat,
   Minds books, when he has other diet.

But more of trap and bait, Sir,
   Why fhou'd I fing, or either?
Since the rat, who knew the fleight,
Came in the dead of night,
   And dragg'd 'em away together:

Both trap and bait were vanifh'd,
   Thro' a fracture in the flooring;
Which, tho' fo trim
It now may feem,
   Had then—a dozen or more in.

Then

Then anfwer this, ye fages!
 Nor deem I mean to wrong ye,
Had the rat which thus did feize on
The trap, lefs claim to reafon,
 Than many a fcull among ye?

DAN PRIOR's mice, I own it,
 Were vermin of condition;
But this rat, who merely learn'd
What rats alone concern'd,
 Was the greater politician.

That England's topfy-turvy,
 Is clear from thefe mifhaps, Sir;
Since traps, we may determine,
Will no longer take our vermin,
 But vermin * take our traps, Sir.

Let fophs, by rats infefted,
 Then truft in cats to catch 'em;
Left they grow as learn'd as we,
In our ftudies; where, d'ye fee,
 No mortal fits to watch 'em.

Good luck betide our captains;
 Good luck betide our cats, Sir;
And grant that the one
May quell the Spanifh Don,
 And the other deftroy our rats, Sir.

On

* Written at the time of the Spanifh depredations.

On certain P A S T O R A L S.

SO rude and tunefels are thy lays,
  The weary audience vow,
'Tis not th' Arcadian fwain that fings,
  But 'tis his herds that low.

+++

On Mr. C—— of KIDDERMINSTER's Poetry.

THY verfes, friend, are KIDDERMINSTER * fluff,
  And I muft own you've meafur'd out enough.

+++

To the V I R T U O S O S.

HAIL curious wights! to whom fo fair ;
  The form of mortal flies is!
Who deem thofe grubs beyond compare,
  Which common fenfe defpifes.

Whether o'er hill, morafs or mound,
  You make your fportfman fallies ;
Or that your prey in gardens found
  Is urg'd thro' walks and allies,

                                   Yet,

* KIDDERMINSTER, famous for a coarfe woollen manufacture.

Yet, in the fury of the chace,
　　No flope cou'd e'er retard you;
Bleft if one fly repay the race,
　　Or painted wing reward you.

Fierce as CAMILLA * o'er the plain
　　Purfu'd the glitt'ring ftranger;
Still ey'd the purple's pleafing ftain,
　　And knew not fear nor danger.

'Tis you difpenfe the fav'rite meat
　　To nature's filmy people;
Know what conferves they chufe to eat,
　　And what liqueurs to tipple.

And, if her brood of infects dies,
　　You fage affiftance lend her;
Can ftoop to pimp for am'rous flies,
　　And help 'em to engender.

'Tis you protect their pregnant hour;
　　And, when the birth's at hand,
Exerting your obftetric pow'r,
　　Prevent a mothlefs land.

Yet oh! howe'er your tow'ring view
　　Above grofs objects rifes,
Whate'er refinements you purfue,
　　Hear, what a friend advifes:

　　　　　　　　　　　　　　　A friend,

* See VIRGIL.

A friend, who, weigh'd with yours, muſt prize
   DOMITIAN's idle paſſion;
That wrought the death of teazing flies,
   But ne'er their propagation.

Let FLAVIA's eyes more deeply warm,
   Nor thus your hearts determine,
To ſlight dame nature's faireſt form
   And ſigh for nature's vermin.

And ſpeak with ſome reſpect of beaux,
   No more as triflers treat 'em;
'Tis better learn to ſave one's cloaths,
   Than cheriſh moths, that eat 'em.

The EXTENT of COOKERY.

Aliuſque et idem.

EXPLANATION.

Another and the ſame.

WHEN TOM to CAMBRIDGE firſt was ſent
   A plain brown bob he wore;
Read much, and look'd as tho' he meant
   To be a fop no more.

See him to LINCOLN's-INN repair,
   His reſolution flag;
He cheriſhes a length of hair,
   And tucks it in a bag.

Nor COKE nor SALKELD he regards,
　　But gets into the houfe,
And foon a judge's rank rewards
　　His pliant votes and bows.

Adieu ye bobs! ye bags give place!
　　Full bottoms come inftead!
Good L——d! to fee the various ways
　　Of dreffing—a calve's-head!

━━━━━━━━━━━━━━━━━━━━━━━━━━━━━━━

The PROGRESS of ADVICE.
A Common CASE.

Suade, nam certum eft.

EXPLANATION.
Advife it, for 'tis fix'd.

SAYS RICHARD to THOMAS (and feem'd half afraid)
　"I am thinking to marry thy miftrefs's maid:
Now, becaufe Mrs. LUCY to thee is well known,
I will do't if thou bid'ft me, or let it alone.

Nay don't make a jeft on't; 'tis no jeft to me;
For 'faith I'm in earneft, fo prithee be free.
I have no fault to find with the girl fince I knew her,
But I'd have thy advice, ere I tye myfelf to her."

Said THOMAS to RICHARD, "To fpeak my opinion,
There is not fuch a bitch in King GEORGE's dominion,
And I firmly believe, if thou knew'ft her as I do,
Thou wou'dft chufe out a whipping-poft, firft, to be ty'd to.

She's

She's peevifh, fhe's thievifh, fhe's ugly, fhe's old,
And a lyar, and a fool, and a flut, and a fcold,"
Next day RICHARD haften'd to church and was wed,
And ere night had inform'd her what THOMAS had faid.

✦✦✦

A BALLAD.

Trahit fua quemque voluptas.   HOR.

PROVERBIALIZ'D.

Every one to his liking.

FROM Lincoln to London rode forth our young fquire,
To bring down a wife, whom the fwains might ad-
But in fpite of whatever the mortal cou'd fay,   [mire;
The goddefs objected the length of the way !

To give up the op'ra, the park, and the ball,
For to view the ftag's horns in an old country hall;
To have neither China nor India to fee !
Nor a laceman to plague in a morning—not fhe !

To forfake the dear play-houfe, Quin, Garrick, and Clive,
Who by dint of mere humour had kept her alive;
To forego the full box for his lonefome abode,
O heav'ns ! fhe fhou'd faint, fhe fhou'd die on the road !

To forget the gay fafhions and geftures of France,
And to leave dear Augufte in the midft of the dance,
And Harlequin to !—'twas in vain to require it ;
And fhe wonder'd how folks had the face to defire it.

She

She might yield to refign the fweet-fingers of Ruckholt,
Where the citizen-matron feduces her cuckold ;
But Ranelagh foon would her footfteps recall,
And the mufic, the lamps, and the glare of Vauxhall.

To be fure fhe cou'd breathe no where elfe than in town,
Thus fhe talk'd like a wit, and he look'd like a clown ;
But the while honeft Harry defpair'd to fucceed,
A coach with a coronet trail'd her to Tweed.

++

SLENDER's Ghoft. *vid.* SHAKESPEAR.

BEneath a church-yard yew,
  Decay'd and worn with age,
At dufk of eve methought I fpy'd
Poor SLENDER's ghoft, that whimp'ring cry'd,
  O fweet O fweet ANNE PAGE!

Ye gentle bards ! give ear !
  Who talk of am'rous rage,
Who fpoil the lily, rob the rofe,
Come learn of me to weep your woes :
  O fweet O fweet ANNE PAGE!

Why fhou'd fuch labour'd ftrains
  Your formal Mufe engage ?
I never dreamt of flame or dart,
That fir'd my breaft, or pierc'd my heart,
  But figh'd, O fweet ANNE PAGE!

And you! whofe love-fick minds,
   No med'cine can affuage!
Accufe the leech's art no more,
But learn of SLENDER to deplore;
   O fweet O fweet ANNE PAGE!

And ye! whofe fouls are held,
   Like linnets in a cage!
Who talk of fetters, links and chains,
Attend, and imitate my ftrains!
   O fweet O fweet ANNE PAGE!

And you who boaft or grieve,
   What horrid wars ye wage!
Of wounds receiv'd from many an eye;
Yet mean as I do, when I figh
   O fweet O fweet ANNE PAGE!

Hence ev'ry fond conceit
   Of fhepherd or of fage;
'Tis SLENDER's voice, 'tis SLENDER's way
Expreffes all you have to fay,
   O fweet O fweet ANNE PAGE!

✦✦✦✦✦✦✦✦✦✦✦✦✦✦✦✦✦✦✦✦✦✦✦✦✦✦✦✦✦✦✦✦

The INVIDIOUS.   MART.

O Fortune! if my pray'r of old
   Was ne'er folicitous for gold,
With better grace thou may'ft allow
My fuppliant wifh, that afks it now.

                          Yet

Yet think not, goddefs! I require it
For the fame end your clowns defire it.
In a well-made effectual ftring,
Fain would I fee LIVIDIO fwing!
Hear him, from Tyburn's height haranguing,
But fuch a cur's not worth one's hanging.
Give me, O goddefs! ftore of pelf,
And he will tye the knot himfelf.

<hr />

The PRICE of an EQUIPAGE.

Servum fi potes, Ole, non habere,
Et regem potes, Ole, non habere.   MART.

"If thou from Fortune doft no fervant crave,
"Believe me, thou no mafter need'ft to have."

I Afk'd a friend, amidft the throng,
  Whofe coach it was that trail'd along:
" The gilded coach there—don't ye mind?
That, with the footmen ftuck behind."

  O Sir! fays he, what! han't you feen it?
'Tis DAMON's coach, and DAMON in it.
'Tis odd methinks you have forgot
Your friend, your neighbour, and—what not!
Your old acquaintance DAMON!—"True;
But faith his equipage is new."

  " Blefs me, faid I, where can it end?
What madnefs has poffefs'd my friend?
Four powder'd flaves, and thofe the talleft,
Their ftomachs doubtlefs not the fmalleft!

O 2   Can

Can DAMON's revenue maintain
In lace and food, fo large a train?
I know his land—each inch o' ground—
'Tis not a mile to walk it round—
If DAMON's whole eftate can bear
To keep his lad, and one-horfe chair,
I own 'tis paft my comprehenfion."
Yes, Sir, but DAMON has a penfion—
　　Thus does a falfe ambition rule us,
Thus pomp delude, and folly fool us;
To keep a race of flick'ring knaves,
He grows himfelf the worft of flaves.

✦✦✦✦✦✦✦✦✦✦✦✦✦✦✦✦✦✦✦✦✦✦✦✦✦✦✦✦✦✦✦✦✦✦

HINT from VOITURE.

LET SOL his annual journeys run,
　And when the radiant tafk is done,
Confefs, thro' all the globe, 'twould pofe him,
To match the charms that CELIA fhews him.

And fhou'd he boaft he once had feen
As juft a form, as bright a mien,
Yet muft it ftill for ever pofe him,
To match—what CELIA never fhews him.

✦✦✦✦✦✦✦✦✦✦✦✦✦✦✦✦✦✦✦✦✦✦✦✦✦✦✦✦✦✦✦✦✦✦

INSCRIPTION.

To the memory
Of A. L. Efquire,
Juftice of the peace for this county:

Who,

Who, in the whole courfe of his pilgrimage
Thro' a trifling ridiculous world,
Maintaining his proper dignity,
Notwithstanding the fcoffs of ill-difpos'd perfons,
And wits of the age,
That ridicul'd his behaviour,
Or cenfur'd his breeding;
Following the dictates of nature,
Defiring to eafe the afflicted,
Eager to fet the prifoners at liberty,
Without having for his end
The noife, or report fuch things generally caufe
. In the world,
(As he was feen to perform them of none)
But the fole relief and happinefs
Of the party in diftrefs;
Himfelf refting eafy,
When he cou'd render that fo;
Not griping, or pinching himfelf,
To hoard up fuperfluities;
Not coveting to keep in his poffeffion
What gives more difquietude, than pleafure;
But charitably diffufing it
To all round about him:
Making the moft forrowful countenance
To fmile,
In his prefence;
Always beftowing more than he was afk'd,
Always imparting before he was defir'd;
Not proceeding in this manner,

O 3   Upon

Upon every trivial fuggeftion,
But the moft mature, and folemn deliberation;
With an incredible prefence, and undauntednefs
Of mind;
With an inimitable gravity and œconomy
Of face;
Bidding loud defiance
To politenefs and the fafhion,
Dar'd let a f—t.

+

To a FRIEND.

HAVE you ne'er feen, my gentle fquire,
  The humours of your kitchen fire?
Says NED to SAL, "I lead a fpade,
Why don't ye play?—the girl's afraid—
Play fomething—any thing—but play—
'Tis but to pafs the time away—
Phoo—how fhe ftands—biting her nails—
As tho' fhe play'd for half her vails—
Sorting her cards, hagling and picking—
We play for nothing, do us, chicken?
That card will do—'blood, never doubt it,
It's not worth while to think about it."
  SAL thought, and thought, and mifs'd her aim,
And NED, ne'er ftudying, won the game.
  Methinks, old friend, 'tis wond'rous true,
That verfe is but a game at loo.

While many a bard, that shews so clearly
He writes for his amusement merely,
Is known to study, fret, and toil;
And play for nothing all the while:
Or praise at most; for wreaths of yore
Ne'er signify'd a farthing more:
'Till having vainly toil'd to gain it,
He sees your flying pen obtain it.

   Thro' fragrant scenes the trifler roves,
And hallow'd haunts that PHOEBUS loves:
Where with strange heats his bosom glows,
And mystic flames the God bestows.
You now none other flame require,
Than a good blazing parlour fire;
Write verses—to defy the scorners,
In shit-houses and chimney-corners.

   SAL found her deep-laid schemes were vain—
The cards are cut—come deal again—
No good comes on it when one lingers—
I'll play the cards come next my fingers—
Fortune could never let NED loo her,
When she had left it wholly to her.

   Well, now who wins?—why, still the same—
For SAL has lost another game.

   " I've done; (she mutter'd) I was saying,
It did not argufy my playing.
Some folks will win, they cannot chuse,
But think or not think—some must lose.
I may have won a game or so—
But then it was an age ago—

It

It ne'er will be my lot again—
I won it of a baby then—
Give me an ace of trumps and fee,
Our NED will beat me with a three.
'Tis all by luck that things are carry'd—
He'll fuffer for it, when he's marry'd."

Thus SAL, with tears in either eye;
While victor NED fate titt'ring by.

Thus I, long envying your fuccefs,
And bent to write, and ftudy lefs,
Sate down, and fcribbled in a trice,
Juft what you fee—and you defpife.

You, who can frame a tuneful fong,
And hum it as you ride along;
And, trotting on the king's highway,
Snatch from the hedge a fprig of bay;
Accept this verfe, howe'er it flows,
From one that is your friend in profe.

What is this wreath, fo green! fo fair!
Which many wifh, and few muft wear?
Which fome men's indolence can gain,
And fome men's vigils ne'er obtain?
For what muft SAL or poet fue,
Ere they engage with NED or you?
For luck in verfe, for luck at loo?

Ah no! 'tis genius gives you fame.
And NED, thro' fkill, fecures the game.

The

The POET and the DUN. 1741.

Thefe are meffengers
That feelingly perfuade me what I am.
                                SHAKESPEAR.

COMES a dun in the morning and raps at my door—
    "I made bold to call—'tis a twelvemonth and more—
I'm forry, believe me, to trouble you thus, Sir,—
But Job wou'd be paid, Sir, had Job been a mercer."
My friend, have but patience—" Ay thefe are your ways."
I have got but one fhilling to ferve me two days—
But, Sir—prithee take it, and tell your attorney,
If I han't paid your bill, I have paid for your journey.
    Well, now thou art gone, let me govern my paffion,
And calmly confider—confider? vexation !
What whore that muft paint, and muft put on falfe locks,
And counterfeit joy in the pangs of the pox !
What beggar's wife's nephew, now ftarv'd, and now beaten,
Who, wanting to eat, fears himfelf fhall be eaten !
What porter, what turnfpit, can deem his cafe hard !
Or what dun boaft of patience that thinks of a bard !
Well, I'll leave this poor trade, for no trade can be poorer,
Turn fhoe-boy, or courtier, or pimp, or procurer ;
Get love, and refpect, and good living, and pelf,
And dun fome poor dog of a poet myfelf.
One's credit, however, of courfe will grow better ;
Here enters the footman, and brings me a letter.
                                " Dear

" Dear Sir ! I receiv'd your obliging epiftle,
Your fame is fecure—bid the critics go whiftle.
I read over with wonder the poem you fent me ;
And I muft fpeak your praifes, no foul fhall prevent me.
The audience, believe me, cry'd out ev'ry line
Was ftrong, was affecting, was juft, was divine ;
All pregnant, as gold is, with worth, weight and beauty,
And to hide fuch a genius was—far from your duty.
I forefee that the court will be hugely delighted :
Sir RICHARD, for much a lefs genius, was knighted.
Adieu, my good friend, and for high life prepare ye ;
I cou'd fay much more, but you're modeft, I fpare ye."
Quite fir'd with the flatt'ry, I call for my paper,
And wafte that, and health, and my time, and my taper :
I fcribble 'till morn, when with wrath no fmall ftore,
Comes my old friend the mercer, and raps at my door.
" Ah ! friend, 'tis but idle to make fuch a pother,
Fate, fate has ordain'd us, to plague one another."

✦✦✦✦✦✦✦✦✦✦✦✦✦✦✦✦✦✦✦✦✦✦✦✦✦✦✦✦✦✦✦✦✦✦

Written at an Inn at HENLEY.

TO thee, fair freedom ! I retire
    From flattery, cards, and dice, and din ;
Nor art thou found in manfions higher.
    Than the low cott, or humble inn.

'Tis here with boundlefs pow'r I reign ;
    And every health which I begin,
Converts dull port to bright champaigne ;
    Such freedom crowns it, at an inn.

I fly from pomp, I fly from plate!
  I fly from falſehood's ſpecious grin!
Freedom I love, and form I hate,
  And chuſe my lodgings at an inn.

Here, waiter! take my ſordid ore,
  Which lacqueys elſe might hope to win;
It buys, what courts have not in ſtore;
  It buys me freedom at an inn.

Whoe'er has travell'd life's dull round,
  Where'er his ſtages may have been,
May ſigh to think he ſtill has found
  The warmeſt welcome, at an inn.

‡‡‡‡‡‡‡‡‡‡‡‡‡‡‡‡‡‡‡‡‡‡‡‡‡‡‡‡‡‡‡‡‡‡‡‡‡‡‡

A SIMILE.

WHAT village but has ſometimes ſeen
    The clumſy ſhape, the frightful mien,
Tremendous claws, and ſhagged hair,
Of that grim brute yclep'd a bear?
He from his dam, the learn'd agree,
Receiv'd the curious form you ſee;
Who with her plaſtic tongue alone,
Produc'd a viſage—like her own—
And thus they hint, in myſtic faſhion,
The pow'rful force of education*—
Perhaps yon croud of ſwains is viewing
E'en now, the ſtrange exploits of Bruin;

Who

* Of a fond matron's education.

Who plays his antics, roars aloud ;
The wonder of a gaping croud !

   So have I known an awkward lad,
Whofe birth has made a parifh glad,
Forbid, for fear of fenfe, to roam,
And taught by kind mamma at home ;
Who gives him many a well-try'd rule,
With ways and means—to play the fool.
In fenfe the fame, in ftature higher,
He fhines, ere long, a rural fquire,
Pours forth unwitty jokes, and fwears,
And bawls, and drinks, but chiefly ftares:
His tenants of fuperior fenfe
Caroufe, and laugh, at his expence ;
And deem the paftime I'm relating,
To be as pleafant, as bear-baiting.

✦✦✦✦✦✦✦✦✦✦✦✦✦✦✦✦✦✦✦✦✦✦✦✦✦✦✦✦✦✦✦✦✦

The CHARMS of PRECEDENCE.
A TALE.

" SIR, will you pleafe to walk before ?"
   —No, pray Sir—you are next the door.
—" Upon mine honour, I'll not ftir—"
Sir, I'm at home, confider, Sir—
" Excufe me, Sir, I'll not go firft."
Well, if I muft be rude, I muft—
But yet I wifh I cou'd evade it—
'Tis ftrangely clownifh, be perfuaded—
   Go forward, cits ! go forward, fquires !
Nor fcruple each, what each admires.

Life

Life fquares not, friends, with your proceeding ;
It flies, while you difplay your breeding ;
Such breeding as one's granam preaches,
Or fome old dancing-mafter teaches.
O for fome rude tumultuous fellow,
Half crazy, or, at leaft, half mellow,
To come behind you unawares,
And fairly pufh you both down ftairs !
But death's at hand—let me advife ye,
Go forward, friends, or he'll furprize ye.

    Befides, how infincere you are !
Do ye not flatter, lye, forfwear,
And daily cheat, and weekly pray,
And all for this—to lead the way ?

    Such is my theme, which means to prove,
That tho' we drink, or game, or love,
As that or this is moft in fafhion,
Precedence is our ruling paffion.

    When college-ftudents take degrees,
And pay the beadle's endlefs fees,
What moves that fcientific body,
But the firft cutting at a gawdy ?
And whence fuch fhoals, in bare conditions,
That ftarve and languifh as phyficians,
Content to trudge the ftreets, and ftare at
The fat apothecary's chariot ?
But that, in CHARLOT's chamber (fee
MOLIERE's Medicin malgre lui)
The leach, howe'er his fortunes vary,
Still walks before the apothecary.

               FLAVIA

FLAVIA in vain has wit and charms,
And all that shines, and all that warms;
In vain all human race adore her,
For—lady MARY ranks before her.

O CELIA, gentle CELIA! tell us,
You who are neither vain, nor jealous!
The softest breast, the mildest mien!
Wou'd you not feel some little spleen,
Nor bite your lip, nor furl your brow,
If FLORIMEL, your equal now,
Shou'd, one day, gain precedence of ye?
First ferv'd—tho' in a difh of coffee?
Plac'd first, altho' where you are found,
You gain the eyes of all around?
Nam'd first, tho' not with half the fame,
That waits my charming CELIA's name?

Hard fortune! barely to infpire
Our fix'd esteem, and fond defire!
Barely, where'er you go, to prove
The source of universal love!—
Yet be content, obferving this,
Honour's the offspring of caprice:
And worth, howe'er you have pursu'd it,
Has now no pow'r—but to exclude it.
You'll find your general reputation
A kind of supplemental station.

Poor SWIFT, with all his worth, cou'd ne'er,
He tells us, hope to rise a peer;
So, to supply it, wrote for fame:
And well the wit fecur'd his aim.

A com-

A common patriot has a drift,
Not quite fo innocent as SWIFT:
In BRITAIN's caufe he rants, he labours;
" He's honeft, faith"—Have patience, neighbours,
For patriots may fometimes deceive,
May beg their friends' reluctant leave,
To ferve them in a higher fphere;
And drop their virtue, to get there.—

    As LUCIAN tells us, in his fafhion,
How fouls put off each earthly paffion,
Ere on ELYSIUM's flow'ry ftrand,
Old CHARON fuffer'd 'em to land;
So ere we meet a court's careffes,
No doubt our fouls muft change their dreffes:
And fouls there be, who, bound that way,
Attire themfelves ten times a day.

    If then 'tis rank which all men covet,
And faints alike and finners love it;
If place, for which our courtiers throng
So thick, that few can get along;
For which fuch fervile toils are feen,
Who's happier than a king?—a queen.

    Howe'er men aim at elevation,
'Tis properly a female paffion:
Women, and beaux, beyond all meafure
Are charm'd with rank's extatic pleafure.

    Sir, if your drift I rightly fcan,
You'd hint a beau were not a man:
Say, women then are fond of places;
I wave all difputable cafes.

A man

A man perhaps would fomething linger,
Were his lov'd rank to coft—a finger;
Or were an ear or toe the price on't,
He might delib'rate once or twice on't;
Perhaps afk GATAKER's advice on't.
And many, as their frame grows old,
Would hardly purchafe it with gold.

But women wifh precedence ever;
'Tis their whole life's fupreme endeavour;
It fires their youth with jealous rage,
And ftrongly animates their age.
Perhaps they would not fell outright
Or maim a limb—that was in fight;
Yet on worfe terms they fometimes chufe it;
Nor ev'n in punifhments, refufe it.

Pre-eminence in pain! you cry,
All fierce and pregnant with reply.
But lend your patience, and your ear,
An argument fhall make it clear.
But hold, an argument may fail,
Befide my title fays, a tale.

Where AVON rolls her winding ftream,
AVON, the mufes' fav'rite theme!
AVON, that fills the farmers' purfes,
And decks with flow'rs both farms, and verfes,
She vifits many a fertile vale—
Such was the fcene of this my tale.
For 'tis in EV'SHAM's vale, or near it,
That folks with laughter tell, and hear it.

The foil with annual plenty bleft
Was by young CORYDON poffeft.

His

His youth alone I lay before ye,
As moſt material to my ſtory:
For ſtrength and vigour too, he had 'em,
And 'twere not much amiſs, to add 'em.
   Thrice happy lout! whoſe wide domain
Now green with graſs, now gilt with grain,
In ruſſet robes of clover deep,
Or thinly veil'd, and white with ſheep;
Now fragrant with the bean's perfume,
Now purpled with the pulſe's bloom,
Might well with bright alluſion ſtore me;
—But happier bards have been before me!
   Amongſt the various year's increaſe,
The ſtripling own'd a field of peaſe;
Which, when at night he ceas'd his labours,
Were haunted by ſome female neighbours.
Each morn diſcover'd to his ſight
The ſhameful havoc of the night;
Traces of this they left behind 'em,
But no inſtructions where to find 'em.
The devil's works are plain and evil,
But few or none have ſeen the devil.
Old NOLL, indeed, if we may credit
The words of ECHARD, who has ſaid it,
Contriv'd with SATAN how to fool us;
And bargain'd face to face to rule us;
But then old Noll was one in ten,
And fought him more than other men.
Our ſhepherd too, with like attention,
May meet the female fiends we mention.

He rose one morn at break of day,
And near the field in ambush lay:
When lo! a brace of girls appears,
The third, a matron much in years.
Smiling, amidst the pease the finners
Sate down to cull their future dinners;
And, caring little who might own 'em,
Made free as tho' themselves had sown 'em.

'Tis worth a sage's observation
How love can make a jest of passion.
Anger had forc'd the swain from bed,
His early dues to love unpaid!
And love, a god that keeps a pother,
And will be paid one time or other,
Now banish'd anger out o' door;
And claim'd the debt withheld before.
If anger bid our youth revile,
Love form'd his features to a smile:
And knowing well, 'twas all grimace,
To threaten with a smiling face,
He in few words express'd his mind—
And none would deem them much unkind.
    The am'rous youth, for their offence,
Demanded instant recompence:
That recompence from each, which shame
Forbids a bashful muse to name.
Yet, more this sentence to discover,
'Tis what B—T— ** grants her lover,
When he, to make the strumpet willing,
Has spent his fortune—to a shilling.

Each

Each stood a while, as 'twere suspended,
And loth to do, what—each intended.

At length with soft pathetic sighs,
The matron, bent with age, replies.

'Tis vain to strive—justice, I know,
And our ill stars will have it so——
But let my tears your wrath assuage,
And shew some deference for age!
I from a distant village came,
Am old, G— knows, and something lame;
And if we yield, as yield we must,
Dispatch my crazy body first.

Our shepherd, like the Phrygian swain,
When circled round on IDA's plain,
With goddesses, he stood suspended,
And PALLAS's grave speech was ended,
Own'd what she ask'd might be his duty;
But paid the compliment to beauty.

+++

ODE

To be performed by Dr. BRETTLE, and a Chorus of HALES-OWEN CITIZENS.

The Instrumental Part, a Viol d'Amour.

AIR by the DOCTOR.

AWAKE! I say, awake good people!
And be for once alive and gay;
Come let's be merry; stir the tipple;
How can you sleep,
Whilst I do play? how can you sleep, &c.

CHORUS

CHORUS of CITIZENS.

Pardon, O pardon, great mufician !
On drowfy fouls fome pity take !
For wond'rous hard is our condition,
 To drink thy beer,
 Thy ftrains to hear ;
  To drink,
  To hear,
 And keep awake !

SOLO by the DOCTOR.

Hear but this ftrain—'twas made by HANDEL,
 A wight of fkill, and judgment deep !
Zoonters, they're gone—SAL, bring a candle——
 No, here is one, and he's afleep.

DUETTE.

DR.—How cou'd they go   Soft mufic.
   Whilft I do play ?
SAL.—How cou'd they go ?   Warlike mufic.
   How fhou'd they ftay ?

E P I-

EPILOGUE to the Tragedy of CLEONE.

WELL, ladies—fo much for the tragic ftile—
And now the cuftom is to make you fmile.
To make us fmile!—methinks I hear you fay—
Why, who can help it, at fo ftrange a play?
The captain gone three years!—and then to blame
The faultlefs conduct of his virtuous dame!
My ftars!—what gentle belle would think it treafon,
When thus provok'd, to give the brute fome reafon?
Out of my houfe!—this night, forfooth, depart!
A modern wife had faid—" With all my heart—
But think not, haughty Sir, I'll go alone!
Order your coach—conduct me fafe to town—
Give me my jewels, wardrobe, and my maid—
And pray take care my pin-money be paid."

 Such is the language of each modifh fair;
Yet memoirs, not of modern growth, declare
The time has been when modefty and truth
Were deem'd additions to the charms of youth:
When women hid their necks, and veil'd their faces, ⎫
Nor romp'd, nor rak'd, nor ftar'd at public places, ⎬
Nor took the airs of amazons for graces: ⎭
Then plain domeftic virtues were the mode,
And wives ne'er dreamt of happinefs abroad;
They lov'd their children, learnt no flaunting airs,
But with the joys of wedlock mixt the cares.

Thofe

Thofe times are paft—yet fure they merit praife,
For marriage triumph'd in thofe golden days:
By chafte decorum they affection gain'd;
By faith and fondnefs what they won, maintain'd.

'Tis yours, ye fair, to bring thofe days agen,
And form anew the hearts of thoughtlefs men;
Make beauty's luftre amiable as bright,
And give the foul, as well as fenfe, delight;
Reclaim from folly a fantaftic age,
That fcorns the prefs, the pulpit, and the ftage.
Let truth and tendernefs your breafts adorn,
The marriage chain with tranfport fhall be worn;
Each blooming virgin rais'd into a bride
Shall double all their joys, their cares divide;
Alleviate grief, compofe the jars of ftrife,
And pour the balm that fweetens human life.

MORAL

MORAL PIECES.

MORAL PIECES

T H E
JUDGMENT of HERCULES.

WHile blooming spring descends from genial skies,
    By whose mild influence instant wonders rise;
From whose soft breath Elysian beauties flow,
The sweets of HAGLEY, or the pride of STOWE;
Will LYTTELTON the rural landskip range,
Leave noisy fame, and not regret the change?
Pleas'd will he tread the garden's early scenes,
And learn a moral from the rising greens?
There, warm'd alike by Sol's enliv'ning pow'r,
The weed, aspiring, emulates the flow'r:
The drooping flow'r, its fairer charms display'd,
Invites, from grateful hands, their gen'rous aid:

                       Soon,

Soon, if none check th' invafive foe's defigns,
The lively luftre of thefe fcenes declines!

'Tis thus, the fpring of youth, the morn of life,
Rears in our minds the rival feeds of ftrife.
Then páffion riots, reafon then contends;
And, on the conqueft, ev'ry blifs depends:
Life, from the nice decifion, takes its hue:
And bleft thofe judges who decide like you!
On worth like theirs fhall ev'ry blifs attend:
The world their fav'rite, and the world their friend,

There are, who blind to thought's fatiguing ray,
As fortune gives examples urge their way:
Not virtue's foes, though they her paths decline,
And fcarce her friends, tho' with her friends they join,
In her's, or vice's cafual road advance
Thoughtlefs, the finners or the faints of chance!
Yet fome more nobly fcorn the vulgar voice;
With judgment fix, with zeal purfue their choice,
When ripen'd thought, when reafon born to reign,
Checks the wild tumults of the youthful vein;
While paffion's lawlefs tides, at their command,
Glide thro' more ufeful tracts, and blefs the land.

Happieft of thefe is he whofe matchlefs mind,
By learning ftrengthen'd, and by tafte refin'd,
In virtue's caufe effay'd its earlieft pow'rs;
Chofe virtue's paths, and ftrew'd her paths with flow'rs.
The firft alarm'd, if freedom waves her wings:
The fitteft to adorn each art fhe brings:
Lov'd by that prince whom ev'ry virtue fires:
Prais'd by that bard whom ev'ry mufe infpires:

Bleft

Bleſt in the tuneful art, the ſocial flame;
In all that wins, in all that merits fame!
　'Twas youth's perplexing ſtage his doubts inſpir'd,
When great ALCIDES to a grove retir'd.
Thro' the lone windings of a devious glade,
Reſign'd to thought, with ling'ring ſteps he ſtray'd;
Bleſt with a mind to taſte ſincerer joys:
Arm'd with a heart each falſe one to deſpiſe.
Dubious he ſtray'd, with wav'ring thoughts poſſeſt,
Alternate paſſions ſtruggling ſhar'd his breaſt;
The various arts which human cares divide,
In deep attention all his mind employ'd:
Anxious, if fame an equal bliſs ſecur'd;
Or ſilent eaſe with ſofter charms allur'd.
The ſilvan choir whoſe numbers ſweetly flow'd,
The fount that murmur'd, and the flow'rs that blow'd;
The ſilver flood that in meanders led
His glitt'ring ſtreams along th' enliven'd mead;
The ſoothing breeze, and all thoſe beauties join'd,
Which, whilſt they pleaſe, effeminate the mind,
In vain! while diſtant, on a ſommit rais'd,
Th' imperial tow'rs of fame attractive blaz'd.
　　While thus he trac'd thro' fancy's puzzling maze
The ſep'rate ſweets of pleaſure, and of praiſe;
Sudden the wind a fragrant gale convey'd,
And a new luſtre gain'd upon the ſhade.
At once, before his wond'ring eyes were ſeen
Two female forms, of more than mortal mien.
Various their charms; and in their dreſs and face,
Each ſeem'd to vie with ſome peculiar grace.

　　　　　　　　　　　　　　This,

This, whofe attire lefs clogg'd with art appear'd,
The fimple fweets of innocence endear'd.
Her fprightly bloom, her quick fagacious eye,
Shew'd native merit mix'd with modefty.
Her air diffus'd a mild yet aweful ray,
Severely fweet, and innocently gay.
Such the chafte image of the martial maid,
In artlefs folds of virgin white array'd!
She let no borrow'd rofe her cheeks adorn,
Her blufhing cheeks, that fham'd the purple morn.
Her charms nor had, nor wanted artful foils,
Or ftudy'd geftures, or well-practis'd fmiles.
She fcorn'd the toys which render beauty lefs;
She prov'd th' engaging chaftity of drefs;
And while fhe chofe in native charms to fhine,
Ev'n thus fhe feem'd, nay more than feem'd, divine.
One modeft em'rald clafp'd the robe fhe wore,
And, in her hand, th' imperial fword fhe bore.
Sublime her height, majeftic was her pace,
And match'd the aweful honours of her face.
The fhrubs, the flow'rs, that deck'd the verdant ground,
Seem'd, where fhe trod, with rifing luftre crown'd.
Still her approach with ftronger influence warm'd;
She pleas'd, while diftant, but, when near, fhe charm'd.
So ftrikes the gazer's eye, the filver gleam
That glitt'ring quivers o'er a diftant ftream:
But from its banks we fee new beauties rife,
And, in its cryftal bofom, trace the fkies.

With other charms the rival vifion glow'd;
And from her drefs her tinfel beauties flow'd.

A flutt'ring

A flutt'ring robe her pamper'd ſhape conceal'd,
And ſeem'd to ſhade the charms it beſt reveal'd.
Its form, contriv'd her faulty ſize to grace;
Its hue, to give freſh luſtre to her face.
Her plaited hair diſguis'd with brilliants glar'd;
Her cheeks the ruby's neighb'ring luſtre ſhar'd;
The gaudy topaz lent its gay ſupplies,
And ev'ry gem that ſtrikes leſs curious eyes;
Expos'd her breaſt with foreign ſweets perfum'd;
And, round her brow, a roſeate garland bloom'd.
Soft ſmiling, bluſhing lips conceal'd her wiles;
Yet ah! the bluſhes artful as the ſmiles.
Oft-gazing on her ſhade, th' enraptur'd fair
Decreed the ſubſtance well deſerv'd her care:
Her thoughts, to others' charms malignly blind,
Center'd in that, and were to that confin'd;
And if on others' eyes a glance were thrown,
'Twas but to watch the influence of her own.
Much like her guardian, fair CYTHERA's queen,
When for her warrior ſhe refines her mien;
Or when, to bleſs her DELIAN fav'rite's arms,
The radiant fair invigorates her charms.
Much like her pupil, EGYPT's ſportive dame,
Her dreſs expreſſive, and her air the ſame,
When her gay bark o'er ſilver CYDNOS roll'd,
And all th' emblazon'd ſtreamers wav'd in gold.
Such ſhone the viſion: nor forbore to move
The fond contagious airs of lawleſs love.
Each wanton eye deluding glances fir'd,
And am'rous dimples on each cheek conſpir'd.

Lifeleſs

Lifeless her gait, and slow, with seeming pain,
She dragg'd her loitering limbs along the plain; }
Yet made some faint efforts, and first approach'd the swain.
So glaring draughts, with taudry lustre bright,
Spring to the view, and rush upon the sight:
More slowly charms a RAPHAEL's chaster air,
Waits the calm search, and pays the searcher's care.

Wrap'd in a pleas'd suspence, the youth survey'd
The various charms of each attractive maid:
Alternate each he view'd, and each admir'd,
And found, alternate, varying flames inspir'd.
Quick o'er their forms his eyes with pleasure ran,
When she, who first approach'd him, first began.

"Hither, dear boy, direct thy wand'ring eyes;
'Tis here the lovely vale of pleasure lies.
Debate no more, to me thy life resign;
Each sweet which nature can diffuse is mine.
For me the nymph diversifies her pow'r,
Springs in a tree, or blossoms in a flow'r;
To please my ear, she tunes the linnet's strains;
To please my eye, with lilies paints the plains;
To form my couch, in mossy beds she grows;
To gratify my smell, perfumes the rose;
Reveals the fair, the fertile scene you see,
And swells the vegetable world, for me.

Let the gull'd fool the toils of war pursue,
Where bleed the many to enrich the few:
Where chance from courage claims the boasted prize;
Where, tho' she give, your country oft denies.
Industrious thou shalt CUPID's wars maintain,
And ever gently fight his soft campaign.

His

His darts alone fhalt wield, his wounds endure,
Yet only fuffer, to enjoy the cure.
Yield but to me—a choir of nymphs fhall rife,
And fire thy breaft, and blefs thy ravifh'd eyes.
Their beauteous cheeks a fairer rofe fhall wear,
A brighter lily on their necks appear;
Where fondly thou thy favour'd head fhalt reft,
Soft as the down that fwells the cygnet's neft?
While PHILOMEL in each foft voice complains,
And gently lulls thee with mellifluous ftrains:
Whilft, with each accent, fweeteft odours flow;
And fpicy gums round ev'ry bofom glow.
Not the fam'd bird Arabian climes admire,
Shall in fuch luxury of fweets expire.
At floth let war's victorious fons exclaim;
In vain! for pleafure is my real name;
Nor envy thou the head with bays o'er-grown;
No, feek thou rofes to adorn thy own:
For well each op'ning fcene, that claims my care,
Suits and deferves the beauteous crown I wear.

   Let others prune the vine; the genial bowl
Shall crown thy table, and enlarge thy foul.
Let vulgar hands explore the brilliant mine,
So the gay produce glitter ftill on thine.
Indulgent BACCHUS loads his lab'ring tree,
And, guarding, gives its cluft'ring fweets to me.
For my lov'd train, APOLLO's piercing beam
Darts thro' the paffive glebe, and frames the gem.
See in my caufe confenting gods employ'd,
Nor flight thofe gods, their bleffings unenjoy'd!

For

For thee the poplar shall its amber drain;
For thee, in clouded beauty, spring the cane;
Some costly tribute ev'ry clime shall pay;
Some charming treasure ev'ry wind convey;
Each object round some pleasing scene shall yield;
Art build thy dome, while nature decks thy field;
Of CORINTH's order shall the structure rise;
The spiring turrets glitter thro' the skies;
Thy costly robe shall glow with Tyrian rays;
Thy vase shall sparkle, and thy car shall blaze;
Yet thou, whatever pomp the sun display,
Shalt own the am'rous night exceeds the day.

When melting flutes, and sweetly-sounding lyres
Wake the gay loves, and cite the young desires;
Or, in th' Ionian dance, some fav'rite maid
Improves the flame her sparkling eyes convey'd;
Think, can'st thou quit a glowing DELIA's arms,
To feed on virtue's visionary charms;
Or slight the joys which wit and youth engage,
For the faint honour of a frozen sage?
To find dull envy ev'n that hope deface,
And, where you toil'd for glory, reap disgrace?

O! think that beauty waits on thy decree,
And thy lov'd loveliest charmer pleads with me.
She, whose soft smile, or gentler glance to move,
You vow'd the wild extremities of love;
In whose endearments years, like moments flew;
For whose endearments millions seem'd too few;
She, she implores; she bids thee seize the prime,
And tread with her the flow'ry tracts of time;

Nor

Nor thus her lovely bloom of life beſtow
On ſome cold lover, or inſulting foe.
Think, if againſt that tongue thou canſt rebel,
Where love yet dwelt, and reaſon ſeem'd to dwell;
What ſtrong perſuaſion arms her ſofter ſighs!
What full conviction ſparkles in her eyes!
 See nature ſmiles, and birds ſalute the ſhade,
Where breathing jaſmin ſcreens the ſleeping maid:
And ſuch her charms, as to the vain may prove,
Ambition ſeeks more humble joys than love!
There buſy toil ſhall ne'er invade thy reign,
Nor ſciences perplex thy lab'ring brain:
Or none, but what with equal ſweets invite;
Nor other arts, but to prolong delight:
Sometimes thy fancy prune her tender wing,
To praiſe a pendant, or to grace a ring;
To fix the dreſs that ſuits each varying mien;
To ſhew where beſt the cluſtering gems are ſeen;
To ſigh ſoft ſtrains along the vocal grove,
And tell the charms, the ſweet effects of love!
Nor fear to find a coy diſdainful muſe;
Nor think the ſiſters will their aid refuſe.
Cool grots, and tinkling rills, or ſilent ſhades;
Soft ſcenes of leiſure! ſuit th' harmonious maids;
And all the wiſe, and all the grave decree
Some of that ſacred train ally'd to me.
 But if more ſpecious eaſe thy wiſhes claim,
And thy breaſt glow with faint deſire of fame,
Some ſofter ſcience ſhall thy thoughts amuſe,
And learning's name a ſolemn ſound diffuſe:

To thee all nature's curious stores I'll bring,
Explain the beauties of an insect's wing;
The plant, which nature, less diffusely kind,
Has to few climes with partial care confin'd;
The shell she scatters with more careless air,
And, in her frolics, seems supremely fair;
The worth that dazzles in the tulip's stains,
Or lurks beneath a pebble's various veins.

    Sleep's downy god, averse to war's alarms,
Shall o'er thy head diffuse his softest charms;
Ere anxious thought thy dear repose assail,
Or care, my most destructive foe, prevail.
The wat'ry nymphs shall tune the vocal vales,
And gentle zephyrs harmonize their gales,
For thy repose, inform, with rival joy,
Their streams to murmur, and their winds to sigh.
Thus shalt thou spend the sweetly-flowing day,
'Till lost in bliss thou breathe thy soul away;
'Till she t' Elysian bow'rs of joy repair,
Nor find my charming scenes exceeded there."

    She ceas'd; and on a lily'd bank reclin'd,
Her flowing robe wav'd wanton with the wind:
One tender hand her drooping head sustains;
One points, expressive, to the flow'ry plains.
Soon the fond youth perceiv'd her influence roll
Deep in his breast, to melt his manly soul:
As when FAVONIUS joins the solar blaze,
And each fair fabric of the frost decays.
Soon, to his breast, the soft harangue convey'd
Resolves too partial to the specious maid.

He

He figh'd, he gaz'd, fo fweetly fmil'd the dame;
Yet fighing, gazing, feem'd to fcorn his flame,
And, oft as virtue caught his wand'ring eye,
A crimfon blufh condemn'd the rifing figh.
'Twas fuch the ling'ring TROJAN's fhame betray'd,
When MAIA's fon the frown of JOVE difplay'd:
When wealth, fame, empire, could no balance prove,
For the foft reign of DIDO, and of love.
Thus ill with arduous glory love confpires;
Soft tender flames with bold impetuous fires!

   Some hov'ring doubts his anxious bofom mov'd,
And virtue, zealous fair! thofe doubts improv'd.

   " Fly, fly, fond youth, the too indulgent maid,
Nor err, by fuch fantaftic fcenes betray'd.
Tho' in my path the rugged thorn be feen,
And the dry turf difclofe a fainter green;
Tho' no gay rofe, or flow'ry product fhine,
The barren furface ftill conceals the mine.
Each thorn that threatens, ev'n the weed that grows
In virtue's path, fuperior fweets beftows—
Yet fhou'd thofe boafted, fpecious toys allure,
Whence cou'd fond floth the flatt'ring gifts procure?
The various wealth that tempts thy fond defire,
'Tis I alone, her greateft foe, acquire.
I from old ocean rob the treafur'd ftore;
I thro' each region latent gems explore;
'Twas I the rugged brilliant firft reveal'd,
By num'rous ftrata deep in earth conceal'd;
'Tis I the furface yet refine, and fhow
The modeft gem's intrinfic charms to glow.

Q 2

Nor

Nor fwells the grape, nor fpires its feeble tree
Without the firm fupports of induftry.

But grant we floth the fcene herfelf has drawn,
The moffy grotto, and the flow'ry lawn ;
Let PHILOMELA tune th' harmonious gale,
And with each breeze eternal fweets exhale ;
Let gay POMONA flight the plains around,
And chufe, for faireft fruits, the favour'd ground;
To blefs the fertile vale fhou'd virtue ceafe,
Nor moffy grots, nor flow'ry lawns cou'd pleafe ;
Nor gay POMONA's lufcious gifts avail,
The found harmonious, or the fpicy gale.

Seeft thou yon rocks in dreadful pomp arife,
Whofe rugged cliffs deform th' encircling fkies ?
Thofe fields, whence PHOEBUS all their moifture drains,
And, too profufely fond, difrobes the plains ?
When I vouchfafe to tread the barren foil,
Thofe rocks feem lovely, and thofe deferts fmile.
The form thou view'ft, to ev'ry fcene with eafe
Transfers its charms, and ev'ry fcene can pleafe.
When I have on thofe pathlefs wilds appear'd,
And the lone wand'rer with my prefence chear'd;
Thofe cliffs the exile has with pleafure view'd,
And call'd that defert blifsful folitude !

Nor I alone to fuch extend my care :
Fair-blooming health furveys her altars there.
Brown exercife will lead thee where fhe reigns,
And with reflected luftre gild the plains.
With her, in flow'r of youth, and beauty's pride,
Her offspring, calm content and peace, refide.

One

One ready off'ring suits each neighb'ring shrine;
And all obey their laws, who practise mine.

But health averse from sloth's smooth region flies;
And, in her absence, pleasure droops and dies.
Her bright companions, mirth, delight, repose,
Smile where she smiles, and sicken when she goes.
A galaxy of pow'rs! whose forms appear
For ever beauteous, and for ever near.

Nor will soft sleep to sloth's request incline,
He from her couches flies unbid to mine.

Vain is the sparkling bowl, the warbling strain,
Th' incentive song, the labour'd viand vain!
Where she relentless reigns without controul,
And checks each gay excursion of the soul:
Unmov'd, tho' beauty, deck'd in all its charms,
Grace the rich couch, and spread the softest arms:
'Till joyless indolence suggests desires;
Or drugs are sought to furnish languid fires;
Such languid fires as on the vitals prey,
Barren of bliss, but fertile of decay.
As artful heats, apply'd to thirsty lands,
Produce no flow'rs, and but debase the sands.

But let fair health her chearing smiles impart,
How sweet is nature, how superfluous art!
'Tis she the fountain's ready draught commends,
And smooths the flinty couch which fortune lends,
And when my hero from his toils retires,
Fills his gay bosom with unusual fires,
And, while no checks th' unbounded joy reprove,
Aids and refines the genuine sweets of love.

His

His faireſt proſpect riſing trophies frame;
His ſweeteſt muſic is the voice of fame:
Pleaſures to ſloth unknown! ſhe never found
How fair the proſpect, or how ſweet the ſound.

   See fame's gay ſtructure from yon ſummit charms,
And fires the manly breaſt to arts or arms:
Nor dread the ſteep aſcent, by which you riſe
From grov'ling vales to tow'rs which reach the ſkies.

   Love, fame, eſteem, 'tis labour muſt acquire;
The ſmiling offspring of a rigid ſire!
To fix the friend, your ſervice muſt be ſhewn;
All, ere they lov'd your merit, lov'd their own.
That wond'ring GREECE your portrait may admire,
That tuneful bards may ſtring for you their lyre,
That books may praiſe, or coins record your name,
Such, ſuch rewards 'tis toil alone can claim!
And the ſame column which diſplays to view
The conqu'ror's name, diſplays the conqueſt too.

   'Twas ſlow experience, tedious miſtreſs! taught
All that e'er nobly ſpoke, or bravely fought.
'Twas ſhe the patriot, ſhe the bard refin'd,
In arts that ſerve, protect, or pleaſe mankind.
Not the vain viſions of inactive ſchools,
Not fancy's maxims, not opinion's rules,
E'er form'd the man whoſe gen'rous warmth extends
T' enrich his country, or to ſerve his friends.
On active worth the laurel war beſtows:
Peace rears her olive for induſtrious brows:
Nor earth, uncultur'd, yields its kind ſupplies:
Nor heav'n, its ſhow'rs without a ſacrifice.

See

See far below, such grov'ling scenes of shame,
As lull to reft IONAVIA's slumb'ring dame.
Her friends, from all the toils of fame secure,
Alas! inglorious, greater toils endure.
Doom'd all to mourn, who in her cause engage,
A youth enervate, and a painful age;
A sickly sapless mass, if reason flies;
And, if she linger, impotently wise!
A thoughtless train, who, pamper'd, sleek, and gay,
Invite old age, and revel youth away;
From life's fresh vigour move the load of care,
And idly place it where they least can bear.
When to the mind, diseas'd, for aid they fly,
What kind reflection shall the mind supply?
When, with lost health, what shou'd the loss allay,
Peace, peace is lost: a comfortless decay!
But to my friends, when youth, when pleasure flies,
And earth's dim beauties fade before their eyes,
Thro' death's dark vista flowery tracks are seen,
Elysian plains, and groves for ever green.
If o'er their lives a refluent glance they cast,
Their's is the present who can praise the past.
Life has its bliss for these, when past its bloom,
As wither'd roses yield a late perfume.

  Serene, and safe from passion's stormy rage,
How calm they glide into the port of age!
Of the rude voyage less depriv'd than eas'd;
More tir'd than pain'd, and weaken'd than diseas'd.
For health on age, 'tis temp'rance must bestow;
And peace from piety alone can flow;

And

And all the incense bounteous JOVE requires,
Has sweets for him who feeds the sacred fires.—
   Sloth views the tow'rs of fame with envious eyes;
Desirous still, still impotent to rise.
Oft, when resolv'd to gain those blissful tow'rs,
The pensive queen the dire ascent explores,
Comes onward, wasted by the balmy trees,
Some silvan music, or some scented breeze:
She turns her head, her own gay realm she spies,
And all the short-liv'd resolution dies.
Thus some fond insect's fault'ring pinions wave,
Clasp'd in its fav'rite sweets, a lasting slave:
And thus in vain these charming visions please
The wretch of glory, and the slave of ease:
Doom'd ever in ignoble state to pine,
Boast her own scenes, and languish after mine.
   But shun her snares: nor let the world exclaim,
Thy birth, which was thy glory, prov'd thy shame.
With early hope thine infant actions fir'd;
Let manhood crown what infancy inspir'd.
Let gen'rous toils reward with health thy days,
Prolong thy prime, and eternize thy praise.
The bold exploit that charms th' attesting age,
To latest times shall gen'rous hearts engage;
And with that myrtle shall thy shrine be crown'd,
With which, alive, thy graceful brows were bound:
'Till time shall bid thy virtues freely bloom,
And raise a temple where it found a tomb.
   Then in their feasts thy name shall GRECIANS join;
Shall pour the sparkling juice to JOVE's and thine.
                                  Thine,

Thine, us'd in war, fhall raife their native fire;
Thine, us'd in peace, their mutual faith infpire.
Dulnefs perhaps, thro' want of fight, may blame,
And fpleen, with odious induftry, defame;
And that, the honours giv'n, with wonder view,
And this, in fecret fadnefs own them due:
Contempt and envy were by fate defign'd
The rival tyrants which divide mankind;
Contempt, which none, but who deferve, can bear;
While envy's wounds the fmiles of fame repair.
For know, the gen'rous thine exploits fhall fire,
Thine ev'ry friend it fuits thee to require,
Lov'd by the gods, and, till their feats I fhew,
Lov'd by the good, their images below."

Ceafe, lovely maid, fair daughter of the fkies!
My guide! my queen! th' extatic youth replies.
In thee I trace a form defign'd for fway;
Which chiefs may court, and kings with pride obey.
And, by thy bright immortal friends I fwear,
Thy fair idea fhall no toils impair.
Lead me! O lead me where whole hofts of foes,
Thy form depreciate, and thy friends oppofe!
Welcome all toils th' inequal fates decree,
While toils endear thy faithful charge to thee.
Such be my cares, to bind th' oppreffive hand,
And crufh the fetters of an injur'd land:
To fee the monfter's noxious life refign'd,
And tyrants quell'd, the monfters of mankind!
Nature fhall fmile to view the vanquifh'd brood,
And none, but envy, riot unfubdu'd.

In

In cloifter'd ftate let felfifh fages dwell,
Proud that their heart is narrow as their cell!
And boaft their mazy labyrinth of rules,
Far lefs the friends of virtue, than the fools:
Yet fuch in vain thy fav'ring fmiles pretend;
For HE is thine, who proves his country's friend.
Thus when my life well-fpent the good enjoy,
And the mean envious labour to deftroy;
When, ftrongly lur'd by fame's contiguous fhrine,
I yet devote my choicer vows to thine;
If all my toils thy promis'd favour claim,
O lead thy fav'rite thro' the gates of fame!

He ceas'd his vows, and, with difdainful air,
He turn'd to blaft the late exulting fair.
But vanifh'd, fled to fome more friendly fhore,
The confcious phantom's beauty pleas'd no more:
Convinc'd, her fpurious charms of drefs and face
Claim'd a quick conqueft, or a fure difgrace.
Fantaftic pow'r! whofe tranfient charms allur'd,
While error's mift the reas'ning mind obfcur'd:
Not fuch the victrefs, virtue's conftant queen,
Endur'd the teft of truth, and dar'd be feen.
Her bright'ning form and features feem'd to own,
'Twas all her wifh, her int'reft to be known:
And when his longing view the fair declin'd,
Left a full image of her charms behind.

Thus reigns the moon, with furtive fplendor crown'd,
While glooms opprefs us, and thick fhades furround.
But let the fource of light its beams difplay,
Languid and faint the mimic flames decay,
And all the fick'ning fplendor fades away.

The

The Progress of TASTE;

or,

The Fate of DELICACY.

A POEM on the Temper and Studies of the Author; and how great a Misfortune it is, for a
Man of small Estate to have much Taste.

PART the FIRST.

PERHAPS some cloud eclips'd the day,
   When thus I tun'd my pensive lay.
" The ship is launch'd—we catch the gale—
On life's extended ocean sail :
For happiness our course we bend,
Our ardent cry, our general end!
Yet ah ! the scenes which tempt our care
Are like the forms dispers'd in air,
Still dancing near disorder'd eyes ;
And weakest his, who best descries !

   Yet let me not my birthright barter,
(For wishing is the poet's charter ;
All bards have leave to wish what's wanted,
Tho' few e'er found their wishes granted ;
Extensive field ! where poets pride them
In singing all that is deny'd them.)

   For humble ease, ye pow'rs ! I pray ;
That plain warm suit for ev'ry day !
And pleasure, and brocade, bestow ;
To flaunt it—once a month, or so.

The

The firſt for conſtant wear we want;
The firſt, ye pow'rs! for ever grant!
But conſtant wear the laſt beſpatters,
And turns the tiſſue into tatters.

Where'er my vagrant courſe I bend,
Let me ſecure one faithful friend.
Let me, in public ſcenes, requeſt
A friend of wit and taſte, well dreſs'd:
And, if I muſt not hope ſuch favour,
A friend of wit and taſte, however.

Alas! that wiſdom ever ſhuns
To congregate her ſcatter'd ſons;
Whoſe nervous forces well combin'd,
Would win the field, and ſway mankind.
The fool will ſqueeze, from morn to night,
To fix his follies full in ſight;
The note he ſtrikes, the plume he ſhows,
Attract whole flights of fops and beaux;
And kindred-fools, who ne'er had known him,
Flock at the ſight, careſs, and own him;
But ill-ſtar'd ſenſe, nor gay nor loud,
Steals ſoft on tip-toe, thro' the crowd:
Conveys his meagre form between;
And ſlides like pervious air, unſeen:
Contracts his known tenuity,
As though 'twere ev'n a crime, to be:
Nor ev'n permits his eyes to ſtray,
And win acquaintance in their way.

In company, ſo mean his air,
You ſcarce are conſcious he is there:

'Till

' ill from some nook, like sharpen'd steel,
Occurs his face's thin profile.
Still seeming, from the gazer's eye,
Like VENUS, newly bath'd, to fly.
Yet while reluctant he displays
His real gems before the blaze,
The fool hath, in its center, plac'd
His tawdry stock of painted paste.
Disus'd to speak, he tries his skill;
Speaks coldly, and succeeds but ill;
His pensive manner, dulness deem'd;
His modesty, reserve esteem'd;
His wit unknown, his learning vain,
He wins not one of all the train.
And those who, mutually known,
In friendship's fairest list had shone,
Less prone, than pebbles, to unite,
Retire to shades from public sight;
Grow savage, quit their social nature;
And starve, to study mutual satire.

But friends, and fav'rites, to chagrin them,
Find counties, countries, seas between them:
Meet once a year, then part, and then
Retiring, wish to meet again.

Sick of the thought, let me provide
Some human form to grace my side;
At hand, where'er I shape my course;
An useful, pliant, stalking-horse!

No gesture free from some grimace;
No seam, without its share of lace;

But,

But, mark'd with gold or silver either,
Hint where his coat was piec'd together.
His legs be lengthen'd, I advise,
And stockings roll'd abridge his thighs.
What tho' VANDYCK had other rules,
What had VANDYCK to do with fools?
Be nothing wanting, but his mind;
Before, a solitaire; behind,
A twisted ribbon, like the track
Which nature gives an ass's back.
Silent as midnight! pity 'twere
His wisdom's slender wealth to share!
And, whilst in flocks our fancies stray,
To wish the poor man's lamb away.

   This form attracting ev'ry eye,
I stroll all unregarded by:
This wards the jokes of ev'ry kind,
As an umbrella sun or wind;
Or, like a spunge, absorbs the sallies,
And pestilential fumes of malice;
Or like a splendid shield is fit
To screen the templar's random wit;
Or what some gentler cit lets fall,
As wool-packs quash the leaden ball.

   Allusions these of weaker force,
And apter still the stalking-horse!

   O let me wander all unseen,
Beneath the sanction of his mien!
As lilies soft, as roses fair!
Empty as air-pumps drain'd of air!

With

With steady eye and pace remark
The speckled flock that haunts the park * ;
Level my pen with wond'rous heed
At follies, flocking there to feed :
And, as my satire bursts amain,
See feather'd fopp'ry strew the plain.

But when I seek my rural grove,
And share the peaceful haunts I love,
Let none of this unhallow'd train
My sweet sequester'd paths profane.
Oft may some polish'd virtuous friend
To these soft-winding vales descend ;
And love with me inglorious things,
And scorn with me the pomp of kings :
And check me, when my bosom burns
For statues, paintings, coins and urns.
For I in DAMON's pray'r cou'd join,
And DAMON's wish might now be mine—
But all dispers'd ! the wish, the pray'r,
Are driv'n to mix with common air.

PART the SECOND.

HOW happy once was DAMON's lot,
While yet romantic schemes were not !
Ere yet he sent his weakly eyes,
To plan frail castles in the skies ;
Forsaking pleasures cheap and common,
To court a blaze, still flitting from one.

Ah happy DAMON ! thrice and more,
Had taste ne'er touch'd thy tranquil shore.

Oh

* St. JAMES's.

Oh days! when to a girdle ty'd
The couples jingled at his fide;
And DAMON fwore he would not barter
The fportfman's girdle, for a garter!

    Whoever came to kill an hour,
Found eafy DAMON in their pow'r;
Pure focial nature all his guide,
" DAMON had not a grain of pride."

    He wifh'd not to elude the fnares
Which knav'ry plans, and craft prepares;
But rather wealth to crown their wiles,
And win their univerfal fmiles:
For who are chearful, who at eafe,
But they who cheat us as they pleafe?

    He wink'd at many a grofs defign,
The new-fall'n calf might countermine:
Thus ev'ry fool allow'd his merit;
" Yes! DAMON had a gen'rous fpirit!"

    A coxcomb's jeft, however vile,
Was fure, at leaft, of DAMON's fmile:
That coxcomb ne'er deny'd him fenfe;
For why? it prov'd his own pretence:
All own'd, were modefty away,
DAMON cou'd fhine as much as they.

    When wine and folly came in feafon,
DAMON ne'er ftrove to fave his reafon;
Obnoxious to the mad uproar:
A fpy upon a hoftile fhore!
'Twas this his company endear'd:
Mirth never came till he appear'd:

His

His lodgings—ev'ry draw'r cou'd fhew 'em;
The flave was kick'd, who did not know 'em.

   Thus DAMON, ftudious of his eafe,
And pleafing all, whom mirth cou'd pleafe;
Defy'd the world, like idle COLLEY,
To fhew a fofter word than folly.
Since wifdom's gorgon-fhield was known
To ftare the gazer into ftone;
He chofe to truft in folly's charm,
To keep his breaft alive and warm.

   At length grave learning's fober train
Remark'd the trifler with difdain;
The fons of tafte contemn'd his ways,
And rank'd him with the brutes that graze:
While they to nobler heights afpir'd,
And grew belov'd, efteem'd, admir'd.

   Hence with our youth, not void of fpirit;
His old companions loft their merit:
And ev'ry kind well-natur'd fot
Seem'd a dull play, without a plot;
Where ev'ry yawning gueft agrees,
The willing creature ftrives to pleafe:
But temper never could amufe;
It barely led us to excufe;
'Twas true, converfing they aver'd,
All they had feen, or felt, or heard:
Talents of weight! for wights like thefe,
The law might chufe for witneffes:
But fure th' attefting dry narration
Ill fuits a judge of converfation.

* What were their freedoms? mere excuses
To vent ill manners, blows and bruises.
Yet freedom, gallant freedom! hailing,
At form, at form, inceffant railing,
Would they examine each offence,
Its latent caufe, its known pretence,
Punctilio ne'er was known to breed 'em,
So fure as fond prolific freedom.
Their courage? but a loaded gun;
Machine the wife wou'd wifh to fhun;
Its guard unfafe, its lock an ill one,
Where accident might fire and kill one.

In fhort, difgufted out of meafure,
Thro' much contempt, and flender pleafure,
His fenfe of dignity returns;
With native pride his bofom burns;
He feeks refpect—but how to gain it?
Wit, focial mirth, cou'd ne'er obtain it:
And laughter, where it reigns uncheck'd,
Difcards and diffipates refpect.
The man who gravely bows, enjoys it;
But fhaking hands, at once, deftroys it.
Precarious plant, which, frefh and gay,
Shrinks at the touch, and fades away!

Come then, referve! yet from thy train
Banifh contempt, and curft difdain.
Teach me, he cry'd, thy magic art
To act the decent diftant part:
To hufband well my complaifance,
Nor let ev'n wit too far advance;

But

* Boifterous mirth.

But chufe calm reafon for my theme.
In thefe her royal realms fupreme ;
And o'er her charms, with caution fhewn,
Be ftill a graceful umbrage thrown ;
And each abrupter period crown'd,
With nods, and winks, and fmiles profound,
'Till refcu'd from the crow'd beneath,
No more with pain to move or breathe,
I rife with head elate, to fhare
Salubrious draughts of purer air.
Refpect is won by grave pretence
And filence, furer ev'n than fenfe—

'Tis hence the facred grandeur fprings
Of Eaftern—and of other kings,
Or whence this awe to virtue due,
While virtue's diftant as PERU ?
The fheathlefs fword the guard difplays,
Which round emits its dazzling rays :
The ftately fort, the turrets tall,
Portcullis'd gate, and battled wall,
Lefs fcreens the body, than controuls,
And wards contempt from royal fouls.

The crowns they wear but check the eye,
Before it fondly pierce too nigh ;
That dazzled crowds may be employ'd
Around the furface of—the void.
O ! 'tis the ftatefman's craft profound
To fcatter his amufements round ;
To tempt us from their confcious breaft,
Where full-fledg'd crimes enjoy their neft.

Nor

Nor awes us every worth reveal'd,
So deeply, as each vice conceal'd.

The lordly log, difpatch'd of yore,
That the frog people might adore,
With guards to keep them at a diftance,
Had reign'd, nor wanted wit's affiftance:
Nay—had addreffes from his nation,
In praife of log-adminiftration.

PART the THIRD.

THE buoyant fires of youth were o'er,
And fame and finery pleas'd no more;
Productive of that gen'ral ftare,
Which cool reflection ill can bear!
And, crowds commencing mere vexation,
Retirement fent its invitation.

Romantic fcenes of pendent hills,
And verdant vales, and falling rills,
And moffy banks the fields adorn,
Where DAMON, fimple fwain, was born.

The dryads rear'd a fhady grove;
Where fuch as think, and fuch as love,
May fafely figh their fummer's day;
Or mufe their filent hours away.

The oreads lik'd the climate well;
And taught the level plain to fwell
In verdant mounds, from whence the eye
Might all their larger works defcry.

The naiads pour'd their urns around,
From nodding rocks o'er vales profound.

They

They form'd their ftreams to pleafe the view,
And bade them wind, as ferpents do :
And having fhewn them where to ftray,
Threw little pebbles in their way.

Thefe fancy, all-fagacious maid,
Had at their feveral tafks furvey'd :
She faw and fmil'd ; and oft would lead
Our DAMON's foot o'er hill and mead ;
There, with defcriptive finger, trace
The genuine beauties of the place ;
And when fhe all its charms had fhewn,
Prefcribe improvements of her own.

" See yonder hill, fo green, fo round,
Its brow with ambient beeches crown'd !
'Twould well become thy gentle care
To raife a dome to VENUS there :
Pleas'd would the nymphs thy zeal furvey ;
And VENUS, in their arms, repay.
'Twas fuch a fhade, and fuch a nook,
In fuch a vale, near fuch a brook ;
From fuch a rocky fragment fpringing ;
That fam'd APOLLO chofe, to fing in.
There let an alter wrought with art
Engage thy tuneful patron's heart.
How charming there to mufe and warble
Beneath his buft of breathing marble !
With laurel wreath and mimic lyre,
That crown a poet's vaft defire.
Then, near it, fcoop the vaulted cell
Where mufic's * charming maids may dwell ;

* The mufes.

R 3

Prone

Prone to indulge thy tender paffion,
And make thee many an affignation.
Deep in the grove's obfcure retreat
Be plac'd MINERVA's facred feat;
There let her aweful turrets rife,
(For wifdom flies from vulgar eyes :)
There her calm dictates fhalt thou hear
Diftinctly ftrike thy lift'ning ear :
And who would fhun the pleafing labour,
To have MINERVA for his neighbour ?"

   In fhort, fo charm'd each wild fuggeftion,
Its truth was little call'd in queftion :
And DAMON dreamt he faw the Fauns,
And Nymphs, diftinctly, fkim the lawns;
Now trac'd amid the trees, and then
Loft in the circling fhades again.
With leer oblique their lover viewing—
And CUPID—panting—and purfuing—
Fancy, enchanting fair, he cry'd,
Be thou my goddefs! thou my guide!
For thy bright vifions I defpife
What foes may think, or friends advife.
The feign'd concern, when folks furvey
Expence, time, ftudy caft away;
The real fpleen, with which they fee :
I pleafe myfelf, and follow thee.

   Thus glow'd his breaft by fancy warm'd;
And thus the fairy landfkip charm'd,
But moft he hop'd his conftant care
Might win the favour of the fair;

And,

And, wand'ring late thro' yonder glade,
He thus the foft defign betray'd.

   " Ye doves! for whom I rear'd the grove,
With melting lays falute my love!
My DELIA with your notes detain,
Or I have rear'd the grove in vain!
Ye flow'rs! which early fpring fupplies,
Difplay at once your brighteft dyes!
That fhe your op'ning charms may fee;
Or what were elfe your charms to me?
Kind zephyr! brufh each fragrant flow'r,
And fhed its odours round my bow'r,
Or ne'er again, O gentle wind!
Shall I, in thee, refrefhment find.
Ye ftreams, if e'er your banks I lov'd,
If e'er your native founds improv'd,
May each foft murmur foothe my fair;
Or oh 'twill deepen my defpair!
Be fure, ye willows! you be feen
Array'd in livelieft robes of green;
Or I will tear your flighted boughs,
And let them fade around my brows.
And thou, my grott! whofe lonely bounds
The malancholy pine furrounds!
May fhe admire thy peaceful gloom,
Or thou fhalt prove her lover's tomb."

   And now the lofty domes were rear'd;
Loud laugh'd the fquires, the rabble ftar'd.

   " See, neighbours, what our DAMON's doing!
I think fome folks are fond of ruin!

        I faw

I faw his fheep at random ftray—
But he has thrown his crook away—
And builds fuch huts, as, in foul weather,
Are fit for fheep nor fhepherd neither."
    Whence came the fober fwain mifled?
Why, PHOEBUS put it in his head.
PHOEBUS befriends him, we are told;
And PHOEBUS coins bright tuns of gold,
'Twere prudent not to be fo vain on't, .
I think he'll never touch a grain on't,
And if, from PHOEBUS, and his mufe,
Mere earthly lazinefs enfues;
'Tis plain, for aught that I can fay,
The dev'l infpires, as well as they.
So they—while fools of groffer kind,
Lefs weeting what our bard defign'd,
Impute his fchemes to real evil;
That in thefe haunts he met the devil.

    He own'd, tho' their advice was vain,
It fuited wights who trod the plain:
For dullnefs—tho' he might abhor it—
In them, he made allowance for it.
Nor wonder'd, if beholding mottos,
And urns, and domes, and cells, and grottos,
Folks, little dreaming of the mufes,
Were plagu'd to guefs their proper ufes.

    But did the mufes haunt his cell;
Or in his dome did VENUS dwell?
Did PALLAS in his counfels fhare?
The Delian god reward his pray'r?
Or did his zeal engage the fair?

When

When all the ftructure fhone compleat;
Not much convenient, wond'rous neat;
Adorn'd with gilding, painting, planting,
And the fair guefts alone were wanting;
Ah me! ('twas DAMON's own confeffion)
Came poverty and took poffeffion.

PART the FOURTH.

WHY droops my DAMON, whilft he roves
Thro' ornamented meads and groves?
Near columns, obelifks, and fpires,
Which ev'ry critic eye admires?
'Tis poverty, detefted maid,
Sole tenant of their ample fhade!
'Tis fhe, that robs him of his eafe;
And bids their very charms difpleafe.
But now, by fancy long controul'd,
And with the fons of tafte enroll'd,
He deem'd it fhameful, to commence
Firft minifter to common-fenfe:
Far more elated, to purfue
The loweft talk of dear vertû,

And now behold his lofty foul,
That whilom flew from pole to pole,
Settle on fome elaborate flow'r;
And, like a bee, the fweets devour!
Now, of a rofe enamour'd, prove
The wild folicitudes of love!
Now, in a lily's cup enfhrin'd,
Forego the commerce of mankind!

As in thefe toils he wore away
The calm remainder of his day;
Conducting fun, and fhade, and fhow'r,
As moft might glad the new-born flow'r,
So fate ordain'd—before his eye—
Starts up the long-fought butterfly !
While flutt'ring round, her plumes unfold
Celeftial crimfon, dropt with gold.

Adieu, ye bands of flow'rets fair !
The living beauty claims his care:
For this he ftrips—nor bolt, nor chain,
Cou'd DAMON's warm purfuit reftrain.

See him o'er hill, morafs, or mound,
Where'er the fpeckled game is found,
Tho' bent with age, with zeal purfue ;
And totter tow'rds the prey in view.

Nor rock, nor ftream, his fteps retard
Intent upon the bleft reward !
One vaffal fly repays the chace !
A wing, a film, rewards the race !
Rewards him, tho' difeafe attend,
And in a fatal furfeit end.
So fierce CAMILLA fkim'd the plain,
Smit with the purple's pleafing ftain,
She ey'd intent the glitt'ring ftranger,
And knew, alas ! nor fear, nor danger:
'Till deep within her panting heart.
Malicious fate impell'd the dart !

How ftudious he what fav'rite food
Regales dame nature's tiny brood !

What

What junkets fat the filmy people !
And what liqueurs they chufe to tipple !

Behold him, at fome crife, prefcribe,
And raife with drugs the fick'ning tribe !
Or haply, when their fpirits fau'ter,
Sprinkling my Lord of CLOYNE's tar-water.

When nature's brood of infects dies,
See how he pimps for am'rous flies !
See him the timely fuccour lend her,
And help the wantons to engender !

Or fee him guard their pregnant hour;
Exert his foft obftetric power :
And, lending each his lenient hand,
With new-born grubs enrich the land !

* O WILKS ! what poet's loftieft lays
Can match thy labours, and thy praife ?
Immortal fage ! by fate decreed
To guard the moth's illuftrious breed;
'Till flutt'ring fwarms on fwarms arife,
And all our wardrobes teem with flies !

And muft we praife this tafte for toys ?
Admire it then in girls and boys.
Ye youths of fifteen years, or more,
Refign your moths—the feafon's o'er.
'Tis time more focial joys to prove;
'Twere now your nobler tafk—to love.
Let * * * *'s eyes more deeply warm;
Nor flighting nature's faireft form,

The

* Alluding to moths and butterflies delineated by BENJAMIN
WILKS. See his very expenfive propofals.

The bias of your souls determine
Tow'rds the mean love of nature's vermin.

But ah! how wond'rous few have known,
To give each ftage of life its own.

'Tis the pretexta's utmoft bound,
With radiant purple edg'd around,
To pleafe the child; whofe glowing dyes
Too long delight maturer eyes:
And few, but with regret, affume
The plain-wrought labours of the loom.
Ah! let not me by fancy fteer,
When life's autumnal clouds appear;
Nor ev'n in learning's long delays
Confume my faireft, fruitlefs days:
Like him, who fhould in armour fpend
The fums that armour fhould defend.

Awhile, in pleafure's myrtle bow'r,
We fhare her fmiles, and blefs her pow'r:
But find at laft, we vainly ftrive
To fix the worft coquette alive.

O you! that with affiduous flame
Have long purfu'd the faithlefs dame;
Forfake her foft abodes awhile,
And dare her frown, and flight her fmile.
Nor fcorn, whatever wits may fay,
The foot-path road, the king's highway.
No more the fcrup'lous charmer teaze,
But feek the roofs of honeft eafe;
The rival fair, no more purfu'd,
Shall there with forward pace intrude;

Shall

Shall there her ev'ry art effay,
To win you to her flighted fway;
And grant your fcorn a glance more fair
Than e'er fhe gave your fondeft pray'r.

But would you happinefs purfue?
Partake both eafe, and pleafure too?
Would you, thro' all your days, difpenfe
The joys of reafon, and of fenfe?
Or give to life the moft you can?
Let focial virtue fhape the plan.
For does not to the virtuous deed
A train of pleafing fweets fucceed?
Or like the fweets of wild defire,
Did focial pleafures ever tire?

Yet midft the groupe be fome preferr'd,
Be fome abhorr'd—for DAMON err'd:
And fuch there are—of fair addrefs—
As 'twere unfocial to carefs.
O learn by reafon's equal rule
To fhun the praife of knave, or fool!
Then, tho' you deem it better ftill
To gain fome ruftic 'fquire's good will;
And fouls, however mean or vile,
Like features, brighten by a fmile;
Yet reafon holds it for a crime,
The trivial breaft fhould fhare thy time:
And virtue, with reluctant eyes,
Beholds this human facrifice!

Thro' deep referve, and air erect,
Miftaken DAMON won refpect;

But

But cou'd the fpacious homage pafs,
With any creature, but an afs?
If confcious, they who fear'd the fkin,
Wou'd fcorn the fluggifh brute within.
What awe-ftruck flaves the tow'rs enclofe,
Where Perfian monarchs eat, and doze!
What proftrate rev'rence all agree,
To pay a prince they never fee!
Mere vaffals of a royal throne!
The fophi's virtues muft be fhewn,
To make the reverence his own.

　　As for THALIA—wouldft thou make her
Thy bride without a portion? take her.
She will with duteous care attend,
And all thy penfive hours befriend;
Will fwell thy joys, will fhare thy pain;
With thee rejoice, with thee complain;
With fmooth thy pillow, pleat thy bow'rs,
And bind thine aching head with flow'rs.
But be this previous maxim known—
If thou can'ft feed on love alone:
If, bleft with her, thou canft fuftain
Contempt, and poverty, and pain:
If fo—then rifle all her graces—
And fruitful be your fond embraces!

　　Too foon, by caitliff-fpleen infpir'd,
Sage DAMON to his groves retir'd:
The path difclaim'd by fober reafon;
Retirement claims a later feafon;
Ere active youth and warm defires
Have quite withdrawn their ling'ring fires.

With

With the warm bofom, ill agree,
Or limpid ftream, or fhady tree.
Love lurks within the rofy bow'r,
And claims the fpeculative hour;
Ambition finds his calm retreat,
And bids his pulfe too fiercely beat;
Ev'n focial friendfhip duns his ear,
And cites him to the public fphere.
Does he refift their genuine force?
His temper takes fome froward courfe;
'Till paffion, mifdirected, fighs
For weeds, or fhells, or grubs, or flies!

 Far happieft he; whofe early days
Spent in the focial paths of praife,
Leave, fairly printed on his mind,
A train of virtuous deeds behind:
From this rich fund, the mem'ry draws
The lafting meed of felf-applaufe.

 Such fair ideas lend their aid
To people the fequefter'd fhade.
Such are the naiads, nymphs, and fauns,
That haunt his floods, or chear his lawns.
If where his devious ramble ftrays,
He virtue's radiant form furveys;
She feems no longer now to wear
The rigid mien, the frown fevere; *
To fhew him her remote abode;
To point the rocky arduous road:
But from each flower, his fields allow,
She twines a garland for his brow.

OECO-

* Alluding to—the allegory in CEBES's tablet.

OECONOMY,

A RHAPSODY, addreſſed to young Poets.

Inſanis ; omnes gelidis quicunque lacernis
Sunt tibi, Naſones Virgilioſque vides.   Mart.

IMITATION.

———— Thou know'ſt not what thou ſay'ſt,
In garments that ſcarce fence them from the cold,
Our Ovids and our Virgils you behold.

PART the FIRST.

TO you ye bards ! whoſe laviſh breaſt requires
        This monitory lay, the ſtrains belong ;
Nor think ſome miſer vents his ſapient ſaw,
Or ſome dull cit unfeeling of the charms
That tempt profuſion, ſings ; while friendly zeal,
To guard from fatal ills the tribe he loves,
Inſpires the meaneſt of the muſe's train !
Like you I loathe the groveling progeny,
Whoſe wily arts, by creeping time matur'd,
Advance them high on pow'r's tyrannic throne ;
To lord it there in gorgeous uſeleſſneſs,
And ſpurn ſucceſsleſs worth that pines below !

  See the rich churl, amid the ſocial ſons
Of wine and wit, regaling ! hark he joins
In the free jeſt delighted ! ſeems to ſhew
A meliorated heart ! he laughs ! he ſings !
Songs of gay import, madrigals of glee,

                                            And

And drunken anthems, fet agape the board.
Like * Demea, in the play, benign and mild,
And pouring forth benevolence of foul,
'Till Micio wonders : or, in Shakespear's line,
Obftrep'rous Silence † ; drowning Shallow's voice,
And ftartling Falstaff, and his mad compeers.

He owns 'tis prudence, ever and anon,
To fmoothe his careful brow ; to let his purfe
Ope to a fixpence's diameter ;
He likes our ways ; he owns the ways of wit
Are ways of pleafaunce, and deferve regard,
True, we are dainty good fociety,
But what art thou ? alas ! confider well,
Thou bane of focial pleafure, know thyfelf.
Thy fell approach, like fome invafive damp
Breath'd thro' the pores of earth from Stygian caves,
Deftroys the lamp of mirth ; the lamp which we
Its flamens boaft to guard : we know not how,
But at thy fight the fading flame affumes
A ghaftly blue, and in a ftench expires.

True, thou feem'ft chang'd ; all fainted, all enfky'd ;
The trembling tears that charge thy melting eyes
Say thou art honeft, and of gentle kind ;
But all is falfe ! an intermitting figh
Condemns each hour, each moment giv'n to fmiles,
And deems thofe only loft, thou doft not lofe.
Ev'n for a demi-groat, this open'd foul,
This boon companion, this elaftic breaft

* In Terence's Adelphi.
† Juftice Silence, in Shakefpeare's Henry IVth, fecond part.

Revibrates quick; and fends the tuneful tongue
To lavifh mufic on the rugged walls
Of fome dark dungeon.   Hence thou caitiff, fly !
Touch not my glafs, nor drain my facred bowl,
Monfter, ingrate ! beneath one common fky
Why fhould'ft thou breathe; beneath one common roof
Thou ne'er fhalt harbour; nor my little boat
Receive a foul with crimes to prefs it down.
Go to thy bags, thou recreant ! hourly go,
And gazing there, bid them be wit, be mirth,
Be converfation.   Not a face that fmiles
Admit thy prefence ! not a foul that glows
With focial purport, bid or ev'n or morn
Inveft thee happy ! but when life declines,
May thy fure heirs ftand titt'ring round thy bed,   —
And ufh'ring in their fav'rites, burft thy locks,
And fill their laps with gold; 'till want and care
With joy depart, and cry, " We afk no more."
    Ah never never may th' harmonious mind
Endure the worldly ! poets ever void
Of guile, diftruftlefs, fcorn the treafur'd gold,
And fpurn the mifer, fpurn his deity.
Ballanc'd with friendfhip, in the poet's eye
The rival fcale of intereft kicks the beam,
Than lightning fwifter.   From his cavern'd ftore
The fordid foul, with felf-applaufe, remarks
The kind propenfity; remarks and fmiles,
And hies with impious hafte to fpread the fnare.
Him we deride, and in our comic fcenes
Contemn the niggard form MOLIERE has drawn.
We loathe with juftice; but alas the pain

To

To bow the knee before this calf of gold;
Implore his envious aid, and meet his frown!
   But 'tis not GOMEZ, 'tis not he whose heart
Is crufted o'er with drofs, whofe callous mind
Is fenfelefs as his gold, the flighted mufe
Intenfely loathes. 'Tis fure no equal tafk
To pardon him, who lavifhes his wealth
On racer, fox-hound, hawk or fpaniel, all
But human merit; who with gold effays
All, but the nobleft pleafure, to remove
The wants of genius, and its fmiles enjoy.
   But you, ye titled youths! whofe nobler zeal
Would burnifh o'er your coronets with fame;
Who liften pleas'd when poet tunes his lay;
Permit him not, in diftant folitudes
To pine, to languifh out the fleeting hours
Of active youth! then virtue pants for praife,
That feafon unadorn'd, the carelefs bard
Quits your worn threfhold, and like honeft GAY
Contemns the niggard boon ye time fo ill.
Your favours then, like trophies giv'n the tomb,
Th' enfranchis'd fpirit foaring not perceives,
Or fcorns perceiv'd; and execrates the fmile
Which bade his vig'rous bloom, to treacherous hopes
And fervile cares a prey, expire in vain!——
   Two lawlefs pow'rs, engag'd by mutual hate
In endlefs war, beneath their flags enroll
The vaffal world. This avarice is nam'd,
That luxury; 'tis true their partial friends
Affign them fofter names; ufurpers both!

      That

That fhare by dint of arms the legal throne
Of juft œconomy ; yet both betray'd
By fraudful minifters.   The niggard chief
Lift'ning to want, all faithlefs, and prepar'd
To join each moment in his rival's train,
His conduct models by the needlefs fears
The flave infpires ; while luxury, a chief
Of ampleft faith, to plenty's rule refigns
His whole campaign.   'Tis plenty's flatt'ring founds
Engrofs his ear ; 'tis plenty's fmiling form
Moves ftill before his eye.   Difcretion ftrives,
But ftrives in vain, to banifh from the throne
The perjur'd minion.   He, fecure of truft,
With latent malice to the hoftile camp
Day, night, and hour, his monarch's wealth conveys.
     Ye tow'ring minds ! ye fublimated fouls !
Who carelefs of your fortunes, feal and fign,
Set, let, contract, acquit, with eafier mien
Than fops take fnuff ! whofe œconomic care
Your green-filk purfe engroffes ! eafy, pleas'd,
To fee gold fparkle thro' the fubtle folds ;
Lovely, as when th' Hefperian fruitage fmil'd
Amid the verd'rous grove ! who fondly hope
Spontaneous harvefts ! harvefts all the year !
Who fcatter wealth, as tho' the radiant crop
Glitter'd on ev'ry bough ; and ev'ry bough,
Like that the Trojan gather'd, once avuls'd
Were by a fplendid fucceffor fupply'd
Inftant, fpontaneous ! liften to my lays.
For 'tis not fools, whate'er proverbial phrafe

Have

Have long decreed, that quit with greatest eafe
The treafur'd gold. Of words indeed profufe,
Of gold tenacious, their torpefcent foul
Clenches their coin, and what electral fire
Shall folve the frofty gripe, and bid it flow?
'Tis genius, fancy, that to wild expence
Of health! of treafure! ftimulates the foul:
Thefe, with officious care, and fatal art,
Improve the vinous flavour; thefe the fmile
Of CLOE foften; thefe the glare of drefs
Illume; the glitt'ring chariot gild anew,
And add ftrange wifdom to the furs of pow'r.

   Alas! that he, amid the race of men,
That he, who thinks of pureft gold with fcorn,
Shou'd with unfated appetite demand;
And vainly court the pleafure it procures!
When fancy's vivid fpark impels the foul
To fcorn quotidian fcenes, to fpurn the blifs
Of vulgar minds, what noftrum fhall compofe
Its fatal tenfion? in what lonely vale
Of balmy med'cine's various field, afpires
The bleft refrigerant? Vain, ah vain the hope
Of future peace, this orgafm uncontroul'd!
Impatient, hence, of all the frugal mind
Requires; to eat, to drink, to fleep, to fill
A cheft with gold, the fprightly breaft demands
Inceffant rapture; life, a tedious load
Deny'd its continuity of joy.
But whence obtain? philofophy requires
No lavifh coft; to crown its utmoft pray'r

Suffice

Suffice the root-built-cell, the fimple fleece,
The juicy viand, and the cryftal ftream.
Ev'n mild ftupidity rewards her train
With cheap contentment. Tafte alone requires
Entire profufion ! Days and nights, and hours
Thy voice, hydropic fancy ! calls aloud
For coftly draughts, inundant bowls of joy,
Rivers of rich regalement ! feas of blifs !
Seas without fhore ! infinity of fweets !

And yet, unlefs fage reafon join her hand
In pleafure's purchafe, pleafure is unfure :
And yet, unlefs œconomy's confent
Legitimate expence, fome gracelefs mark,
Some fymptom ill-conceal'd, fhall, foon or late,
Burft like a pimple from the vicious tide
Of acid blood, proclaiming want's difeafe,
Amidft the bloom of fhew. The fcanty ftream
Slow-loitering in its channel, feems to vie
With VAGA's depth; but fhould the fedgy pow'r
Vain-glorious empty his penurious urn
O'er the rough rock, how muft his fellow ftreams
Deride the tinklings of the boaftive rill !

I not afpire to mark the dubious path
That leads to wealth, to poets mark'd in vain !
But ere felf-flattery foothe the vivid breaft
With dreams of fortune near ally'd to fame,
Refleft how few, who charm'd the lift'ning ear
Of fatrap or of king, her fmiles enjoy'd !
Confider well, what meagre alms repay'd
The great Mæonian, fire of tuneful fong,

And prototype of all that foar'd fublime,
And left dull cares below; what griefs impell'd
The modeft bard of learn'd ELIZA's reign
To fwell with tears his MULLA's parent ftream,
And mourn aloud the pang " to ride, to run,
To fpend, to give, to want, to be undone."
Why fhou'd I tell of COWLEY's penfive mufe
Belov'd in vain ? too copious is my theme !
Which of your boafted race might hope reward
Like loyal BUTLER, when the lib'ral CHARLES,
The judge of wit, perus'd the fprightly page
Triumphant o'er his foes ? Believe not hope,
The poet's parafite ; but learn alone
To fpare the fcanty boon the fates decree.
Poet and rich ! 'tis folecifm extreme !
'Tis heighten'd contradiction ! in his frame,
In ev'ry nerve and fibre of his foul,
The latent feeds and principles of want
IIas nature wove ; and fate confirm'd the clue.
   Nor yet defpair to fhun the ruder gripe
Of penury ; with nice precifion learn
A dollar's value.   Foremoft in the page
That marks th' expence of each revolving year,
Place inattention.   When the luft of praife,
Or honour's falfe idea, tempts thy foul
To flight frugality, affure thine heart
That danger's near.   This perifhable coin
Is no vain ore.   It is thy liberty,
It fetters mifers, but it muft alone
Enfranchife thee.   The world, the cit-like world,

Bids

Bids thee beware ; thy little craft eſſay ;
Nor, pidling with a tea-ſpoon's ſlender form,
See with ſoup-ladles devils gourmandize.

    Œconomy ! thou good old aunt ! whoſe mien
Furrow'd with age and care the wiſe adore,
The wits contemn ! reſerving ſtill thy ſtores
To chear thy friends at laſt ! why with the cit,
Or bookleſs churl, with each ignoble name,
Each earthly nature, deign'ſt thou to reſide ?
And ſhunning all, who by thy favours crown'd
Might glad the world, to ſeek ſome vulgar mind,
Inſpiring pride, and ſelfiſh ſhapes of ill ?

    Why with the old, infirm, and impotent,
And childiſh, love to dwell, yet leave the breaſt
Of youth unwarn'd, unguided, uninform'd ?
Of youth, to whom thy monitory voice
Were doubly kind ? for ſure to youthful eyes,
(How ſhort ſoe'er it prove) the road of life
Appears protracted ; fair on either ſide
The loves, the graces play, on fortune's child
Profuſely ſmiling ; well might youth eſſay
The frugal plan, the lucrative employ,
Source of their favour all the live-long day.
But fate aſſents not. Age alone contracts
His meagre palm, to clench the tempting bane
Of all his peace, the glitt'ring ſeeds of care !

    O that the muſe's voice might pierce the ear
Of gen'rous youth ! for youth deſerves her ſong.
Youth is fair virtue's ſeaſon, virtue then
Requires the pruner's hand ; the ſequent ſtage,

It

It barely vegetates; nor long the fpace
Ere robb'd of warmth its arid trunk difplay
Fell winter's total reign.   O lovely fource
Of gen'rous foibles, youth! when op'ning minds
Are honeft as the light, lucid as air,
As foft'ring breezes kind, as linnets gay,
Tender as buds, and lavifh as the fpring !
Yet, haplefs ftate of man ! his earlieft youth
Cozens itfelf; his age defrauds mankind.

   Nor deem it ftrange that rolling years abrade
The focial biafs.   Life's extenfive page,
What does it but unfold repeated proofs
Of gold's omnipotence ? With patriots, friends,
Sick'ning beneath its ray, enervate fome,
And others dead, whofe putrid name exhales
A noifome fcent, the bulky volume teems.
With kinfmen, brothers, fons, moift'ning the fhroud,
Or honouring the grave, with fpecious grief
Of fhort duration; foon in fortune's beams
Alert, and wond'ring at the tears they fhed.

   But who fhall fave by tame profaic ftrain
That glowing breaft, where wit with youth confpires
To fweeten luxury ?   The fearful mufe
Shall yet proceed, tho' by the fainteft gleam
Of hope infpir'd, to warn the train fhe loves.

PART the SECOND.

IN some dark season, when the misty show'r
   Obscures the sun, and saddens all the sky;
When linnets drop the wing, nor grove nor stream
Invites thee forth, to sport thy drooping muse;
Seize the dull hour, nor with regret assign
To worldly prudence. She nor nice nor coy
Accepts the tribute of a joyless day:
She smiles well-pleas'd, when wit and mirth recede,
And not a grace, and not a muse will hear.
Then, from majestic MARO's aweful strain,
Or tow'ring HOMER, let thine eye descend
To trace, with patient industry, the page
Of income and expence. And oh! beware,
Thy breast, self-flatt'ring, place no courtly smile,
No golden promise of your faithless muse,
Nor latent mine which fortune's hand may shew,
Amid thy solid store. The siren's song
Wrecks not the list'ning sailor, half so sure.
See by what avenues, what devious paths,
The foot of want, detested, steals along,
And bars each fatal pass! Some few short hours
Of punctual care, the refuse of thy year,
On frugal schemes employ'd, shall give the muse
To sing intrepid many a chearful day.
   But if too soon before the tepid gales
Thy resolution melt; and ardent vows
In wary hours preferr'd, or die forgot,

Or

Or feem the forc'd effect of hazy fkies;
Then, ere furprize, by whofe impetuous rage
The maffy fort with which thy gentler breaft
I not compare, is won, the fong proceeds.

   Know too by nature's undiminifh'd law,
Throughout her realms obey'd, the various parts
Of deep creation, atoms, fyftems, all !
Attract and are attracted ; nor prevails the law
Alone in matter ; foul alike with foul
Afpires to join ; nor yet in fouls alone,
In each idea it imbibes, is found
The kind propenfity.   And when they meet,
And grow familiar, various tho' their tribe,
Their tempers various, vow perpetual faith :
That, fhou'd the world's disjointed frame once more
To chaos yield the fway, amid the wreck
Their union fhou'd furvive ; with Roman warmth,
By facred hofpitable laws endear'd,
Shou'd each idea recollect its friend.

   Here then we fix ; on this perennial bafe
Erect thy fafety, and defy the ftorm.
Let foft profufion's fair idea join
Her hand with poverty ; nor here defift,
'Till, o'er the groupe that forms their various train
Thou fing loud hymeneals.   Let the pride
Of outward fhew in lafting leagues combine
With fhame thread-bare ; the gay vermilion face
Of rafh intemp'rance, be difcreetly pair'd
With fallow hunger ; the licentious joy,
With mean dependence ; ev'n the dear delight

                                      Of

Of fculpture, paint, intaglios, books, and coins,
Thy breaſt, ſagacious prudence ! ſhall conneſt
With filth and beggary ; nor diſdain to link
With black inſolvency. Thy ſoul alarm'd
Shall ſhun the ſiren's voice ; nor boldly dare
To bid the ſoft enchantreſs ſhare thy breaſt,
With ſuch a train of horrid fiends conjoin'd.

    Nor think, ye ſordid race ! ye groveling minds !
I frame the ſong for you ! for you, the muſe
Cou'd other rules impart. The friendly ſtrain
For gentler boſoms plan'd, to yours wou'd prove
The juice of lurid aconite, exceed
Whatever CoLcHos bore ; and in your breaſt
Compaſſion, love, and friendſhip all deſtroy !

    It greatly ſhall avail, if e'er thy ſtores
Increaſe apace, by periodic days
Of annual payment, or thy patron's boon,
The lean reward of groſs unbounded praiſe !
It much avails, to ſeize the preſent hour,
And, undeliberating, call around
Thy hungry creditors ; their horrid rage
When once appeas'd, the ſmall remaining ſtore
Shall riſe in weight tenfold, in luſtre riſe,
As gold improv'd by many a fierce aſſay.
'Tis thus the frugal huſbandman direſts
His narrow ſtream, if o'er its wonted banks
By ſudden rains impell'd, it proudly ſwell ;
His timely hand thro' better tracks conveys
The quick-decreaſing tide ; ere borne along
Or thro' the wild moraſs, or cultur'd field,

                                             Or

Or bladed grafs mature, or barren fands,
It flow deftructive, or it flow in vain!
But happieft he who fanctifies expence
By prefent pay! who fubjects not his fame
To tradefmen's varlets, nor bequeaths his name,
His honour'd name, to deck the vulgar page
Of bafe mechanic, fordid, unfincere!
There haply, while thy mufe fublimely foars
Beyond this earthly fphere, in heav'n's abodes,
And dreams of nectar and ambrofial fweets,
Thy growing debt fteals unregarded o'er
The punctual record; 'till nor PHOEBUS' felf,
Nor fage MINERVA's art can aught avail
To foothe the ruthlefs dun's detefted rage.
Frantic and fell, with many a curfe profane
He loads the gentle mufe; then hurls thee down
To want, remorfe, captivity and fhame.

Each public place, the glitt'ring haunts of men,
With horror fly. Why loiter near thy bane?—
Why fondly linger on a hoftile fhore
Difarm'd, defencelefs? why require to tread
The precipice? or why, alas! to breathe
A moment's fpace, where ev'ry breeze is death?
Death to thy future peace! Away, collect
Thy diffipated mind; contract thy train
Of wild ideas, o'er the flow'ry fields
Of fhew diffus'd, and fpeed to fafer climes.
Œconomy prefents her glafs, accept
The faithful mirror; powerful to difclofe
A thoufand forms; unfeen by carelefs eyes,

That

That plot thy fate.   Temptation in a robe
Of Tyrian dye, with every fweet perfum'd,
Befets thy fenfe; extortion follows clofe
Her wanton ftep, and ruin brings the rear.
Thefe and the reft fhall her myfterious glafs
Embody to thy view; like VENUS kind,
When to her lab'ring fon, the vengeful pow'rs
That urg'd the fall of ILIUM, fhe difplay'd.
He, not imprudent, at the fight declin'd
Th' inequal conflict, and decreed to raife
The Trojan welfare on fome happier fhore.
For here to drain thy fwelling purfe await
A thoufand arts, a thoufand frauds attend :
" The cloud-wrought canes, the gorgeous fnaff-boxes:
The twinkling jewels, and the gold etwee,
With all its bright inhabitants, fhall wafte
Its melting ftores, and in the dreary void
Leave not a doit behind."   Ere yet exhauft
Its flimfy-folds offend thy penfive eye, .
Away ! embofom'd deep in diftant fhades,
Nor feen nor feeing, thou may'ft vent thy fcorn
Of lace, embroidery, purple, gems, and gold!
There of the farded fop and effenc'd beau,
Ferocious with a ftoic's frown difclofe
Thy manly fcorn, averfe to tinfel pomp ;
And fluent thine harangue, But can thy foul
Deny thy limbs the radiant grace of drefs,
Where drefs is merit ! where thy graver friend
Shall wifh thee burnifh'd ! where the fprightly fair
Demand embellifhment ! ev'n DELIA's eye,

As in a garden, roves, of hues alone
Inquirent, curious? Fly the curft domain;
Thefe are the realms of luxury and fhew,
No claffic foil; away! the bloomy fpring
Attracts thee hence; the waning autumn warns;
Fly to thy native fhades, and dread ev'n there,
Left bufy fancy tempt thy narrow ftate
Beyond its bounds.   Obferve FLORELIO's mien.
Why treads my friend with melancholy ftep
That beauteous lawn? why penfive ftrays his eye
O'er ftatues, grottoes, urns by critic art
Proportion'd fair? or from his lofty dome
Bright glitt'ring through the grove, returns his eye
Unpleas'd, difconfolate? And is it love,
Difaftrous love, that robs the finifh'd fcenes
Of all their beauty? cent'ring all in her
His foul adores? or from a blacker caufe
Springs this remorfeful gloom? is confcious guilt
The latent fource of more than love's defpair?
It cannot be within that polifh''d breaft
Where fcience dwells, that guilt fhould harbour there.
No! 'tis the fad furvey of prefent want,
And paft profufion! Loft to him the fweets
Of yon pavilion, fraught with ev'ry charm
For other eyes; or, if remaining, proofs
Of criminal expence! Sweet interchange
Of river, valley, mountain, woods and plains!
How gladfome once he rang'd your native turf,
Your fimple fcenes, how raptur'd! ere expence
Had lavifh'd thoufand ornaments, and taught

Convenience

Convenience to perplex him, art to pall,
Pomp to dejeĉt, and beauty to difpleafe.

   Oh ! for a foul to all the glare of wealth,
To fortune's wide exhauftlefs treafury,
Nobly fuperior ! but let caution guide
The coy difpofal of the wealth we fcorn,
And prudence be our Almoner ! Alas !
The pilgrim wand'ring o'er fome diftant clime,
Sworn foe of avarice ! not difdains to learn
Its coin's imputed worth ; the deftin'd means
To fmoothe his paffage to the favour'd fhrine.
Ah let not us, who tread this ftranger-world,
Let none who fojourn on the realms of life.
Forget the land is merc'nary ; nor wafte
His fare, cre landed on no venal fhore.

   Let never bard confult PALLADIO's rules ;
Let never bard, O BURLINGTON ! furvey
Thy learned art, in CHISWICK's dome difplay'd :
Dang'rous incentive ! nor with ling'ring eye
Survey the window VENICE calls her own.
Better for him, with no ingrateful mufe,
To fing a requiem to that gentle foul
Who plan'd the fky-light ; which to lavifh bards
Conveys alone the pure etherial ray :
For garrets him, and fqualid walls await,
Unlefs, prefageful, from this friendly ftrain,
He glean advice, and fhun the fcribbler's doom.

PART

PART the THIRD.

YET once again, and to thy doubtful fate
    The trembling mufe configns thee. Ere contempt,
Or want's empoifon'd arrow, ridicule,
Transfix thy weak unguarded breaft, behold!
The poet's roofs, the carelefs poet's, his
Who fcorns advice, fhall clofe my ferious lay.

    When GULLIVER, now great, now little deem'd,
The play-thing of comparifon, arriv'd
Where learned bofoms their aerial fchemes
Projected, ftudious of the public weal;
'Mid thefe, one fubtler artift he defcry'd,
Who cherifh'd in his dufty tenement
The fpider's web, injurious, to fupplant
Fair ALBION's fleeces! Never, never may
Our monarch on fuch fatal purpofe fmile,
And irritate MINERVA's beggar'd fons
The MELKSHAM weavers! Here in ev'ry nook
Their wefts they fpun; here revell'd uncontroul'd,
And, like the flags from WESTMINSTER's high roof
Dependant, here their fluttering textures wav'd.
Such, fo adorn'd, the cell I mean to fing!
Cell ever fqualid! where the fneerful maid
Will not fatigue her hand! broom never comes,
That comes to all! o'er whofe quiefcent walls
ARACHNE's unmolefted care has drawn
Curtains fubfufk, and fave th' expence of art.

    Survey thofe walls, in fady texture clad,

Where wand'ring ſnails in many a ſlimy path,
Free, unreſtrain'd, their various journeys crawl;
Peregrinations ſtrange, and labyrinths
Confus'd inextricable! ſuch the clue
Of Cretan ARIADNE ne'er explain'd!
Hooks! angles! crooks! and involutions wild!
Mean time, thus ſilver'd with meanders gay,
In mimic pride the ſnail-wrought tiſſue ſhines,
Perchance of tabby, or of harrateen,
Not ill expreſſive! ſuch the pow'r of ſnails.

Behold his chair, whoſe fractur'd ſeat infirm
An aged cuſhion hides! replete with duſt
The foliag'd velvet; pleaſing to the eye
Of great ELIZA's reign, but now the ſnare
Of weary gueſt that on the ſpecious bed
Sits down confiding. Ah! diſaſtrous wight!
In evil hour and raſhly doſt thou truſt
The fraudful couch! for tho' in velvet cas'd,
The fated thigh ſhall kiſs the duſty floor.
The trav'ler thus, that o'er Hibernian plains
Hath ſhap'd his way; on beds profuſe of flow'rs
Cowſlip, or primroſe, or the circ'lar eye
Of daiſie fair, decrees to baſk ſupine.
And ſee! delighted, down he drops, ſecure
Of ſweet refreſhment, eaſe without annoy,
Or luſcious noon-day nap. Ah much deceiv'd,
Much ſuff'ring pilgrim! thou nor noon-day nap,
Nor ſweet repoſe ſhalt find; the falſe morafs
In quiv'ring undulations yields beneath
Thy burden, in the miry gulph encloſ'd!

And

And who would truſt appearance ? caſt thine eye
Where 'mid machines of het'rogeneous form
His coat depends ; alas ! his only coat,
Eldeſt of things ! and napleſs, as an heath
Of ſmall extent by fleecy myriads graz'd.
Not diff'rent have I ſeen in dreary vault
Diſplay'd, a coffin ; on each ſable ſide
The texture unmoleſted ſeems entire.
Fraudful, when touch'd it glides to duſt away !
And leaves the wond'ring ſwain to gape, to ſtare,
And with expreſſive ſhrug, and piteous ſigh,
Declare the fatal force of rolling years,
Or dire extent of frail mortality.
This aged veſture, ſcorn of gazing beaux,
And formal cits, (themſelves too haply ſcorn'd)
Both on its ſleeve and on its ſkirt, retains
Full many a pin wide-ſparkling : for, if e'er
Their well-known creſt met his delighted eye,
Tho' wrapt in thought, commercing with the ſky,
He, gently ſtooping, ſcorn'd not to upraiſe,
And on each ſleeve, as conſcious of their uſe,
Indenting fix them ; nor, when arm'd with theſe,
The cure of rents and ſeparations dire,
And chaſms enormous, did he view diſmay'd
Hedge, bramble, thicket, buſh, portending fate
To breeches, coat and hoſe ! had any wight
Of vulgar ſkill, the tender texture own'd ;
But gave his mind to form a ſonnet quaint
Of Silvia's ſhoe-ſtring, or of Cloe's fan,
Or ſweetly-faſhion'd tip of Celia's ear.

Alas !

Alas! by frequent use decays the force
Of mortal art! the refractory robe
Eludes the taylor's art, eludes his own;
How potent once, in union quaint conjoin'd!

   See near his bed (his bed too falsely call'd
The place of rest, while it a bard sustains;
Pale, meagre, muse-rid wight! who reads in vain
Narcotic volumes o'er) his candlestick,
Radiant machine, when from the plastic hand
Of MULCIBER, the may'r of BIRMINGHAM,
The engine issu'd; now alas disguis'd
By many an unctuous tide, that wand'ring down
Its sides congeal; what he, perhaps, essays
With humour forc'd, and ill-dissembled smile,
Idly to liken to the poplar's trunk
When o'er its bark the lucid amber, wound
In many a pleasing fold, incrusts the tree.
Or suits him more the winter's candy'd thorn,
When from each branch, anneal'd, the works of frost
Pervasive, radiant icicles depend!

   How shall I sing the various ill that waits
The careful sonneteer? or who can paint
The shifts enormous, that in vain he forms
To patch his panelefs window; to cement
His batter'd tea-pot, ill-retentive vase?
To war with ruin? anxious to conceal
Want's fell appearance, of the real ill
Nor foe, nor fearful. Ruin unforeseen
Invades his chattles; ruin will invade;
Will claim his whole invention to repair,

                                    Nor,

Nor, of the gift, for tuneful ends defign'd,
Allow one part to decorate his fong.
While ridicule, with ever-pointing hand
Confcious of ev'ry fhift, of ev'ry fhift
Indicative, his inmoft plot betrays,
Points to the nook, which he his ftudy calls
Pompous and vain! for thus he might efteem
His cheft, a wardrobe; purfe, a treafury;
And fhews, to crown her full difplay, himfelf.
One whom the pow'rs above, in place of health,
And wonted vigour; of paternal cot,
Or little farm; of bag, or fcrip, or ftaff,
Cup, difh, fpoon, plate, or worldly utenfil,
A poet fram'd; yet fram'd not to repine,
And wifh the cobler's loftieft fite his own;
Nor, partial as they feem, upbraid the fates,
Who to the humbler mechanifm, join'd
Goods fo fuperior, fuch exalted blifs!
  See with what feeming eafe, what labour'd peace
He, haplefs hypocrite! refines his nail,
His chief amufement! then how feign'd, how forc'd,
That care-defying fonnet, which implies
His debts difcharg'd, and he of half a crown
In full poffeffion, uncontefted right
And property! Yet ah! whoe'er this wight
Admiring view, if fuch there be, diftruft
The vain pretence; the fmiles that harbour grief,
As lurks the ferpent deep in flow'rs enwreath'd.
Forewarn'd, be frugal; or with prudent rage
Thy pen demolifh; chufe the truftier flail,

And

And bleſs thoſe labours which the choice inſpir'd.
But if thou view'ſt a vulgar mind, a wight
Of common ſenſe, who ſeeks no brighter name,
Him envy, him admire, him, from thy breaſt,
Preſcient of future dignities, ſalute
Sheriff, or may'r, in comfortable furs
Enwrapt, ſecure: nor yet the laureat's crown
In thought exclude him ! He perchance ſhall riſe
To nobler heights than foreſight can decree.

    When fir'd with wrath, for his intrigues diſplay'd
In many an idle ſong, Saturnian Jove
Vow'd ſure deſtruction to the tuneful race;
Appeas'd by ſuppliant Phoebus, "Bards, he ſaid,
Henceforth of plenty, wealth, and pomp debarr'd,
But fed by frugal cares, might wear the bay
Secure of thunder."—Low the Delian bow'd,
Nor at th' invidious favour dar'd repine.

❖❖❖

The RUIN'D ABBY;

OR,

The EFFECTS of SUPERSTITION.

AT length fair peace with olive crown'd regains
    Her lawful throne, and to the ſacred haunts
Of wood or fount the frighted muſe returns,
    Happy the bard, who, from his native hills,
Soft muſing on a ſummer's eve, ſurveys

His

His azure ſtream, with penſile woods encloſ'd!
Or o'er the glaſſy ſurface, with his friend,
Or faithful fair, thro' bord'ring willows green
Wafts his ſmall frigate. Fearleſs he of ſhouts,
Or taunts, the rhetoric of the wat'ry crew
That ape confuſion from the realms thy rule!
Fearleſs of theſe; who ſhares the gentler voice
Of peace and muſic; birds of ſweeteſt ſong
Attune from native boughs their various lay,
And chear the foreſt; birds of brighter plume
With buſy pinion ſkim the glitt'ring wave,
And tempt the ſun; ambitious to diſplay
Their ſeveral merit, while the vocal flute,
Or number'd verſe, by female voice endear'd,
Crowns his delight, and mollifies the ſcene.
    If ſolitude his wand'ring ſteps invite
To ſome more deep receſs, (for hours there are,
When gay, when ſocial minds to friendſhip's voice,
Or beauty's charm, her wild abodes prefer)
How pleas'd he treads her venerable ſhades,
Her ſolemn courts! the center of the grove!
The root-built cave, by far extended rocks
Around emboſom'd, how it ſoothes the ſoul!
If ſcoop'd at firſt by ſuperſtitious hands
The rugged cell receiv'd alone the ſhoals
Of bigot minds, religion dwells not here,
Yet virtue pleas'd, at intervals, retires;
Yet here may wiſdom, as ſhe walks the maze,
Some ſerious truths collect, the rules of life,
And ſerious truths of mightier weight than gold!

I aſk

I afk not wealth; but let me hoard with care,
With frugal cunning, with a niggard's art,
A few fix'd principles; in early life,
Ere indolence impede the fearch, explor'd.
Then like old LATIMER, when age impairs
My judgment's eye, when quibbling fchools attack
My grounded hope, or fubtler wits deride,
Will I not blufh to fhun the vain debate,
And this mine anfwer; "Thus, 'twas thus I thought,
" My mind yet vigorous, and my foul entire;
" Thus will I think, averfe to liften more
" To intricate difcuffion, prone to ftray.
" Perhaps my reafon may but ill defend
" My fettled faith; my mind, with age impair'd,
" Too fure its own infirmities declare.
" But I am arm'd by caution, ftudious youth,
" And early forefight; now the winds may rife,
" The tempeft whiftle, and the billows roar;
" My pinnace rides in port, defpoil'd and worn,
" Shatter'd by time and ftorms, but while it fhuns
" Th' inequal conflict, and declines the deep,
" Sees the ftrong veffel fluctuate lefs fecure."
    Thus while he ftrays, a thoufand rural fcenes
Suggeft inftruction, and inftructing pleafe.
And fee betwixt the grove's extended arms
An abby's rude remains attract thy view,
Gilt by the mid-day fun: with ling'ring ftep
Produce thine axe, (for, aiming to deftroy
Tree, branch, or fhade, for never fhall thy breaft
Too long deliberate) with timorous hand

                                    Remove

Remove th' obstructive bough; nor yet refuse,
Tho' sighing, to destroy that fav'rite pine,
Rais'd by thine hand, in its luxuriant prime
Of beauty fair, that screens the vast remains.
Aggriev'd, but constant as the Roman sire,
The rigid Manlius, when his conqu'ring son
Bled by a parent's voice; the cruel meed
Of virtuous ardor, timelessly display'd;
Nor cease 'till, thro' the gloomy road, the pile
Gleam unobstructed; thither oft thine eye
Shall sweetly wander; thence returning, soothe
With pensive scenes thy philosophic mind.

 'These were thy haunts, thy opulent abodes,
O superstition! hence the dire disease
(Ballanc'd with which the fam'd Athenian pest
Were a short head-ach, were the trivial pain
Of transient indigestion) seiz'd mankind.

 Long time she rag'd, and scarce a southern gale
Warm'd our chill air, unloaded with the threats
Of tyrant Rome; but futile all, 'till she,
Rome's abler legate, magnify'd their pow'r,
And in a thousand horrid forms attir'd.

 Where then was truth, to sanctify the page
Of British annals? if a foe expir'd,
The perjur'd monk suborn'd infernal shrieks,
And fiends to snatch at the departing soul
With hellish emulation. If a friend,
High o'er his roof exultant angels tune
Their golden lyres, and waft him to the skies.

 What then were vows, were oaths, were plighted faith?
The

The fovereign's juft, the fubject's loyal pact
To cherifh mutual good, annull'd and vain,
By Roman magic, grew an idle fcroll
Ere the frail fanction of the wax was cold.

    With thee, * PLANTAGENET, from civil broils
The land awhile refpir'd, and all was peace.
Then BECKET rofe, and impotent of mind,
From regal courts with lawlefs fury march'd
The church's blood-ftain'd convicts, and forgave ;
Bid murd'rous priefts the fov'reign frown contemn,
And with unhallow'd crofier bruis'd the crown.

    Yet yielded not fuplinely tame a prince
Of HENRY's virtues ; learn'd, courageous, wife,
Of fair ambition.   Long his regal foul
Firm and erect the peevifh prieft exil'd,
And brav'd the fury of revengeful ROME.
In vain ! let one faint malady diffufe
The penfive gloom which fuperftition loves,
And fee him, dwindled to a recreant groom,
Rein the proud palfrey while the prieft afcends !

    Was † COEUR-DE-LION bleft with whiter days ?
Here the cowl'd zealots with united cries
Urged the crufade ; and fee, of half his ftores
Defpoil'd the wretch, whofe wifer bofom chofe
To blefs his friends, his race, his native land.

    Of ten fair funs that roll'd their annual race,
Not one beheld him on his vacant throne :
While haughty ‡ LONGCHAMP, 'mid his liv'ry'd files
Of wanton vaffals, fpoil'd his faithful realm,

Battling

* HENRY II.　　† RICHARD I.　　‡ Bifhop of ELY, Lord
Chancellor.

Battling in foreign fields ; collecting wide
A laurel harveft for a pillag'd land,
 Oh dear-bought trophies ! when a prince deferts
His drooping realm, to pluck the barren fprays !
 When faithlefs JOHN ufurp'd the fully'd crown,
What ample tyranny ! the groaning land
Deem'd earth, deem'd heav'n its foe ! fix tedious years
Our helplefs fathers in defpair obey'd
The papal interdict ; and who obey'd,
The fovereign plunder'd.   O inglorious days !
When the French tyrant by the futile grant
Of papal refcript, claim'd BRITANNIA's throne,
And durft invade ; be fuch inglorious days
Or hence forgot, or not recall'd in vain !
 Scarce had the tortur'd ear dejected heard
ROME's loud anathema, but heartlefs, dead
To ev'ry purpofe, men nor wifh'd to live,
Nor dar'd to die.   The poor laborious hind
Heard the dire curfe, and from his trembling hand
Fell the neglected crook that rul'd the plain.
Thence journeying home, in ev'ry cloud he fees
A vengeful angel, in whofe waving fcroll
He reads damnation ; fees its fable train
Of grim attendants pencil'd by defpair !
 The weary pilgrim from remoter climes
By painful fteps arriv'd ; his home, his friends,
His offspring left, to lavifh on the fhrine
Of fome far-honour'd faint his coftly ftores,
Inverts his footftep ; fickens at the fight
Of the barr'd fane, and filent fheds his tear.

The

The wretch whofe hope by ftern oppreffion chas'd
From ev'ry earthly blifs, ftill as it faw
Triumphant wrong, took wing and flew to heav'n
And refted there, now mourn'd his refuge loft
And wonted peace.   The facred fane was barr'd,
And the lone alter, where the mourners throng'd
To fupplicate remiffion, fmok'd no more ;
While the green weed, luxuriant round uprofe.
Some from their death-bed, whofe delirious faith
Thro' ev'ry ftage of life to ROME's decrees
Obfequious, humbly hop'd to die in peace,
Now faw the ghaftly king approach, begirt
In tenfold terrors ; now expiring heard
The laft loud clarion found, and heav'n's decree
With unremitting vengeace bar the fkies.
Nor light the grief, by fuperftition weigh'd,
That their difhonour'd corfe, fhut from the verge
Of hallow'd earth, or tutelary fane,
Muft fleep with brutes their vaffals ; on the field ;
Unneath fome path, in marle unexorcifed !
No folemn bell extort a neighbour's tear !
No tongue of prieft pronounce their foul fecure !
Nor fondeft friend affure their peace obtain'd !

The prieft ! alas fo boundlefs was the ill !
He, like the flock he pillag'd, pin'd forlorn ;
The vivid vermeil fled his fady cheek,
And his big paunch, diftended with the fpoils
Of half his flock : emaciate, groan'd beneath
Superior pride, and mightier luft of pow'r !
'Twas now ROME's fondeft friend, whofe meagre hand
Told

'Told to the midnight lamp his holy beads
With nice precifion, felt the deeper wound
As his gull'd foul rever'd the conclave more.

    Whom did the ruin fpare? for wealth, for pow'r,
Birth, honour, virtue, enemy, and friend,
Sunk helplefs in the dreary gulph involv'd;
And one capricious curfe envelop'd all!

    Were kings fecure? in tow'ring ftations born,
In flatt'ry nurs'd, inur'd to fcorn mankind,
Or view diminifh'd from their fite fublime;
As when a fhepherd, from the lofty brow
Of fome proud cliff, furveys his lefs'ning flock
In fnowy groups diffufive, fcud the vale.

    Awhile the furious menace JOHN return'd,
And breath'd defiance loud.　Alas! too foon
Allegiance fick'ning faw its fov'reign yield,
An angry prey to fcruples not his own.
The loyal foldier, girt around with ftrength,
Who ftole from mirth and wine his blooming years,
And feiz'd the fauchion, refolute to guard
His fovereign's right, impalfy'd at the news,
Finds the firm bias of his foul revers'd
For foul defertion; drops the lifted fteel,
And quits fame's noble harveft, to expire
The death of monks, of furfeit and of floth!

    At length fatigu'd with wrongs the fervile king
Drain'd from his land its fmall remaining ftores
To buy remiffion.　But could thefe obtain?
No! refolute in wrongs the prieft obdur'd;
'Till crawling bafe to ROME's deputed flave

His

His fame, his people, and his crown he gave.
Mean monarch ! slighted, brav'd, abhor'd before !
   And now, appeas'd by delegated sway,
The wily pontiff scorns not to recall
His interdictions.   Now the sacred doors
Admit repentant multitudes, prepar'd
To buy deceit; admit obsequious tribes
Of satraps ! princes ! crawling to the shrine
Of sainted villainy ! the pompous tomb
Dazzling with gems and gold, or in a cloud
Of incense wreath'd, amidst a drooping land
That sigh'd for bread ! 'Tis thus the Indian clove
Displays its verdant leaf, its crimson flow'r,
And sheds its odours ; while the flocks around
Hungry and faint the barren sands explore
In vain ! nor plant nor herb endears the soil ;
Drain'd and exhaust to swell its thirsty pores,
And furnish luxury—Yet, yet in vain
BRITANNIA strove; and whether artful ROME
Caress'd or curs'd her, superstition rag'd
And blinded, fetter'd and despoil'd the land.
   At length some murd'rous monk, with pois'nous art
Expell'd the life his brethren robb'd of peace.
   Nor yet surceas'd with JOHN's disastrous fate
Pontific fury ! English wealth exhaust,
The sequent reign * beheld the beggar'd shore
Grim with Italian usurers ; prepar'd
To lend, for griping unexampled hire,
To lend—what Rome might pillage uncontroul'd.
   For now with more extensive havock rag'd

Relentless

* Henry III. who cancell'd the Magna Charta.

Relentless GREG'RY, with a thousand arts,
And each rapacious, born to drain the world!
Nor shall the muse repeat, how oft he blew
The croise's trumpet; then for sums of gold
Annull'd the vow, and bade the false alarm
Swell the gross hoards of HENRY, or his own.
Nor shall she tell, how pontiffs dar'd repeal
The best of charters! dar'd absolve the tye
Of British kings by legal oath restrain'd.
Nor can she dwell on argosies of gold
From ALBION's realm to servile shores convey'd,
Wrung from her sons, and speeded by her kings!
Oh irksome days! when wicked thrones combine
With papal craft, to gull their native land!

　　Such was our fate, while ROME's director taught
Of subjects, born to be their monarch's prey,
To toil for monks, for gluttony to toil,
For vacant gluttony; extortion, fraud,
For av'rice, envy, pride, revenge, and shame!
O doctrine breath'd from Stygian caves! exhal'd
From inmost EREBUS!—Such HENRY's reign!
Urging his loyal realm's reluctant hand
To wield the peaceful sword, by JOHN erewhile
Forc'd from its scabbard; and with burnish'd lance
Essay the savage cure, domestic war!

　　And now some nobler spirits chas'd the mist
Of general darkness. GROSTED * now adorn'd
The mitred wreath he wore, with reason's sword

Stag-

* Bishop of LINCOLN, called Malleus Romanorum.

Stagg'ring delufion's frauds; at length beneath
ROME's interdict expiring calm, refign'd
No vulgar foul, that dar'd to Heav'n appeal!
But ah this fertile glebe, this fair domain
Had well nigh ceded to the flothful hands
Of monks libidinous; ere EDWARD's care
The lavifh hand of death-bed fear reftrain'd.
Yet was he clear of fuperftition's taint?
He too, mifdeemful of his wholefome law,
Ev'n he, expiring, gave his treafur'd gold
To fatten monks on SALEM's diftant foil!

  Yes, the third EDWARD's breaft, to papal fway
So little prone, and fierce in honour's caufe,
Cou'd fuperftition quell! before the tow'rs
Of haggard PARIS, at the thunder's voice
He drops the fword, and figns ignoble peace!

  But ftill the night by Romifh art diffus'd
Collects her clouds, and with flow pace recedes.
When, by foft BOURDEAU's braver queen approv'd,
Bold WICKLIFF rofe: and while the bigot pow'r
Amidft her native darknefs fkulk'd fecure,
The demon vanifh'd as he fpread the day.
So from his bofom CACUS breath'd of old
The pitchy cloud, and in a night of fmoke
Secure awhile his recreant life fuftain'd;
Till fam'd ALCIDES, o'er his fubtleft wiles
Victorious, chear'd the ravag'd nations round.

  Hail, honour'd WICKLIFF! enterprizing fage!
An Epicurus in the caufe of truth!
For 'tis not radiant funs, the jovial hours

Of youthful fpring, an æther all ferene,
Nor all the verdure of CAMPANIA's vales,
Can chafe religious gloom! 'Tis reafon, thought,
The light, the radiance that pervades the foul,
And fheds its beams on heav'n's myfterious way!
As yet this light but glimmer'd, and again
Error prevail'd; while kings by force uprais'd
Let loofe the rage of bigots on their foes,
And feek affection by the dreadful boon
Of licens'd murder. Ev'n the kindeft prince,
The moft extended breaft, the royal HAL!
All unrelenting heard the Lollards' cry
Burft from the center of remorfelefs flames;
Their fkrieks endur'd! O ftain to martial praife!
When COBHAM, gen'rous as the noble peer
That wears his honours, pay'd the fatal price
Of virtue blooming, ere the ftorms were laid!

'Twas thus, alternate, truth's precarious flame
Decay'd or flourifh'd. With malignant eye
The pontiff faw BRITANNIA's golden fleece,
Once all his own, inveft her worthier fons!
Her verdant valleys, and her fertile plains,
Yellow with grain, abjure his hateful fway!
Effay'd his utmoft art, and inly own'd
No labours bore proportion to the prize.

So when the tempter view'd, with envious eye,
The firft fair pattern of the female frame,
All nature's beauties in one form difplay'd,
And cent'ring there, in wild amaze he ftood;

VOL. I.   U   Then

Then only envying heav'n's creative hand;
Wish'd to his gloomy reign his envious arts
Might win this prize, and doubled ev'ry snare.

And vain were reason, courage, learning, all,
Till pow'r accede: till TUDOR's wild caprice
Smile on their cause; TUDOR, whose tyrant reign
With mental freedom crown'd, the best of kings
Might envious view, and ill prefer their own!
Then WOLSEY rose, by nature form'd to seek
Ambition's trophies, by address to win,
By temper to enjoy—whose humbler birth
Taught the gay scenes of pomp to dazzle more.

Then from its tow'ring height with horrid sound
Rush'd the proud abby. Then the vaulted roofs,
Torn from their walls, disclos'd the wanton scene
Of monkish chastity! Each angry friar
Crawl'd from his bedded strumpet, mutt'ring low
An ineffectual curse. The pervious nooks
That, ages past, convey'd the guileful priest
To play some image on the gaping crowd,
Imbibe the novel day-light; and expose
Obvious, the fraudful engin'ry of ROME.
As tho' this op'ning earth to nether realms
Shou'd flash meridian day, the hooded race
Shudder abash'd to find their cheats display'd:
And conscious of their guilt, and pleas'd to wave
Its fearful meed, resign'd their fair domain.

Nor yet supine, nor void of rage, retir'd
The pest gigantic; whose revengeful stroke

Ting'd

Ting'd the red annals of MARIA's reign.
When from the tenderest breast, each wayward priest
Cou'd banish mercy and implant a fiend!
When cruelty the fun'ral pyre uprear'd,
And bound religion there, and fir'd the base!
When the same blaze, which on each tortur'd limb
Fed with luxuriant rage, in ev'ry face
Triumphant faith appear'd, and smiling hope.
O blest ELIZA! from thy piercing beam
Forth flew this hated fiend, the child of ROME;
Driv'n to the verge of ALBION, linger'd there,
Then with her JAMES receding, cast behind
One angry frown, and sought more servile climes.
Henceforth they ply'd the long-continued task
Of righteous havoc, cov'ring distant fields
With the wrought remnants of the shatter'd pile.
While thro' the land the musing pilgrim sees
A tract of brighter green, and in the midst
Appears a mouldering wall, with ivy crown'd;
Or gothic tarret, pride of ancient days!
Now but of use to grace a rural scene;
To bound our vistas, and to glad the sons
Of GEORGE's reign, reserv'd for fairer times!

LOVE

LOVE and HONOUR.

Sed neque Medorum silvæ, ditissima terra
Nec pulcher Ganges, atque auro turbidus Hæmus,
Laudibus Angligenûm certent : non Bactra, nec Indi,
Totaque turriferis Panchaia pinguis arenis.

IMITATION.

Yet let not Median woods (abundant tract !)
Nor Ganges * fair, nor Hæmus †, miser-like,
Proud of his hoarded gold, presume to vie
With Britain's boast and praise ; nor Persian Bactra ‡,
Nor India's coasts, nor all Panchaia's ‖ sands,
Rich, and exulting in their lofty towers.

L ET the green olive glad Hesperian shores ;
  Her tawny citron, and her orange-groves,
These let IBERIA boast ; but if in vain,
To win the stranger plant's diffusive smile,
The BRITON labours, yet our native minds,
Our constant bosoms, these, the dazzled world
May view with envy ; these, Iberian dames
Survey with fixt esteem and fond desire.

Hap-

---

* *Ganges*—the greatest river, which divides the Indies in two parts.
† *Hæmus*—an high mountain dividing Thrace and Thessaly.
‡ *Bactra*—the Bactrians, provincials of Persia.
‖ *Panchaia*—a country of Arabia Felix, fruitful in frankincense, and
   various spices, remarkable also for its many towers, and lofty
   buildings.

Haplefs ELVIRA ! thy difaftrous fate
May well this truth explain ; nor ill adorn
The Britifh lyre ; then chiefly, if the mufe,
Nor vain nor partial, from the fimple guife
Of ancient record catch the penfive lay ;
And in lefs groveling accents give to fame.
ELVIRA ! lovelieft maid ! th' Iberian realm
Could boaft no purer breaft, no fprightlier mind,
No race more fplendent, and no form fo fair.
Such was the chance of war, this peerlefs maid,
In life's luxuriant bloom, enrich'd the fpoil
Of Britifh victors, vict'ry's nobleft pride !
She, fhe alone, amid the wailful train
Of captive maids, affign'd to HENRY's care ;
Lord of her life, her fortune, and her fame !

   He, gen'rous youth, with no penurious hand,
The tedious moments that unjoyous roll
Where freedom's chearful radiance fhines no more,
Effay'd to foften ; confcious of the pang
That beauty feels, to wafte its fleeting hours
In fome dim fort, by foreign rule reftrain'd,
Far from the haunts of men, or eye of day !

   Sometimes, to cheat her bofom of its cares,
Her kind protector number'd o'er the toils
Himfelf had worn : the frowns of angry feas,
Or hoftile rage, or faithlefs friend, more fell
Than ftorm or foe : if haply fhe might find
Her cares diminifh'd ; fruitlefs fond effay !
Now to her lovely hand, with modeft awe
The tender lute he gave ; fhe not averfe,

Nor

Nor deftitute of fkill, with willing hand
Call'd forth angelic ftrains; the facred debt
Of gratitude, fhe faid; whofe juft commands
Still might her hand with equal pride obey!

   Nor to the melting founds the nymph refus'd
Her vocal art; harmonious, as the ftrain ·
Of fome imprifon'd lark, who daily chear'd
By guardian cares, repays them with a fong:
Nor droops, nor deems fweet liberty refign'd.

   The fong, not artlefs, had fhe fram'd to paint
Difaftrous paffion; how, by tyrant laws
Of idiot cuftom fway'd, fome foft-ey'd fair
Lov'd only one: nor dar'd that love reveal!
How the foft anguifh banifh'd from her cheek
The damafk rofe full-blown; a fever came; ·
And from her bofom forc'd the plaintive tale.
Then, fwift as light, he fought the love-lorn maid,
But vainly fought her; torn by fwifter fate
To join the tenants of the myrtle fhade,
Love's mournful victims on the plains below.

   Sometimes, as fancy fpoke the pleafing tafk,
She taught her artful needle to difplay
The various pride of fpring: then fwift upfprung
Thickets of myrtle, eglantine, and rofe:
There might you fee, on gentle toils intent,
A train of bufy loves; fome pluck the flow'r,
Some twine the garland, fome with grave grimace
Around a vacant warrior caft the wreath.
'Twas paint, 'twas life! and fure to piercing eyes
The warrior's face depictur'd HENRY's mien,

Now

Now had the gen'rous chief with joy perus'd
The royal scroll, which to their native home
Their ancient rights, uninjur'd, unredeem'd,
Restor'd the captives. Forth with rapid haste
To glad his fair ELVIRA's ear, he sprung;
Fir'd by the bliss he panted to convey;
But fir'd in vain ! Ah ! what was his amaze,
His fond distress, when o'er her pallid face
Dejection reign'd, and from her lifeless hand!
Down dropt the myrtle's fair unfinish'd flow'r!
Speechless she stood; at length with accents faint,
" Well may my native shore, she said, resound
" Thy monarch's praise ; and ere ELVIRA prove
" Of thine forgetful, flow'rs shall cease to feel
" The fost'ring breeze, and nature change her laws !"
     And now the grateful edict wide alarm'd
The British host. Around the smiling youths
Call'd to their native scenes, with willing haste
Their fleet unmoor; impatient of the love
That weds each bosom to its native soil.
The patriot passion ! strong in ev'ry clime
How justly theirs, who find no foreign sweets
To dissipate their loves, or match their own.
     Not so ELVIRA ! she, disastrous maid,
Was doubly captive ! pow'r nor chance cou'd loose
The subtle bands ; she lov'd her gen'rous foe.
She, where her HENRY dwelt, her HENRY smil'd,
Cou'd term her native shore ; her native shore

By

By him deferted, fome unfriendly ftrand,
Strange, bleak, forlorn! a defert wafte and wild.

　The fleet careen'd, the wind propitious fill'd
The fwelling fails, the glitt'ring tranfports wav'd
'Their pennants gay, and halcyons' azure wing
With flight aufpicious fkim'd the placid main.

　On her lone couch in tears ELVIRA lay,
And chid th' officious wind, the tempting fea,
And wifh'd a ftorm as mercilefs, as tore
Her lab'ring bofom.　Fondly now fhe ftrove
To banifh paffion; now the vaffal days,
The captive moments that fo fmoothly paft,
By many an art recall'd; now from her lute
With trembling fingers call'd the fav'rite founds
Which HENRY deign'd to praife; and now effay'd
With mimic chains of filken fillets wove
To paint her captive ftate; if any fraud
Might to her love the pleafing fcenes prolong,
And with the dear idea feaft the foul.

　But now the chief return'd; prepar'd to launch
On ocean's willing breaft, and bid adieu
To his fair pris'ner.　She, foon as fhe heard
His hated errand, now no more conceal'd
The raging flame; but with a fpreading blufh,
And rifing figh, the latent pang difclos'd.

　" Yes, gen'rous youth! I fee thy bofom glow
With virtuous tranfport, that the tafk is thine
To folve my chains; and to my weeping friends,

And

And every longing relative, reftore
A foft-ey'd maid, a mild offencelefs prey !
But know, my foldier, never youthful mind,
Torn from the lavifh joys of wild expence
By him he loath'd, and in a dungeon bound
To languifh out his bloom, could match the pains
This ill-ftarr'd freedom gives my tortur'd mind.

What call I freedom ? is it that thefe limbs
From rigid bolts fecure, may wander far
From him I love ? Alas ! ere I may boaft
That facred blefling, fome fuperior pow'r
To mortal kings, to fublunary thrones,
Muft loofe my paffion, muft unchain my foul.
Ev'n that I loath ; all liberty I loath !
But moft the joylefs privilege to gaze
With cold indifference, where defert is love.

True, I was born an alien to thofe eyes
I afk alone to pleafe ; my fortune's crime !
And ah ! this flatter'd form by drefs endear'd
To Spanifh eyes, by drefs may thine offend,
Whilft I, ill-fated maid ! ordain'd to ftrive
With cuftom's load, beneath its weight expire.

Yet HENRY's beauties knew in foreign garb
To vanquifh me ; his form, howe'er difguis'd,
To me were fatal ! no fantaftic robe
That e'er caprice invented, cuftom wore,
Or folly fmil'd on, cou'd eclipfe thy charms.

Perhaps by birth decreed, by fortune plac'd
Thy country's foe, ELVIRA's warmeft plea

Seems

Seems but the subtler accent fraud inspires.;
My tenderest glances, but the specious flow'rs
That shade the viper while she plots her wound.
And can the trembling candidate of love
Awake thy fears? and can a female breast,
By ties of grateful duty bound, ensnare?
Is there no brighter mien, no softer smile
For love to wear, to dark deceit unknown?
Heav'n search my soul, and if thro' all its cells
Lurk the pernicious drop of pois'nous guile;
Full on my fenceless head its phial'd wrath
May fate exhaust; and for my happiest hour
Exalt the vengeance I prepare for thee!

Ah me! nor HENRY's, nor his country's foe,
On thee I gaz'd, and reason soon dispell'd
Dim error's gloom, and to thy favour'd isle
Assign'd its total merit, unrestrain'd.
Oh! lovely region to the candid eye!
'Twas there my fancy saw the virtues dwell,
The loves, the graces play; and bless the soil
That nurtur'd thee! for sure the virtues form'd
Thy gen'rous breast; the loves, the graces plan'd
Thy shapely limbs. Relation, birth essay'd
Their partial pow'r in vain: again I gaz'd,
And ALBION's isle appear'd, amidst a tract
Of savage wastes, the darling of the skies!
And thou by nature form'd, by fate assign'd
To paint the genius of thy native shore.

'Tis true, with flow'rs, with many a dazzling scene
Of burnish'd plants, to lure a female eye,

IBERIA

IBERIA glows: but ah! the genial fun,
That gilds the lemon's fruit, or fcents the flow'r,
On Spanifh minds, a nation's nobler boaft!
Beams forth ungentle influences.   There
Sits jealoufy enthron'd, and at each ray
Exultant lights his flow-confuming fires.
Not fuch thy charming region; long before
My fweet experience taught me to decide
Of Englifh worth, the found had pleas'd mine ear.
Is there that favage coaft, that rude fojourn
Stranger to Britifh worth? the worth which forms
The kindeft friends; the moft tremendous foes;
Firft, beft fupports of liberty and love!
No, let fubjected INDIA, while fhe throws
O'er Spanifh deeds the veil, your praife refound.
Long as I heard, or ere in ftory read
Of Englifh fame, my bias'd partial breaft
Wifh'd them fuccefs, and happieft fhe, I cry'd,
Of women happieft fhe, who fhares the love,
The fame, the virtues of an Englifh lord.
And now what fhall I fay? bleft be the hour
Your fair-built veffels touch'd th' Iberian fhores:
Bleft did I fay the time? if I may blefs
That lov'd event, let HENRY's fmiles declare.
Our hearts and cities won, will HENRY's youth
Forego its nobler conqueft? will he flight
The foft endearments of the lovelier fpoil?
And yet IBERIA's fons with every vow
Of lafting faith, have fworn thefe humble charms
Were not excell'd; the fource of all their pains,

And

And love her juſt deſert, who ſues for love;
But ſues to thee, while natives ſigh in vain.

   Perhaps in HENRY's eye (for vulgar minds
Diſſent from his) it ſpreads aú hateful ſtain
On honeſt fame, amid his train to bear
A female friend. Then learn, my gentle youth!
Not love himſelf, with all the pointed pains
That ſtore his quiver, ſhall ſeduce my ſoul
From honour's laws. ELVIRA once deny'd
A conſort's name, more ſwift than lightning flies,
When elements diſcordant vex the ſky,
Shall bluſhing from the form ſhe loves retire.

   Yet if the ſpecious wiſh the vulgar voice
Has titled prudence, ſways a ſoul like thine,
In gems or gold what proud Iberian dame
Eclipſes me ? Nor paint the dreary ſtorms
Or hair-breadth ſcapes that haunt the boundleſs deep,
And force from tender eyes the ſilent tear;
When mem'ry to the penſive maid ſuggeſts
In full contraſt, the ſafe domeſtic ſcene
For theſe reſign'd. Beyond the frantic rage
Of conqu'ring heroes brave, the female mind,
When ſteel'd by love, in love's moſt horrid way
Beholds not danger, or beholding ſcorns.
Heav'n take my life, but let it crown my love."

   She ceas'd, and ere his words her fate decreed,
Impatient, watch'd the language of his eye :
There pity dwelt, and from its tender ſphere
Sent looks of love, and faithleſs hopes inſpir'd.

                                        " Forgive

" Forgive me, gen'rous maid, the youth return'd,
If by thy accents charm'd, thus long I bore
To let such sweetnefs plead, alas! in vain!
Thy virtue merits more than crowns can yield
Of folid blifs, or happieft love beftow.
But ere from native fhores I plough'd the main,
To one dear maid, by virtue and by charms
Alone endear'd, my plighted vows I gave,
To guard my faith, whatever chance fhould wait
My warring fword: if conqueft, fame and fpoil
Grac'd my return, before her feet to pour
The glitt'ring treafure, and the laurel wreath;
Enjoying conqueft then, and fame and fpoil.
If fortune frown'd adverfe; and death forbade
The blifsful union, with my lateft breath
To dwell on MEDWAY's and MARIA's name;
This ardent vow deep-rooted, from my foul
No dangers tore; this vow my bofom fir'd
To conquer danger, and the fpoil enjoy.
Her fhall I leave, with fair events elate,
Who crown'd mine humbleft fortune with her love?
Her fhall I leave, who now perchance alone
Climbs the proud cliff, and chides my flow return?
And fhall that veffel, whofe approaching fails
Shall fwell her breaft with extafies, convey
Death to her hopes, and anguifh to her foul?
No! may the deep my villain-corfe devour,
If all the wealth Iberian mines conceal,
If all the charms Iberian maids difclofe,
If thine, ELVIRA, thine, uniting all!

Thus

Thus far prevail—nor can thy virtuous breast
Demand, what honour, faith, and love denies."
    "Oh! happy she, rejoin'd the pensive maid,
Who shares thy fame, thy virtue, and thy love!
And be she happy! thy distinguish'd choice
Declares her worth, and vindicates her claim.
Farewel my luckless hopes, my flatt'ring dreams
Of rapt'rous days! my guilty suit, farewel!
Yet fond howe'er my plea, or deep the wound
That waits my fame, let not the random shaft
Of censure pierce with me th' Iberian dames:
They love with caution, and with happier stars.
And oh! by pity mov'd, restrain the taunts
Of levity, nor brand ELVIRA's flame;
By merit rais'd; by gratitude approv'd;
By hope confirm'd; with artless truth reveal'd;
Let, let me say, but for one matchless maid
Of happier birth, with mutual ardor crown'd.
    These radiant gems, which burnish happiness,
But mock misfortune, to thy fav'rite's hand
With care convey.   And well may such adorn
Her chearful front, who finds in thee alone
The source of every transport; but disgrace
My pensive breast, which doom'd to lasting woe,
In thee the source of ev'ry bliss resign.
    And now farewel, thou darling youth! the gem
Of English merit! peace, content, and joy,
And tender hopes, and young desires, farewel!
Attend, ye smiling train, this gallant mind

3   Back

Back to his native fhores; there fweetly fmooth
His ev'ning pillow; dance around his groves;
And, where he treads, with vi'lets paint his way.
But leave ELVIRA! leave her, now no more
Your frail companion! in the facred cells
Of fome lone cloifter let me fhroud my fhame:
There, to the matin bell, obfequious, pour
My conftant orifons. The wanton loves
And gay defires fhall fpy the glimm'ring tow'rs,
And wing their flight aloof: but reft confirm'd
That never fhall ELVIRA's tongue conclude
Her fhorteft pray'r ere HENRY's dear fuccefs
The warmeft accent of her zeal employ."

　　Thus fpoke the weeping fair, whofe artlefs mind
Impartial fcorn'd to model her efteem
By native cuftoms; drefs, and face, and air,
And manners, lefs; nor yet refolv'd in vain.
He, bound by prior love, the folemn vow
Giv'n and recciv'd, to foft compaffion gave
A tender tear; then with that kind adieu
Efteem could warrant, weary'd heav'n with pray'r
To fhield that tender breaft he left forlorn.

　　He ceas'd, and to the cloifter's penfive fcene
ELVIRA fhap'd her folitary way.

The SCHOOL-MISTRESS.

In Imitation of SPENSER.

Auditæ voces, vagitus & ingens,
Infantumque animæ flentes in limine primo.   VIRG.

IMITATION.

And mingled founds and infant plaints we hear,
That pierce the entrance fhrill, and wound the tender ear.

ADVERTISEMENT.

What particulars in Spenfer were imagined moft proper
for the Author's imitation on *this occafion*, are his *lan-*
guage, his *fimplicity*, his manner of *defcription*, and a
peculiar *tendernefs* of *fentiment* remarkable throughout
his works.

A H me! full forely is my heart forlorn,
    To think how modeft worth neglected lies ;
While partial fame doth with her blafts adorn.
Such deeds alone, as pride and pomp difguife ;
Deeds of ill fort, and mifchievous emprize :
Lend me thy clarion, goddefs ! let me try
To found the praife of merit, ere it dies ;
Such as I oft have chaunced to efpy,
Loft in the dreary fhades of dull obfcurity.

In

In ev'ry village mark'd with little spire,
Embow'r'd in trees, and hardly known to fame,
There dwells, in lowly shed, and mean attire,
A matron old, whom we school-mistress name;
Who boasts unruly brats with birch to tame;
They grieven sore, in piteous durance pent,
Aw'd by the pow'r of this relentless dame;
And oft-times, on vagaries idly bent,
For unkempt hair, or task unconn'd, are sorely shent.

And all in sight doth rise a birchen tree,
Which learning near her little dome did stowe;
Whilom a twig of small regard to see,
Tho' now so wide its waving branches flow;
And work the simple vassals mickle woe;
For not a wind might curl the leaves that blew,
But their limbs shudder'd, and their pulse beat low;
And as they look'd they found their horror grew,
And shap'd it into rods, and tingled at the view.

So have I seen (who has not, may conceive,)
A lifeless phantom near a garden plac'd;
So doth it wanton birds of peace bereave,
Of sport, of song, of pleasure, of repast;
They start, they stare, they wheel, they look aghast;
Sad servitude! such comfortless annoy
May no bold Briton's riper age e'er taste!
Ne superstition clog his dance of joy;
Ne vision empty, vain, his native bliss destroy.

Near to this dome is found a patch so green,
On which the tribe their gambols do display;
And at the door impris'ning board is seen,
Lest weakly wights of smaller size should stray;
Eager, perdie, to bask in sunny day!
The noises intermix'd, which thence resound,
Do learning's little tenement betray:
Where sits the dame, disguis'd in look profound,
And eyes her fairy throng, and turns her wheel around.

Her cap, far whiter than the driven snow,
Emblem right meet of decency does yield:
Her apron dy'd in grain, as blue, I trowe,
As is the hare-bell that adorns the field:
And in her hand, for scepter, she does wield
Tway birchen sprays; with anxious fear entwin'd,
With dark distrust, and sad repentance fill'd;
And stedfast hate, and sharp affliction join'd,
And fury uncontroul'd, and chastisement unkind.

Few but have ken'd, in semblance meet pourtray'd,
The childish faces of old Eol's train;
Lies, Notus, Auster *: these in frowns array'd,
How then would fare or earth, or sky, or main,
Were the stern god to give his slaves the rein?
And were not she rebellious breasts to quell,
And were not she her statutes to maintain,
The cot no more, I ween, were deem'd the cell,
Where comely peace of mind, and decent order dwell.

A russet

* The south-west wind, south, &c. &c.

A ruffet ftole was o'er her fhoulders thrown;
A ruffet kirtle fenc'd the nipping air;
'Twas fimple ruffet, but it was her own;
'Twas her own country bred the flock fo fair;
'Twas her own labour did the fleece prepare;
And, footh to fay, her pupils, rang'd around,
Thro' pious awe, did term it paffing rare;
For they in gaping wonderment abound,
And think, no doubt, fhe been the greateft wight on
[ground.

Albeit ne flatt'ry did corrupt her truth,
Ne pompous title did debauch her ear;
Goody, good-woman, goffip, n'aunt, forfooth,
Or dame, the fole additions fhe did hear;
Yet thefe fhe challeng'd, thefe fhe held right dear:
Ne would efteem him act as mought behove,
Who fhould not honour'd eld with thefe revere:
For never title yet fo mean could prove,
But there was eke a mind which did that title love.

One ancient hen fhe took delight to feed,
The plodding pattern of the bufy dame;
Which, ever and anon, impell'd by need,
Into her fchool, begirt with chickens, came;
Such favour did her paft deportment claim:
And, if neglect had lavifh'd on the ground
Fragment of bread, fhe would collect the fame;
For well fhe knew, and quaintly could expound,
What fin it were to wafte the fmalleft crumb fhe found.

X 2   Herbs

Herbs too fhe knew, and well of each could fpeak
That in her garden fip'd the filv'ry dew;
Where no vain flow'r difclos'd a gaudy ftreak;
But herbs for ufe, and phyfick, not a few,
Of grey renown, within thofe borders grew:
The tufted bafil, pun-provoking thyme,
Frefh baum, and mary-gold of chearful hue;
The lowly gill, that never dares to climb;
And more I fain would fing, difdaining here to rhyme.

Yet euphrafy may not be left unfung,
That gives dim eyes to wander leagues around;
And pungent radifh, biting infant's tongue;
And plantain ribb'd, that heals the reaper's wound;
And marj'ram fweet, in fhepherds pofie found;
And lavender, whofe fpikes of azure bloom
Shall be, ere-while, in arid bundles bound,
To lurk amidft the labours of her loom,
And crown her kerchiefs clean with mickle rare perfume.

And here trim rofemarine, that whilom crown'd
The daintieft garden of the proudeft peer;
Ere, driven from its envy'd fite, it found
A facred fhelter for its branches here;
Where edg'd with gold its glitt'ring fkirts appear.
Oh waffel days! O cuftoms meet and well!
Ere this was banifh'd from its lofty fphere:
Simplicity then fought this humble cell,
Nor ever would fhe more with thane and lordling dwell.

Here

Here oft the dame, on fabbath's decent eve,
Hymned fuch pfalms as STERNHOLD forth did mete,
If winter 'twere, fhe to her hearth did cleave;
But in her garden found a fummer feat:
Sweet melody! to hear her then repeat
How ISRAEL's fons, beneath a foreign king,
While taunting foe-men did a fong intreat,
All, for the nonce, untuning ev'ry ftring,
Uphung their ufelefs lyres—fmall heart had they to fing.

For fhe was juft, and friend to virtuous lore,
And pafs'd much time in truly virtuous deed;
And, in thofe elfins' ears, would oft deplore
The times, when truth by popifh rage did bleed;
And tortious death was true devotion's meed;
And fimple faith in iron chains did mourn,
That nould on wooden image place her creed;
And lawny faints in fmould'ring flames did burn:
Ah! deareft Lord, forefend, thilk days fhould e'er return.

In elbow chair, like that of Scottifh ftem
By the fharp tooth of cank'ring eld defac'd,
In which, when he receives his diadem,
Our fov'reign prince and liefeft liege is plac'd,
The matron fate; and fome with rank fhe grac'd,
(The fource of children's and of courtier's pride!)
Redrefs'd affronts, for vile affronts there pafs'd;
And warn'd them not the fretful to deride,
But love each other dear, whatever them betide.

X 3   Right

Right well she knew each temper to descry;
To thwart the proud, and the submiss to raise;
Some with vile copper prize exalt on high,
And some entice with pittance small of praise;
And other some with baleful sprig she 'frays:
Ev'n absent, she the reins of pow'r doth hold,
While with quaint arts the giddy crowd she sways;
Forewarn'd, if little bird their pranks behold,
'Twill whisper in her ear, and all the scene unfold.

Lo now with state she utters the command!
Eftsoons the urchins to their tasks repair;
Their books of stature small they take in hand,
Which with pellucid horn secured are;
To save from finger wet the letters fair:
The work so gay, that on their back is seen,
St. George's high atchievements does declare;
On which thilk wight that has y-gazing been
Kens the forth-coming rod, unpleasing sight, I ween!

Ah luckless he, and born beneath the beam
Of evil star! it irks me whilst I write!
As erst the * bard by Mulla's silver stream,
Oft, as he told of deadly dolorous plight,
Sigh'd as he sung, and did in tears indite.
For brandishing the rod, she doth begin
To loose the brogues, the stripling's late delight!
And down they drop; appears his dainty skin,
Fair as the furry coat of whitest ermilin,

O ruth-

* Spenser,

O ruthful scene! when from a nook obscure,
His little sister doth his peril see:
All playful as she sate, she grows demure;
She finds full soon her wonted spirits flee;
She meditates a pray'r to set him free:
Nor gentle pardon could this dame deny,
(If gentle pardon could with dames agree)
To her sad grief that swells in either eye,
And wrings her so that all for pity she could die.

No longer can she now her shrieks command;
And hardly she forbears thro' aweful fear,
To rushen forth, and, with presumptuous hand,
To stay harsh justice in its mid career.
On thee she calls, on thee her parent dear!
(Ah! too remote to ward the shameful blow!)
She sees no kind domestic visage near,
And soon a flood of tears begins to flow;
And gives a loose at last to unavailing woe.

But ah! what pen his piteous plight may trace?
Or what device his loud laments explain?
The form uncouth of his disguised face!
The pallid hue that dyes his looks amain?
The plenteous show'r that does his cheek distain?
When he, in abject wise, implores the dame,
Ne hopeth aught of sweet reprieve to gain;
Or when from high she levels well her aim,
And, thro' the thatch, his cries each falling stroke proclaim.

The

The other tribe, aghaſt, with ſore diſmay,
Attend, and conn their taſks with mickle care:
By turns, aſtony'd, ev'ry twig ſurvey,
And, from their fellow's hateful wounds, beware;
Knowing, I wiſt, how each the ſame may ſhare;
'Till fear has taught them a performance meet,
And to the well-known cheſt the dame repair;
Whence oft with ſugar'd cates ſhe doth 'em greet,
And ginger-bread y-rare; now, certes, doubly ſweet!

See to their ſeats they hye with merry glee,
And in beſeemly order ſitten there;
All but the wight of bum y-galled, he
Abhorreth bench and ſtool, and fourm, and chair;
(This hand in mouth y-fix'd, that rends his hair;)
And eke with ſnubs profound, and heaving breaſt,
Convulſions intermitting! does declare
His grievous wrong; his dame's unjuſt beheſt;
And ſcorns her offer'd love, and ſhuns to be careſs'd,

His face beſprent with liquid cryſtal ſhines,
His blooming face that ſeems a purple flow'r,
Which low to earth its drooping head declines,
All ſmear'd and ſully'd by a vernal ſhow'r.
O the hard boſoms of deſpotic pow'r!
Al!, all, but ſhe, the author of his ſhame,
All, all, but ſhe, regret this mournful hour:
Yet hence the youth, and hence the flow'r, ſhall claim,
If ſo I deem aright, tranſcending worth and fame.

Behind

Behind some door, in melancholy thought,
Mindless of food, he, dreary caitiff! pines;
Ne for his fellow's joyaunce careth aught,
But to the wind all merriment resigns;
And deems it shame, if he to peace inclines;
And many a sullen look ascance is sent,
Which for his dame's annoyance he designs;
And still the more to pleasure him she's bent,
The more doth he, perverse, her haviour past resent.

Ah me! how much I fear lest pride it be!
But if that pride it be, which thus inspires,
Beware, ye dames, with nice discernment see,
Ye quench not too the sparks of nobler fires:
Ah! better far than all the muses' lyres,
All coward arts, is valour's gen'rous heat;
The firm fixt breast which fit and right requires,
Like VERNON's patriot soul; more justly great
Than craft that pimps for ill, or flow'ry false deceit.

Yet nurs'd with skill, what dazzling fruits appear!
Ev'n now sagacious foresight points to show
A little bench of heedless bishops here,
And there a chancellour in embryo,
Or bard sublime, if bard may e'er be so,
As MILTON, SHAKESPEAR, names that ne'er shall die!
Tho' now he crawl along the ground so low,
Nor weeting how the muse shou'd soar on high,
Wisheth, poor starv'ling elf! his paper kite may fly.

And

And this perhaps, who, cens'ring the defign,
  Low lays the houfe which that of cards doth build,
' Shall Dennis be ! if rigid fates incline,
  And many an epic to his rage fhall yield ;
  And many a poet quit th' Aonian field ;
And, four'd by age, profound he fhall appear,
  As he who now with 'fdainful fury thrill'd
Surveys mine work ; and levels many a fneer,
And furls his wrinkly front, and cries, "What ftuff is here ?"

But now Dan Phoebus gains the middle fkie,
  And liberty unbars her prifon-door ;
And like a rufhing torrent out they fly,
  And now the graffy cirque han cover'd o'er
  With boift'rous revel-rout and wild uproar ;
A thoufand ways in wanton rings they run,
  Heav'n fhield their fhort-liv'd paftimes, I implore !
For well may freedom, erft fo dearly won,
Appear to Britifh elf more gladfome than the fun.

Enjoy, poor imps ! enjoy your fportive trade,
  And chafe gay flies, and cull the faireft flow'rs ;
For when my bones in grafs-green fods are laid ;
  For never may ye tafte more carelefs hours
  In knightly caftles, or in ladies bow'rs.
O vain to feek delight in earthly thing !
  But moft in courts where proud ambition tow'rs ;
Deluded wight ! who weens fair peace can fpring
Beneath the pompous dome of kefar or of king.

                         See

See in each fprite fome various bent appear!
Thefe rudely carol moft incondite lay;
Thofe faunt'ring on the green, with jocund leer
Salute the ftranger paffing on his way;
Some builden fragile tenements of clay;
Some to the ftanding lake their courfes bend,
With pebbles fmooth at duck and drake to play;
Thilk to the huxter's fav'ry cottage tend,
In paftry kings and queens th' allotted mite to fpend.

Here, as each feafon yields a different ftore,
Each feafon's ftores in order ranged been;
Apples with cabbage-net y-cover'd o'er,
Galling full fore th' unmoney'd wight, are feen;
And goofe-b'rie clad in liv'ry red or green;
And here of lovely dye, the cath'rine pear,
Fine pear! as lovely for thy juice, I ween:
O may no wight e'er pennylefs come there,
Left fmit with ardent love he pine with hopelefs care!

See! cherries here, ere cherries yet abound,
With thread fo white in tempting pofies ty'd,
Scatt'ring like blooming maid their glances round,
With pamper'd look draw little eyes afide;
And muft be bought, tho' penury betide.
The plumb all azure and the nut all brown,
And here each feafon, do thofe cakes abide,
Whofe honour'd names th' inventive city own,
Rend'ring thro' Britain's ifle Salopia's praifes known. *

Admir'd

* SHREWSBURY cakes.

Admir'd SALOPIA ! that with venial pride
Eyes her bright form in SEVERN's ambient wave,
Fam'd for her loyal cares in perils try'd,
Her daughters lovely, and her ftriplings brave:
Ah ! midft the reft, may flowers adorn his grave,
Whofe art did firft thefe dulcet cates difplay !
A motive fair to learning's imps he gave,
Who chearlefs o'er her darkling region ftray ;
'Till reafon's morn arife, and light them on their way.

CONTENTS.

I. ELEGIES on several Occasions.

ELEGY

CONTENTS.

ELEGY

CONTENTS.

II. ODES, SONGS, BALLADS, &c.

Jemmy

CONTENTS.

THE END OF THE FIRST VOLUME.

www.ingramcontent.com/pod-product-compliance
Lightning Source LLC
Chambersburg PA
CBHW021122270326
41929CB00009B/999